Politics and Post-structuralism
An introduction

edited by
ALAN FINLAYSON and JEREMY VALENTINE

EDINBURGH UNIVERSITY PRESS

© editorial matter and organisation
Alan Finlayson and Jeremy Valentine, 2002.
Copyright in the individual contributions
is retained by the authors

Edinburgh University Press Ltd
22 George Square, Edinburgh

Typeset in Scala by
Koinonia, Manchester, and
printed and bound in Great Britain by
MPG Books Ltd, Bodmin, Cornwall

A CIP Record for this book is available from the British Library

ISBN 0 7486 1296 3 (paperback)

Contents

Acknowledgements   *page* vi
Notes on the Contributors   vii

Introduction   I
Alan Finlayson and Jeremy Valentine

Part One   Politics and the Subject

1 The Subject and Subjectivity   *Caroline Williams*   23
2 The Theoretical Link Between Politics and the Subject   36
   Jeremy Valentine
3 The State and Sovereign Subjectivity   *James Martin*   52
4 After the Subject of International Security   *Jenny Edkins*   66

Part Two   Doing Political Analysis

5 Ideology and Social Movements: the case of the FN   *Steve Bastow*   83
6 The Work of Ideas and Interests in Public Policy   97
   Steven Griggs and David Howarth
7 Globalisation and the Constitution of Political Economy   112
   Glyn Daly
8 Complexity in the Wild: action in local welfare   *Will Medd*   130
9 Political Science and Complexity   *Paul Haynes*   145

Part Three   Critique and Political Thought

10 The Horizon of Community   *Alan Finlayson*   161
11 Critical Theory and Democracy   *Mark Devenney*   176
12 The Singularity of the Political   *Robert Porter*   193
13 Genres, Technologies and Spaces of Being-In-Common   206
    Michael J. Shapiro

Bibliography   223
Index   241

Acknowledgements

The idea for this book grew out of discussions within the *Post-structuralism and Radical Politics Group* of the Political Studies Association UK. The editors would like to acknowledge the participation of its members in the activities of the group.

We would also like to express our gratitude to Nicola Carr of Edinburgh University Press for maintaining goodwill, humour and patience throughout.

Michael Shapiro's essay 'Genres of the Public Interest: Technologies and Spaces of Being in Common' originally appeared in *International Review of Sociology*, 8, 3, 1998.

Notes on the Contributors

Steve Bastow is Senior Lecturer in Politics at Kingston University, London. He has published numerous articles and chapters on the French collaborationist Marcel Déat, under the supeHrvision of the contemporary French extreme right, and third-way discourse in inter-war France. Currently he is working both on the contemporary French radical right and on third-way politics. He is Assistant Editor of the *European Journal of Social Quality*.

Glyn Daly is a Lecturer in the School of Social Studies, University College Northampton. He is the author of three forthcoming books: *Conversations with Slavoj Žižek, Postmarxism*, and *Žižek: the Real, the Subject and Ideology*.

Mark Devenney is Senior Lecturer in the Department of Politics, University of Brighton.

Jenny Edkins is Lecturer in International Politics at the University of Wales Aberystwyth. Already the author of *Post-structuralism and International Politics: Bringing the Political Back In* (1999) *and Whose Hunger: Concepts of Famine, Practices of Aid* (2000), she is currently completing a third book, *Trauma Time and the Memory of Politics*. She would like to acknowledge the financial support of the Leverhulme Trust and the Economic and Social Research Council.

Alan Finlayson is a Lecturer in the Department of Politics at International Relations, University of Wales Swansea, and a co-author of *Contemporary Social and Political Thought: An Introduction* (1998). He is currently working on a book about New Labour and another on political theory and the media.

Steven Griggs is Senior Lecturer in Public Policy at Staffordshire University in the UK. He has published articles on developments in French health policy and politics and is currently studying the mobilisation and decision-making process surrounding direct action campaigns in the UK. His book, *French Politics: Debates and Controversies*, has recently been published (1999).

Paul Haynes recently completed a PhD on Technology and Social Change in the Department of Sociology at Lancaster University. He is currently researching emergent forms of machinic tooling in the West Midlands of England.

David Howarth is Lecturer in Political Theory in the Department of Government at the University of Essex. Recently he has published a book entitled *Discourse* (2000) and has co-edited books entitled *South Africa in Transition: New Theoretical Perspectives* (1998) and *Discourse Theory and Political Analysis* (2000). He has published numerous articles and chapters on theories of discourse, post-Marxist political theory and its application to empirical cases, most notably South African politics and new environmental movements.

James Martin is Lecturer in politics at Goldsmiths College, University of London. He is author of *Gramsci's Political Analysis: A Critical Introduction* (1998) and editor of *Antonio Gramsci: Critical Assessments* (2001).

Will Medd is a Lecturer at the University of Salford, Institute for Public Health Research and Policy. He has published articles on partnership working, complexity theory and methodology and is guest editor of a special edition of *Social Issues* on 'Complexity Theory and Social Policy'. He would like to acknowledge the support of the ESRC, who funded the PhD upon which his chapter is based, and also supervisors and colleagues at Lancaster University, Department of Sociology.

Robert Porter teaches communication and cultural theory in the school of psychology and communication at University of Ulster, Jordanstown.

Michael Shapiro is Professor in the Department of Political Science, University of Hawaii. His most recent publications include *Cinematic Political Thought* (Edinburgh University Press, 1999).

Jeremy Valentine lectures in the Department of Media and Communication, Queen Margaret University College, Edinburgh. He is the co-author of *Polemicization* (Edinburgh University Press, 1999) and co-editor of the series *Taking On The Political*.

Caroline Williams is Lecturer in the Department of Politics, Queen Mary College, University of London. She has written *Contemporary French Philosophy: Modernity and the Persistence of the Subject* (2001).

Introduction

The purpose of this book is quite straightforward. It explores, in a variety of ways, the relationship between the body of theory referred to as post-structuralism and the study of politics. We want to show that post-structuralist theory represents a coherent and significant perspective on the study of politics as well as the practice of political engagement.

The relationship between post-structuralism and political thought is well established. Perhaps Laclau and Mouffe's *Hegemony and Socialist Strategy*, first published in 1985, remains the most condensed example of this relation. This remarkable work provided a theoretical synthesis of the Marxist tradition of Gramsci and Althusser with the structuralism of Saussure and the post-structuralism of Lacan, Foucault and Derrida. Although aspects of the book were, and remain, controversial, its impact was great because it opened up a terrain of engagement between politics and post-structuralism at both the theoretical and empirical levels. The reach of the book extended into and across the European tradition of radical Marxism. In time Laclau and Mouffe's work served to introduce many readers to the work of the Slovenian philosopher Slavoj Žižek, as well as the Parisian post-structuralists, while simultaneously linking into the US radical democratic tradition (see Laclau, 1994; Critchley, 1996; Butler, 2000). Beyond this one text, post-structuralist thought informs many, if not most, contemporary perspectives within the human and social sciences and is, for a variety of reasons, associated with the emergence of 'postmodern' culture and its effects on economic, cultural and other organisational processes.

Despite these enormous influences we should not assume that post-structuralism presents a singular or unified body of thinking. After all, the attempt to specify, once and for all, the precise referent of a term goes against the grain of post-structuralist thinking itself. The variety of contending positions that can operate under the label of post-structuralism are part of what we want to introduce and explore, leaving it to readers to decide what aspects they find illuminating and what they find unhelpful. Not all the contributors to this book agree and if readers find everything here to their taste then we will have failed to present the variety that makes up a field that is always in development.

A jumble of terms – postmodernism, deconstruction, anti-foundationalism, post-metaphysics – are often used indiscriminately and casually as if they referred to one single movement of thought. Numerous writers and philosophers are often thrown about – Derrida, Foucault, Baudrillard, Lacan, Deleuze – as if there is no need to understand the different interests and approaches of these writers. In short 'post-structuralism' has come to refer to a variety of themes, trends, methods, philosophies and orientations that lack the uniformity imposed on them by the name. But the diversity of post-structuralist thinking is part of its productive nature. Research that has arisen from within it has informed and sustained a variety of fields and forms of study such as post-colonialism, film theory and cultural studies. Aspects of these approaches, as this book hopes to show, are of great relevance for political thinking.

But, in politics, as a narrowly and institutionally defined field or discipline, the influence of post-structuralist thinking has not been particularly explicit. Instead the political import of post-structuralism has been recognised primarily by practitioners of literary and cultural studies, for whom it has encouraged a finer attention to the workings and effects of power in texts and social practices, and by some sociologists interested in developing the insights of Michel Foucault into the practice of 'governmentality' (see Rose, 1999). But, in politics, it is still commonplace for political theorists to justify the narrow definition of politics – the representation of the practices of modern liberal regimes – through the exclusion of post-structuralism. The following example from an introductory textbook is typical:

> [other] well known and admired figures have been omitted deliberately, because in my opinion their contributions are not such as to merit inclusion. Legions of neo-Marxists, existentialists, phenomenologists, post-structuralists, postmodernists and deconstructionists are absent for this reason ... the reader will find ... no discussion of, for example, Sartre, Merleau-Ponty, Althusser, Foucault, Rorty or Derrida simply because none of them seems to me to have said anything about politics that is both original and significant – in so far as their writings are comprehensible at all. (Lessnoff, 1999: 4)

What can we make of this defensive response which relies on un-argued judgement? It suggests that, here at least, the specificity of contemporary political thought is established by its exclusion of post-structuralism. There are two ironies with this. Firstly, the question is begged as to why post-structuralism should be included in the first place. If the author is aware of claims that it should be, then these should be examined and refuted in order for the judgement to be persuasive. Secondly, it is a concern with operations of exclusion – logical, ethical, empirical – which characterises post-structuralist approaches to politics. This does not mean that the distinction between exclusion and inclusion should not take place. Rather, the concern is with how this occurs and what are its consequences.

We are not blind to the virtues and value of such polemic. In which spirit, we might point out that, right there, in that opening sentence denying the presence of such authors in his book, Lessnoff introduces them into it. And not just in that sentence where their names are mentioned but, by implication, throughout the book where their very absence (so grandly announced) makes them a permanent presence, haunting this author's attempt to limit the range of acceptable political theory but also acting (in their auspicious exclusion) as the limit for that which he considers proper. Thus, as good post-structuralists, we can say that the absence of these authors renders them a central component in the construction of Lessnoff's limited framework of political ideas. The exclusion fails in the attempt to institute it.

This point is not simply nit-picking. It is true, that, as Paul Patton points out with regard to Deleuze and Guattari, 'It is difficult to read post-stucturalist philosophers as political theorists since their work does not appear to engage with the problems and normative commitments of mainstream political theory' (Patton, 1997: 237) and certainly the same can be said with regard to mainstream political science. But any suggestion that such research has nothing to say about politics begs the question of what counts as politics and of who has the right to decide, in advance, the answer. Consequently, post-structuralist perspectives entail the radical responsibility of critical thought. Derrida has pointed out, in response to some of his more prejudiced critics and in language some might find surprising, that we need to cope with 'the development of research, in the sciences as much as in the humanities, that ... questions ... certainties and axioms of Enlightenment ... in order to think them better and especially to translate and transform them better in the light of what should be the Enlightenment of our time ...'. But, as he adds, this sort of work is 'by definition laborious' and 'These ... activities ... make necessary, questions on the subject of those very principles (the history and foundation of the principle of reason, the history and foundation of the value of truth, of the interpretation of language as communication or as information, of the structure of public space and so forth)' (1995: 428).

In politics textbooks aimed at the undergraduate market, it is, on the whole, still the case that the sorts of topics likely to be encountered can be predicted in advance. Texts on ideology will most likely deal with 'isms' from the obvious and classic (socialism, liberalism, conservatism), to the more contemporary (ecologism and feminism). Texts on general concepts will probably revolve around freedom, sovereignty, rights, justice, equality, citizenship, power and obligation but may, on occasion, open themselves up to concerns such as welfare (often a sub-topic of citizenship), gender (though this may be included in equality) and multiculturalism (though this may be included under rights). Meanwhile textbooks of political science or government (leaving aside area-specific work) will most probably begin by concentrating on the structure of government, the nature of voting systems, significant determinants in voting patterns, party allegiances and so forth before looking at things such as policy formation, the police, the legal system and maybe the media.

These are established core topics but, that they should continue to predominate in standard textbooks, that they should still be the overwhelming convention, is symptomatic of the limits placed on political studies, science or theory at a time when, in real life, the locations of political activity and the range of experiences that demand to be thought politically have been transformed (and are always transforming) because of politics itself. There is nothing given about the elements and forms of the political, the mode in which politics appears. After all, might it not be appropriate for textbooks on political concepts to include chapters on love, emotion, friendship, death or the body? These would not be new topics to the field of political theory. Plato was most certainly concerned with all of them and devoted dialogues or considerable sections of dialogues to each. Love and pity are central to the political philosophy of Rousseau. Death is a fundamental concept within the thought of Thomas Hobbes while a particular sense of the body is crucial to the liberal theory of a thinker such as John Locke. They are also, of course, concepts explored by phenomenologists, existentialists, post-structuralists, postmodernists and deconstructionists.

But contemporary political theory has a tendency to confine itself to a clear set of topics, problems and questions concerning phenomena that can supposedly be clearly located within the field of politics – questions related to the conduct and scope of government, the demands or defences of citizens, the distribution of rights and goods. Debates about utilitarianism, Kantianism, teleological versus deontic theories, theories of the right and the good predominate even though the study of political theory is recognised as not being as clear as it once was. While much of the above still concerns many, and post-Rawlsian normative debates predominate, there is much more fluidity, or uncertainty, within the field. This is a cause for celebration and it is important that this fluidity should itself become one of the things that political theory thinks about – for it is not just the outcome of intellectual trends. It is also the result of changes in the way societies are organised and reproduce their structures of power and hierarchy. Can we talk about debate, dialogue and democracy without thinking about the mass media, the nature of cinema or television, without considering, as political theorists, the meaning and purpose of the internet? Just as our conceptualisations of democracy, justice and equality have to be heightened and 'globalised' in response to the increased scope of world trade and the heightened power of international corporations, so our concepts need to be widened to bring us into contact with the kinds of experiences and phenomena we encounter in the contemporary 'polis'.

It may be the case that one reason why post-structuralism and related approaches have not had a wide or sustained influence on the discipline of politics, remaining confined to scattered and isolated marginal pockets, is that what they tend to look at, as well as how they look at it, is not regarded as properly political or properly the object of political study. It can appear as if post-structuralists are working on topics that do not fall within the purview of the discipline. Perhaps it is the unity of a discipline of politics that post-structuralism threatens and, if it does that, then it certainly also challenges the very idea of what politics is.

This introduction will focus on this question of what politics is, in general and for post-structuralism in particular, since such questioning, as we will show, is something that very broadly unites the body of thought labelled post-structuralism. We will begin with a general consideration of this issue and some of the elements of recent intellectual culture that have fed into it. We will then move on to a more detailed and abstract examination of the roots of post-structuralist philosophy in order to consider the relationship between language, politics, social structure and the idea of political agency. At the end of the introduction we will return to the conceptualisation of politics and argue that giving this dimension of society a certain primacy is central to the importance of post-structuralism for politics.

Post-structuralism and the Idea of Politics

The most significant and interesting currents within post-structuralism, when considered from the standpoint of political studies, are those involved with an ongoing engagement with the understanding and definition of politics itself. The demand that the scope and depth of politics be increased was crucial to the intellectual and social challenges of the 1960s. Most notably, the assertion by feminism that the personal is political formed part of an effort to politicise areas and activities hitherto considered private or simply facts of life – domestic labour, for example, rights and relationships within marriage, sexual activity, as well as our own personality and psychology. This has combined with an increasing recognition of the importance of ethnic identifications which highlighted the wide basis to social and political experience – the way relations of domination extend far beyond the official locations of authority and power.

Within the traditions of sociology and especially British cultural studies, it has been recognised that the ideological nature of contemporary culture must be understood if we are to make sense of and challenge relations of domination that constitute present societies. In part, such a realisation came out of debates within Marxism about the adequacy of a rigid 'base-super-structure' model of social explanation and an increased concern, notably in the work of Althusser, with the way ideological force creates our sense of who and what we are and that this does not so much mask the truth as cause it to appear. Other Marxists came to embrace a version of the work of the Italian

Marxist Antonio Gramsci and so lent greater weight to the sphere of culture as the location of hegemonic political struggles (seen especially in the work of Stuart Hall and the Birmingham Centre for Contemporary Cultural Studies). Such work necessitated a closer consideration of the place of language and communication in politics, the impact of the global expansion of a consumer, capitalist society and the mechanisms by which order is maintained when society seems to be simultaneously more homogenous and more diverse.

Despite their political basis, these ideas (in the Anglo-American context) were, at first, most influential in the humanities rather than the social sciences. They encouraged teachers of literature to politicise their subject and fostered a wealth of critical political study of, for example, film, music and television as well as investigations into the construction of sexuality, gender and the body. All of this represented a radical extension of the referent object of the term politics. In retrospect such an expansion appears to be part of a much longer process embedded in the very notions of enlightenment and democracy. Over centuries the remit of political activity has expanded and the numbers of those deemed capable of participating in politics has grown, usually as the result of radical demands for what is now known as recognition and exclusion but also for things that are now unfashionable such as a decent job, income and general security of existence.

But it is not, in the end, that helpful to simply extend the domain of politics to cover everything. If we do, we only delay the moment of reckoning when we have to, once again, make distinctions between things and try to understand what makes the political moment of a popular television pro-gramme not quite the same as that of an immigration officer detaining an asylum seeker, a protester throwing a brick at a bank or Members of Parlia-ment voting on the budget.

The meaning of 'politics' is usually obtained by specifying its location within a specific domain which modern liberal democracies still tend to contain within the parameters of territorial representation (primarily, but not exclusively, the nation). This domain generally has a public character or a public is constituted through it. It is visible for all to see and all may challenge acts of concealment that occur within it. Doing so is the exercise of the right of the individual citizen-voter and is aligned with a series of other rights through negotiation over their status and relative weight in particular circumstances. Indeed, politics is a name for the wide bartering between such rights and the interests of those individuals who possess them within a demarcated territory. Outside of this public process is the private activity of those individuals which is not a proper matter for political consideration.

From this traditional perspective, politics is largely a matter of the distri-bution or management of power, interests and resources. The sum of the practices of this distribution is usually referred to as the political system and is the object or concern of a political science. This body of knowledge is characterised by the aim of providing confirmation of the objectivity of the political system and has developed various procedures or methods for carrying out this task. These aspire to satisfy propositional criteria analogous to those that characterise the natural sciences – though with variable degrees of success. This is extended to those beliefs, ideas and values that animate these activities, although this generally occurs through some idealised and abstract account of political agents and their ideas. Politics is relegated to the status of a functional sub-system that has the task of regulating the system by which citizens may appear, in public, to each other. Politics is equated with governing through the creation of consent for a distribution of shares and a hierarchy of places and functions (Rancière 1992: 58).

But the authority and objectivity of this sort of political system, and its analysis, have been subjected to heavy criticism. The requirement that politics be a measurable activity, that is itself concerned with measures, cannot deal with the permanent failure of anything like a political object to emerge in a manner which would not in itself be subject to political dispute. Political study thus becomes suspect since it may be an activity based on the systematic mistaking of a process of rationalisation or technologisation for politics itself. It thus renders the ways in which this process is political in itself incompre-hensible and illegitimate, so serving to reinforce the naturalness of the status quo. Which is precisely what the existence of politics puts in question even if, and especially when, the status quo is reinforced by politics. It may be a defin-ing characteristic of modern societies that they appear to be divided into distinct and discrete spheres such that politics is not the same as those spheres designated as economic, juridical, military, civil, cultural and so forth. But how did this division itself come about? How was it instituted? Is it not the case that this very distribution is something that is political or is done by politics?

In classical thought the polis was the city and politics concerned itself with the affairs of the city. The classical works of political theory are not solely concerned with the organisation of the realm of offices but with the form of life they embody and which they in their turn cause to be embodied. They examined (as both Claude Lefort and Leo Strauss have pointed out) 'regimes' in the fullest and broadest sense of that term, as opposed to its contemporary restricted reference. Failing to grasp this aspect of the political, its founda-tional role in constituting the shape of a society and the way in which it distributes activities, persons and processes, naturalises modern liberal governance. In contrast, post-structuralist criticisms politicise politics. They see politics as an indeterminate object, the 'politicality' of which resides in the fact of this indeterminacy. If anything can be said to unite the otherwise diverse perspectives in this book it is this politicisation of politics – a commitment not to let the definition or location of politics be determined in advance and consequently to ask questions about how politics takes place and to see how our answers to these questions have political causes and effects.

That said, it is still incumbent upon us to offer a more general explanation of the broad theory of post-structuralism within which the contributions to the book are to be placed. For the purpose of introductory illumination, we can say that post-structuralism is concerned with the relationship between concepts of structure, language and the subject, or agent, and that it finds the stakes in this relationship to be the fundamentals of politics.

Language, Structure and Politics

Post-structuralism developed out of a series of questions directed at the structuralist account of language developed by Ferdinand de Saussure and his followers who had sought to generalise it into a model for the analysis of the structure of society and culture as a whole (Saussure, 1966; see also: Culler, 1983, 1985; Hawkes, 1977; Lechte, 1994; Sarup, 1993; Sturrock, 1979, 1993).

Saussure's theory concerned the conditions that make the experience of intelligibility or shared meaning possible and his central claim was that language is a systematic structure. Meaning, he argued, does not derive from the outside world it describes but from the system of language itself. Indeed, meaning is only possible because it derives from a system which exists prior to, and independently of, actual acts of speaking.

'Structure' thus refers to the totality of linguistic relations within which an act of language is made possible. Structure is the form of the system. It is enabling but also constraining at the same time. You can say things but you cannot say anything because what you say has to be understood by others who occupy the linguistic system. Structure is understood by Saussure in a *synchronic*, or static, way, distinguished from the temporal or *diachronic* dimension in which things may appear to change. For Saussure it is the synchronic aspect that matters. Of course, language has a history, but this is merely empirical and cannot be linked to the generalisable rules of the system which, alone, can be the object of a science of language.

What does this system consist of? The basic unit is the sign. Language is made up of signs such as the sounds made in the voice box when speaking or these black marks on the page which you are reading. These signs are combined with other signs (to make words and sentences such as this one). But the sign itself is the outcome of the combination of two elements. These are the *signifier*, the material aspect of the sign, its verbal or written form, and the *signified*, the concept or idea with which the *signifier* is associated. Crucially, for Saussure, the connection between these two elements – the word we use for a thing and the thing we mean by that word – is not necessary or natural. It is, as Saussure famously declared, *arbitrary*. The reason a word continues to mean the same thing over time, and is understood by all, has nothing to do with any intrinsic relationship between word and thing. It has to do with the structure and with the conventionality of its usage.

For example, there is no necessary relation between the word 'dog' and the thing with four legs and a tail which is pleased to see you when you come home from the pub. This is why we might refer to it as 'chien' or 'hund' if we are located within a different linguistic system. But, of course, if we did not use one of these words to talk about our dog then nobody would understand us. We are bound to use that word in order to make sense to others. In this sense there is a necessary connection between signifier and signified which means we do not normally notice this dimension of arbitrariness. That necessity is there because the signifier only acquires meaning from its being in relation to other signs. That is to say, the word 'dog' signifies the thing with four legs and a tail because it does not signify something else with four legs and a tail which ignores you unless it wants something – a 'cat'. The relationship that allows meaning to emerge is thus not positive but negative: dog means 'dog' because it does not mean 'cat'. For Saussure, language is a form, not a substance; it is a system structured by arbitrariness and negation.

These factors account for every instance in which language occurs or is used. That a speaker can refer to a dog does not have anything to do with any actual dog that may or may not be present. Meaning can only function precisely because of this separation. If we had a different word for every single dog, and no term to represent them all, communicating about dogs would be a lot harder. An actual dog can only be specified by the further use of signs, such as 'Rex', 'Fido', 'brown' or 'Walthamstow, Saturday, 4:30, 20/1, each way'. Here the act of communication is still contained within the system of language and the dog is specified through negation in as much as it is not 'Rover', 'grey' or 'Hackney, Wednesday, 6:15, 7/4, win'. An act of meaningful speech is the result of a process of selection according to the differential principle of language which Saussure understood in terms of categories with which to organise experience. The world does not organise itself or present itself to us with name tags on. When we refer to what something is in reality, we are actually relying on the system that allows our understanding of it. Normally, our reliance is so secure that we do not need to refer to it when we communicate, except in cases of misunderstandings that give rise to dispute. In fact, we are usually happily unaware of the reality of our communication to the extent that drawing attention to the nature of its existence is often judged to be unhelpful to its practice, rather like the view that belief in God declined as a consequence of the increase in proofs of his existence.

This philosophical diversion into the nature of meaning and the system of language may not appear to have anything of immediate relevance to politics (unless, perhaps, if you live in a land ruled by dogs – a caninocracy). But the link to politics does not require a very great leap. As we have seen, Saussure is interested in meaning, and the meanings with which we invest our social world are clearly of political significance, not least because meaning makes possible the distinction and distribution of value.

Language has always been understood as important to politics. For Aristotle, our capacity for speech differentiated us from other animals and made it possible for people to come to a common view of what was just or unjust. For the inhabitants of democratic Athens, the art of speech, or rhetoric, was central to the exercise of power or influence. Politics was about speaking well in the proper arenas and winning people over. Such a conception of politics implies an 'agent' – the something that makes something happen – and a place where this occurs. Politics occurs through a language deemed to be necessary, in a place specified as political in some way. A structuralist account might help us to understand how this works and how certain utterances are understood as political while others are not. We could, as some historians of political thought have done, examine how important texts, such as Machiavelli's *Prince* (Pocock, 1975 and 1989), Hobbes's *Leviathan* (Skinner, 1989) or Smith's *The Wealth of Nations* (Shapiro, 1993), emerge from and shape political thinking by reworking its language.

But to ask such questions in a rigidly structuralist manner raises questions about how it is that certain things are made to appear necessarily political and others are not and how that distinction is maintained. Since, for the structuralist, there is nothing intrinsic to language that makes one utterance political and another not these would seem like important questions. After all, we might want to change the language of politics. However, strictly speaking, on a structuralist account there can be no rational explanation for such divisions. It just is the case – the nature of the structure. Any explanation of how things got to be that way will be internal to the language of politics itself as it has been constituted at that moment in time. Furthermore, the structuralist claim that language is essentially arbitrary gives us no ultimate justification for any such change in the practice or understanding of politics. Any change would simply be an arbitrary effect which, if it could take place at all, could only do so because it was already a feature of the political language one wished to change in the first place. Our desire to change things would have been included from the start, given by the structural conditions of language within which we are imprisoned. This gives to structuralism a conservative and fatalistic bias that is not suited to making sense of the dynamism of political movement. Critics of structuralism call it 'the prison-house of language' (Jameson, 1972).

However, there is, for politics, an advance here in as much as the potential object of politics has been expanded. We can see how whatever is understood to count as a political act is conditioned by, and related to, the overall social or symbolic order. Indeed, Saussure's structural linguistics opened up a new way of understanding social or cultural structure as a whole, and of identifying the underlying forces and determinants that shape it.

A good example of this opening-up is the translation of anthropology into the terms of structural linguistics by Claude Lévi-Strauss (1997). He took

Saussure's insight that language and society are coextensive to its ultimate conclusion by abolishing the difference between them, arguing that society is structured in the same way as language. Social organisation is characterised by arbitrariness and negativity in the form of a series of fundamental binary oppositions, such as male and female, good and bad, and raw and cooked, which ensured the continuance of the structure by which social order was grounded. In other words, the structure reproduced relations of order and power. But such relations were understood as timeless and ahistorical as well as applicable to all societies, including Lévi-Strauss's own, irrespective of differences in content. For Lévi-Strauss and those influenced by him this structural element explained how societies could reproduce themselves over time and yet remain the same society. Systematic reproduction was the basis of social identity thus making it possible to recognise a particular society as distinct from any other society (or from nature). Again, this leads to a conservative and fatalistic bias, a search for the invariant features of social life that underlie the, only apparently shifting, surface.

Structuralism's theoretical integrity depends on the unchanging existence of its object, or structure as such; on the capacity of a symbolic system to determine acts of meaning and the functional organisation of society. Structuralism assumes that everything has its place and fits together. Social change is simply a matter of readjustment through which societies and their orderings are reproduced. At heart structuralism clings to the assumption that language and society are essentially ordered. The structuralist approach to politics thus broadens our understanding of the meaning and place of politics but then finds the change or transformations of things, to which politics tends, contained within an intrinsically ordered totality. It recognises that society is constituted in a particular way but that act of constitution is not itself thinkable because it is always already there. It is in the rejection of this a priori assumption of order that post-structuralist analysis (as well as the ethics and politics it implies) emerges.

Two Types of Post-structuralism

For post-structuralism the notion of a fundamentally static totality is an incorrect understanding of language and cannot constitute a basis from which to explain the relation between language and society or the symbolic order. But post-structuralism is not simply *anti*-structuralism. It is *post*-structuralism, moving on from its forebear and rejecting the notion of a fundamentally static totality, not simply on a whim or out of annoyance, but for logical reasons.

The ultimate target of post-structuralism is the unity of the symbolic order. It rejects the idea that structures are self-generating or *autopoietic*. But this demands an alternative answer to the question of how structures come to be in the first place. The novelty of post-structuralism lies in the fact that, rather than develop an alternative theory of origin (a metaphysics to explain where everything that is came from), it deals with the problem by raising a different sort of question. Rather than ask why and how there is stability to social systems, it asks why and how structures become undone. This leads to a concern, not with the origin of structures, but with their incompletion.

This approach to the incompletion of structure has given rise to two political positions associated with two types of objection to the assumption of an order to structure. These are often conflated and it is important to distinguish between them. That said, these positions are not always explicitly opposed (both are represented in this book) and our description represents distinctions of difference rather than absolute opposition.

The first of these positions objects to the assumption of structural unity on what are essentially ethical and aesthetic grounds. Structural determinism is morally wrong, a negation of individual freedom which is exemplified by individual creative acts that escape the repetition and reproduction of determinism. This does not falsify the assumption of totality but simply opposes it in the name of asynchronicity and fragmentation. In the fields of politics and culture it elevates rupture, novelty and revolution. But, in so opposing totality, this sort of claim cannot help but reproduce it. Fragmentation makes no sense without its opposite, so we become caught in a strange game of wanting that which oppresses us in order to experience freedom. This position seems to say 'we oppose structures because they exist' and is both arbitrary and impulsive (The classic formulation of this position remains Kristeva (1975; 1998). The most influential translation of this approach into political thought was undertaken by Coward and Ellis (1977.))

Advocates of the ethical-aesthetic values of difference and otherness would, of course, reject such a 'dialectical' objection. They might claim that rupture is external to the totality. It is that which cannot be said or accounted for within the terms of the totality. This leads to an a priori valorisation of that presumed to be exotic and 'other' which is taken to be inherently transgressive and progressive. But the presumption that a position external to structural totality exists is precisely what has to be demonstrated. Besides, if such a place 'outside' does exist already then the determining totality is clearly no such thing and it is not obvious what the aesthete is opposed to, if, indeed, anything at all.

However, it is possible to object to the notion of synchronic-totality on empirical-logical grounds and this is our second form of post-structuralism. Rather than assert the existence of a position external to totality we can ask more about the principle by which a totality is established or accounted for. We can examine how the existence of structure is verified and with which rule or fact this is done. For example, metaphysicians have often had recourse to some extra-real (and hypothetical) phenomenon to account for the origins or point of determination of their theoretical systems. They have come up with prime or unmoved movers (a code word for God), while in politics they have invented mythic figures such as Rousseau's lawgiver or fictional events such as the social contract. In each case, something that is not the structure is given as its empirical cause or logical ground and then re-incorporated within the structure as part of the structure itself. If the principle by which a structure (be it that of language or a social formation) is founded and verified is to be located outside the totality, then it is not a totality and we are back to theology. If it is within the structure, then this means there is something contained within a set of differential relations that is not itself subject to that principle of differentiation. It is thus simultaneously internal and external and the identity of the structure is based on a contradiction. Once again, the structure does not exist (at least not by itself and it cannot account for itself in its own terms).

This is why structural theories, such as some forms of Marxism, become caught in a bind of asserting the economic determination of society at the same time as advocating a radical overthrow of that economic structure by people inside it. Thus they ended up advocating either a 'spontaneous' outbreak of revolt by some radically excluded force or takeover by an elite vanguard in possession of the truth of history. But what if we pursue the logic of structures that can only be presumed to exist on the basis of a violation of their own principles? Here the determining effects of structures are preserved (so avoiding the lapse into the naive voluntarism of ethical-aesthetic objections to structure) but the determination of structure itself is found to be intrinsically indeterminate. Structure is thus not simply rejected or opposed, nor is it falsified by the positing of an alternative ontology. Rather it is turned against itself and found to be, in the jargon, 'undecidable' (not completely inside but not completely outside either, not either/or but both/and). Only in this way can we prevent a lapse back into metaphysics while remaining logical.

This line of critique is known as deconstruction and is associated with the work of Jacques Derrida (1974). Derrida's work is known for posing these problems in the form of paradoxical riddles, such as the question 'Is a window on the outside of a building, or the inside?'. But once the structural nature of a structure is found to be 'undecidable' what becomes of the elements of which the totality was formerly comprised? Contrary to the fears and hopes of many, the undecidability of structure does not entail the terror or freedom of chaos. The sky does not fall down. It does not entail that words will cease to mean anything and communication will come to an end. Rather, undecidability becomes understood as a property of the elements themselves and we are forced to move from a logic of either/or to one that recognises the reality of phenomena that are both/and. This means that we are not faced, as social theorists, with a choice between either rational structural determinism or irrational random events. No event is un-conditioned but there is no absolute conditioning origin (whatever religious sentiment or the self-aggrandisement of artists might demand). This is of capital importance when we think about (or do) politics.

Politics and Post-structuralism

In the field of politics, post-structuralism helps us see how futile it is to pose political issues in terms of either conservation or innovation, of budgetary procedure or revolution, of Burke versus Marx. This is not to say that we simply pick the middle or 'third' way between all extremes. Rather it is to see that these oppositions are themselves part of a wider structure within which all positions must be questioned. In social theory more generally, we come to the question of the relation between structure and agency (in structuralist terms, between language and speech) and we do not have to choose between either. This might lead us to endorse a sociological position in which (in the manner of someone such as Giddens) structure and agent are mutually embedded, the activities of the latter determined by the former but simultaneously reworked in a 'recursive' fashion (see, for example, Giddens 1984; 1990). Such a position runs the risk of falling into a permanent oscillation between the two poles. But, for post-structuralism, as we argued above, it is not only the relationship between structure and agent that is 'undecidable'. The structure and the agent are too. This means, in distinction to something such as Giddens's notion of structuration, we cannot think of the 'agent' as a self-possessed entity acting in response to and upon a structure of social action, since what that agent is is already part of the structure which, being indeterminate, is not itself able to fully determine that subject.

The political space of post-structuralism is less a matter of either/or and more a matter of both/and. Arguably, this rubric describes the political space of postmodernity where, for example, we can find fundamentalist democrats and even democratic fundamentalists. In political science, notions such as 'New Public Management' and concepts from organisation theory such as the 'change agent' (Buchanan and Badham, 1999) are empirical confirmations of the undecidability of structure and agency. Indeed, the notion of *governance* is the name of the response of established political structures to precisely such circumstances. Here we understand the activity of rule, not in terms of the activity of power emanating from a singular, recognised source, but as a practice that operates throughout the social attempting to fix norms, rules, behaviours and so forth, to fix subjects through their very subjectivation in contexts which are constantly changing and conflictual. As Rose puts it:

> Governance directs attention to the nature, problems, means, actions, manners, techniques and objects by which actors place themselves under the control, guidance, sway and mastery of others, or seek to place other actors, organisations, entities or events under their own sway. (Rose, 1999: 16)

Post-structuralism, then, represents an attempt to grapple with and to make sense of the changing operations of power across the field of the social. It does not see politics as something confined to discrete locations but, rather, believes the act of rendering practices, processes or phenomena as political, or not, to be the quintessentially political act. As such, it gives a certain primacy to the political. This is because, in refusing to treat either agents or structures as closed, self-determining, autonomous or unconditioned, at the same time as refusing to make them capable of mutually conditioning each other, post-structuralism leaves them 'undecidable'. Yet decisions are taken and it is this moment of decision that is the moment of the political – the act of leaping one way or the other, of attempting to reassemble elements of the social field into new formations.

But this, in itself, does not represent an answer to the nature of contemporary politics. Rather it produces a terrain of investigation and a new series of questions to be explored. We can continue to ask about the 'who', 'what' and 'where' of politics. Philosophers need not worry as the question 'why' is still to be asked. But to this we add 'how'. How is it that certain things come about in political thought and practice? How is it made possible for political actors to regard themselves and their actions in particular ways? How does politics act on us just as we act in its name and how does it make us what we are and are not? These questions lead to answers that, as ever, necessitate yet more questions. This commitment to the incomplete nature of the task of politics and political analysis is central to post-structuralism.

About This Book

In one way or another, all the contributors to this collection address the location of politics within the field of post-structuralism. The field is divided into four parts.

Part I, 'Politics and the Subject', develops the notion of the subject and especially the Lacanian problematic. In her essay 'The Subject and Subjectivity', Caroline Williams excavates the assumptions concerning the subject that underpin and inform much political theory and analysis. In particular, Williams shows how the post-structuralist critique of these assumptions does not throw agency out of the window but, instead, proposes different and more credible ways of thinking the subject. Subjects are not so much things either determined or determining, but more effects of forces that are always open-ended. Continuing Williams's introduction to the place of the subject within the field of structuralist and post-structuralist thought, Jeremy Valentine considers the precise political dimension of the category of the subject. Following Balibar's location of this dimension within the paradoxical structure of the subject, Valentine examines the relation between the subject and political modernity in the ideas of Descartes and Hobbes. Using Benveniste's account of the linguistic subject, Valentine describes how this political dimension functions in Lacan's theory of the subject. On this basis, Valentine criticises Lacan's account because of its ambivalent relation to modernity. Specifically, for Lacan, modernity undermined the symbolic order on which his account of the subject rests. The chapter concludes with a discussion of the nature of political modernity in a context characterised in terms of the absence of a symbolic structure that would support the political subject.

In his essay 'The State and Sovereign Subjectivity', James Martin looks at this process from the opposite perspective, analysing the closure of the subject in the material form of state sovereignty as a source of both agency and legitimacy. International relations provides a particularly a-critical account of this process and is predisposed to take the state at face value. Typically, the notion of the state as last line of defence against internal or external anarchy is read as a cause rather than a symptom. Hence the personal tone of the legal systems over which states preside and the equivalence between sovereignty, autonomy and agency that states affirm. As an alternative, Martin draws on Laclau and Mouffe's theory of hegemony in order to understand the state as a fluid and dynamic process concerned with projects of stabilisation, as distinct from the reflection of a stabilised subject which the state otherwise appears to be.

Continuing Martin's critique of international relations, Jenny Edkins, in her essay 'After the Subject of International Security', argues that the critique of the state is not the end but the beginning of the matter. After all, the state is one form of response to the development of securitisation, a process that is both empirical and normative. Importantly, the field of this process is constantly expanding such that any domain – or 'object' – can be subject to it. Drawing on Lacan in particular, Edkins locates the origins of this process in an absence of security rather than a threat from some other and external source. In other words, securitisation is founded on the trauma of absence. However, the solution to this problem is not simple resignation and relativism. Rather, Edkins proposes making security more difficult to achieve, requiring decisions in particular cases and an acknowledgement of responsibility. In other words, security is not an expert decision but rather a political moment which requires the democratisation of risk and responsibility.

In Part Two, 'Doing Political Analysis', the contributors show the application of post-structuralism to the empirically rich world of real politics. In his essay 'Ungrounding the Party: The case of the FN', Steve Bastow examines the activity of a core component of modern politics, the party. In this case, Bastow looks at the French far-right Front Nationale. While it is usual for party analysis to explain party activity in terms of its members' and supporters' ideological commitments, in the case of the FN these are varied, conflicted and far from consistent. The FN operates a fluid, dynamic and opportunistic 'strategy of ambiguity' which is imposed by the conditions of the French political system in which it operates. One consequence of this is the almost comical rivalries of the core FN leadership. Yet, behind the buffoonery of the FN, Bastow makes a more serious point. Labelling the FN as fascist, for example, imposes a unity on the party that it does not possess. Rather, these characteristics are more accurately understood as properties of the French party system in which it operates. To use structuralist jargon, the FN is *overdetermined*. Therefore, if such fascistic tendencies are to be denied the veneer of parliamentary legitimacy, then it is this operative context that has to be addressed strategically.

Assumptions about the ideational dimension of politics are also examined in Stephen Griggs and David Howarth's 'The Work of Ideas and Interests in Public Policy'. In particular, Griggs and Howarth are concerned with the so-called 'decision-making process' in public policy, a matter of importance for the contemporary democratic polity. Normally, this is explained as a matter of either individual calculations of advantage or as the effects of institutional and organisational constraints. If this is the case, then the democratic character of policy is tarnished by the opposition between agency and determinism. Policy constitutes a limit of democracy and not a mechanism of its implementation. Griggs and Howarth begin to overcome these limits by distinguishing between decisions within structures and decisions about those structures. The former are largely a matter of repetition but the latter occur in response to systemic crisis. Here signification – or, more precisely, the manner in which meanings (signifieds) are produced through articulations – is what matters. On this basis, Griggs and Howarth argue that the interests of agents are constructed by the context in which a decision is to be made. Political 'ideas' make sense of a situation and, in so doing, define the interests of the agents concerned.

Glyn Daly, in his essay 'Globalisation and the Constitution of Political Economy', examines how the constitution of social and economic processes takes place within the political domain. Following Laclau and Mouffe, Daly takes issue with the property of inevitability usually attributed to the economy – the sense that the economy proceeds all by itself. For Daly, this attribution renders the economy *autopoietic*, as if the economy simply makes itself out of what it is. Here a constant self-making is the location of agency. Daly argues that this view neglects the priority of the political in the constitution of economic subjectivity, or the ways in which the economy only persists by virtue of a political supplement at precisely those points where the economy has no resources to draw on. Strictly speaking, *autopoiesis* is only intelligible with this supplementary dimension. This political supplement is particularly visible in the contemporary discourse of globalisation which tries to square the is/ought circle between 'this is what will happen' and 'we must make this happen'.

How agents make sense of situations is the question addressed by Will Medd's essay 'Complexity in the Wild: Action in local welfare'. Although conventional political scientists often pride themselves on the accuracy of their descriptions of political activity, by relying on assumptions about the nature of both agents and structures, this sense of achievement is misplaced.

As Medd shows, acting is more a matter of uncertainty within conditions characterised by mobility and change, the principles of which are, from a practical point of view, unknown. Taking agency in a local welfare administration as an example, Medd reconstructs the process in which a narrative of uncertainty produces outcomes. To do so, Medd takes an ethnographic approach. Although no political scientist would claim that politics corresponds to the way that she/he describes it, ethnography enjoys the advantage of including the process of description within the description itself.

Paul Hayne's essay 'Political Science and Complexity' develops some of the issues raised by Medd's discussion of complexity. As recent work in science has redescribed systems in terms of their 'complexity', does this mean that these descriptions should be imitated by political thought and analysis in order to support its scientific credentials? To consider this question, Haynes returns to the emergence of modern political science in the dispute between Hobbes and Boyle over the relation between experience and authority. Although Hobbes appeared to support authority, he, in fact, advocated the socially embedded nature of knowledge and the political relations that stem from this. This raises the question of the relation between the political scientist and the object of that science – namely, politics. As the name suggests, complexity theory makes this issue more complex as it incorporates the observer of the system within the system itself. As a post-structuralist approach to politics locates politics within the question of the existence of systems, then the application of complexity theory can only proceed when this critical moment is located in the system's description.

Part Three, 'Critique and Political Thought', is concerned with the importance of political thought in the context of post-structuralism. While some thinkers have advocated withdrawing from the practice of criticism in light of its corrosive effects on fragile and hard won political forms, others criticise post-structuralism for not being critical enough in its alleged failure to produce new political forms ready made for implementation. The contributors to this section avoid this traditional opposition between agreement and rupture that has determined the value and nature of political thought. As initial proof of this point Alan Finlayson, in his essay 'The Horizon of Community', considers the possibilities that arise from the ambivalence of the concept of community. In political thought, the tendency has been to assume community as a fact in which its mythical status as limit is inscribed. Rather than critically dismiss community as an ideological chimera, Finlayson excavates the genealogy of the concept in order to overcome these limits. This is particularly important, given the traditional claims made for the inclusiveness of community. Such claims are always a matter of self-definition which entail exclusion of all that the community is opposed to. It is in this moment of agency that the community is constituted. If this therefore means that community rests on nothing, in what ways is community possible? Finlayson argues that the perspective of politics should shift to the contingency of community itself, and thus to the random facts of being together.

One of the major criticisms of post-structuralism is that it has abandoned the Enlightenment values that would give some substance to critical force it claims for itself. In his essay 'Critical Theory and Democracy', Mark Devenney argues that the criticism of post-structuralism for the abandonment of Enlightenment values is misplaced. In particular, Devenney examines the key modern equivalence of autonomy, sovereignty and authority as states of being that political subjects should aspire to. The problem is that these are not values susceptible to verification or definition and it is thus of the order of a 'category mistake' to seek to do so. Rather, these values are immanent to a project without guarantees or 'warrant'. There is nothing inevitable about it. Thus, to assume the natural or necessary status of such values undermines the chances of their materialisation. In practice, such values can be material-ised precisely because of their undecidability. Indeed, following Laclau, Devenney argues that the universalisation of such values is a consequence of their undecidability. After all, if such values are inherently universal, there would not be a problem in the first place and everyone would be sufficiently satisfied. Thus Enlightenment values cannot be divorced from the political task of implementation.

Robert Porter, in his essay 'The Singularity of the Political', locates this moment in political practice. Contrary to popular belief, this state of affairs does not entail collapse of all social guarantees. While it is not routine, it is nevertheless a central part of political life. Following the philosophers Giles Deleuze and Felix Guattari, Porter argues that the critical political moment arises because of the conceptual resources through which agents understand and have access to political reality. This does not entail repetition but inven-tion or, rather, an improvisation within these concepts. Invention is the singularity of politics in the sense that politics proceeds through the invention of singular cases which cannot be comprehended by concepts. Porter discusses the example of human rights law to illustrate this point. Ultimately, however, these practices depend on a responsibility to desire that which will bring forth the political.

Finally, Michael J. Shapiro addresses the constitutive dimension of expression in political thought. In the essay 'Genres, Technologies and Spaces of Being in Common', he considers the limits of political thought as a genre. This is not to say that political thought can be dismissed as merely literary. Rather, the conventions of the genre prohibit any effective engagement with the terrain it addresses. Political thought becomes normative through avoid-ance and closure. On this basis, Shapiro reverses the problem by discovering the political within other genre forms, notably popular and filmic ones. This approach opens up new possibilities of how we understand film politically by virtue of the properties of film as a technology.

In total these essays, appropriately enough, do not add up to a unified or completed totality. It will not be hard for readers to find differences of opinion and even contradictions between the chapters. This introduction has been markedly 'Derridean' in approach but some of the contributors are quite opposed to this and favour analyses derived from Lacanian psychoanalysis. Other chapters reject both Derrida and Lacan and stress the insights of Foucault or Deleuze. Nevertheless, we are all 'fellow travellers' of the impure roads of contemporary politics. It is hoped that readers will be stimulated to find their own ways through this book and on to those roads.

PART ONE

Politics and the Subject

1

The Subject and Subjectivity

CAROLINE WILLIAMS

Introduction

The question of the status, function and meaning of the subject within theoretical discourse is a problem which has preoccupied philosophers and political theorists for centuries. For the former, the status of knowledge, truth and, indeed, the form of human existence are paramount and all are interwoven with the question of the subject. For the latter, the status of the social contract, the precise ground of freedom, its limits and the origin of political transformation are opened up by posing this insuperable question concerning the status and the function of the subject.

The concept of the subject is a deeply political one whether we are considering its philosophical or political significance. Post-structuralist thought recognises the way in which the philosophical and the political are folded into one another. Conceptual problems which appear to be political in form (for example, the problem of the subject's agency) always rely on philosophical foundations which must be examined carefully. Likewise, conceptual concerns which appear to be dislocated from politics will always have a political resonance. This must be rooted out and its assumptions interrogated. Hence, post-structuralists' reflections on the question of the subject always imbue the concept with a political sense. Indeed, it will be argued here that a regard for the concept of the subject unifies the diverse body of thinking which falls under the banner of post-structuralism. Furthermore, it is through this effort to dislocate and challenge the dominant liberal motif of subjectivity that political theory receives its strongest challenge.

A cursory glance at some of the central problems encountered within modern political thought reveals its central regard for the question of the subject. From the social contract theory of Hobbes, Locke and Kant, to its contemporary presentation in the work of John Rawls, there is a dominant presupposition that the subject is a self-contained, unencumbered, rational and a priori entity who performs a voluntary act of political contract. For each of these political philosophers, an account of the subject's human nature, or sense of moral outlook, is a determining factor. In other words, a theory of human nature, a theory of the essential, original capacities of the human subject, becomes the ordering principle of political systems and institutions, inaugurating the very possibility of social contract. For liberal thinkers in particular, this ontology of human essence or nature also gives rise to a notion of free will and individual sovereignty which, in turn, underscores the liberal conception of freedom. Here, freedom is understood as the conscious and voluntary *potentia* of the subject acting without external impediment. The subject's freedom, we might say, is reflected in its status as sovereign power-holder. Indeed, liberalism shares this foundation view of the subject as original, rational actor with many other political discourses, including behaviourism, empiricism and forms of positivism (see, for example, Ball, 1976).

Radical political thought since Marx has emphasised the limits of this conception of an atomised, contained subject which ignores the latter's socio-economic formation and, for some, its determination by external forces. In post-structuralism, this interrogation of the subject is deepened and the problem of the subject is brought into fresh relief. For Althusser, Foucault, Derrida and Lacan, the subject must be situated in relation to ideology, discourse, power, language and the unconscious. Each of these conceptual fields offers the means to reposition the subject and to raise important epistemological and political questions. For post-structuralism, it is the production of subjectivity and the way(s) in which the subject is dislocated and repositioned which is important. As we shall see in the various presentations of post-structuralism below, the subject cannot be assigned either origin or essence and thus must lose its status as sovereign power and source of knowledge. However, it is sometimes claimed (somewhat superficially) that post-structuralism deprives the subject of its source of agency and its capacity for self-determination. Such critics insist upon the 'death of the subject' in post-structuralism and it is their voices which have often deadened discussions of the political implications of the challenge posed by the post-structuralist critique of the subject.

This chapter explores the specific challenge posed by post-structuralism to the concept of the subject. We shall examine a number of different constructions of the subject in the writings of Althusser, Foucault, Lacan and Derrida, as well as considering some of the ways in which these formulations have been utilised creatively by contemporary political theorists. The course of our analyses will further indicate the shortcomings of reactionary positions which announce the dissolution of the subject and illustrate how their conclusions appear somewhat hasty and misguided. It is clear that post-structuralist thinkers, whatever their particular perspective, by no means abandon the concept of the subject. Rather, they infuse the subject with new meanings and new theoretical possibilities. However, there remains a para-dox in employing the concept of the subject *after* its radical appraisal because the subject is at once a requirement of political analysis *and* something which is radically displaced. This paradox inevitably throws up problems for those trying to analyse its significance. The conclusion of this chapter will examine the implication of the paradox of the subject which is both epistemological and political in form. Let us first turn to the challenge of post-structuralism.

Post-structuralism and the Subject

It is almost impossible to categorise or define post-structuralism because it embraces such a diversity of thinkers who adopt markedly different positions upon the concept of the subject. For example, whilst the writings of Louis Althusser take their primary point of reference from a reading and development of Marx, those of Jacques Derrida may appear, at least on a first reading, to be rather marginal to politics and to political theory. Similarly, the work of Jacques Lacan is essentially of a psychoanalytic form, whilst the writings of Michel Foucault are strongly opposed to what he views as the subjugation and insidious control engendered by psychoanalytic forms of knowledge. Furthermore, it is not only the multiplicity of positions that distinguishes these writers and stalls any easy rendering of post-structuralism. Both Lacan and Althusser *could* be labelled as structuralists, and Derrida and Foucault as post-structuralists. On the other hand, Derrida's early work *Of Grammatology* (1974) is often considered to be a structuralist text, as is Michel Foucault's seminal work *The Order of Things* (1974). To make matters more complicated, Foucault was a student of Althusser and, in one of his many interviews, has noted the importance of his discovery of Lacan's work in the 1950s. Althusser likewise exchanged correspondence with Lacan and invited him to teach at the *Ecole Normale* in Paris. Derrida has also engaged with the writings of all of the aforementioned thinkers and has given testimony to their effects upon his own work. These similarities caution against an overly simple characterisation of one or other of these thinkers as structuralist or post-structuralist. Such classification can only take place retrospectively and it may exclude thinkers who offer important resources for the critique of the subject. Each of the thinkers considered here can be located in the same temporal, historical and intellectual space. It is the mode of questioning of, and preoccupation with, the concept of the subject which unifies these thinkers. What does it mean for the subject to be constructed according to certain presuppositions rather than others? What, moreover, are the philosophical and political effects (and costs) of the constructions of the concept of the subject? These are the questions which interest post-structuralists. Let us examine their particular positions in greater detail.

Louis Althusser: Subjectivity and Ideology

Louis Althusser is best known through his 1966 collaboration with Etienne Balibar, *Reading Capital*. This book claimed to provide a scientific basis for

Marxist theory by breaking with all forms of historicism and empiricism, and with all conceptions of the subject. Althusser's project, in his own words, was 'to draw a line of demarcation between Marxist theory and the forms of philosophical (and political) subjectivism which have compromised or threatened it' (Althusser, 1990: 12). Althusser aimed to read Marx, as Lacan would also read Freud, *symptomatically*, that is, beneath the letter of the text, in order to recover the scientific foundation of Marx's theory which had become shrouded by a latent anthropologism of the subject. One of the central arguments of *Reading Capital* is that historicist and empiricist methods of enquiry both rely upon certain categories of thought, perception and consciousness to motivate and engender their analyses. For such methods, it is the knowing and perceiving subject who identifies the object, or the concrete real, as a form of self-knowledge. It is this idealist principle of subjectivity that Althusser's structuralism will deem ideological and resolutely seek to displace. However, if *Reading Capital* strove to eliminate the phantasm of the ideological subject from the structure of knowledge, Althusser's 1972 essay 'Ideology and Ideological State Apparatuses' (see Althusser, 1984) continued to theorise the construction of the ideological subject.

Althusser's rejection of the subject as the foundation, origin, or essence of a theoretical concept precludes him from establishing an overly simplistic account of ideology as false-consciousness where the subject's experience becomes the source of knowledge necessary to transcend ideology. Likewise, his critique of empiricism obviates against a definition of ideology as an inversion, or as a mystification of the real, as presented by the metaphor of the *camera obscura* in Marx's and Engel's *The German Ideology* (see McClellan, 1988: 164). Althusser is not concerned with investigating what particular subjects may think, or even how, by what means, they carry out the act of thinking. Rather, he is concerned with the *ideological mechanism* according to which thought, perception and subjectivity are *produced*. If this is the function of ideology, how is this function expatiated?

The function of ideology, argues Althusser, is to reproduce the relations of production, to ensure that individuals are constituted as subjects ready to take up their allocated position within the social structure. To this end, ideology operates principally through Ideological State Apparatuses (ISAs), which include institutions like the church, school, family, political parties and so on. The Repressive State Apparatuses (RSAs) secure, by force where necessary, the conditions for the reproduction of the relations of production, and hence the conditions for the actions of the ISAs. For Althusser, ideology is a relatively autonomous level in the structural totality which can act to maintain the economic system by securing certain forms of dominant subjectivity. Giving the example of religion, Althusser notes the modalities of kneeling, the discourse of prayer, the sign of the cross and the gaze of the Absolute, all of which insert the subject into the materiality of religious ideology. These ideological practices work not only to tame and discipline consciousness, but also to normalise and subjugate the body according to certain models of behaviour. Hence Althusser's emphasis not only upon the noun, but also upon the verb 'to subject'. The essay on ideology plays upon these linguistic distinctions (Althusser, 1984: 51–7) with an attention to discipline and subjection that anticipates Foucault's conception of the subject in significant ways.

How does Althusser account for the constitution of the subject by ideology? He claims that ideology *interpellates* individuals as subjects. This is the structure of recognition by which the concrete individual finds a place as a particular kind of social subject. Interpellation performs a vital function of identification, enabling subjects to recognise themselves in the dominant ideology. That such a structure of recognition remains on the level of *misrecognition* is a necessary prerequisite for the subject to acquire consciousness, belief and the possibility of action. If, as Althusser famously writes, 'ideology represents the *imaginary* relation of individuals to their real conditions of existence' (Althusser, 1984: 36), this subject lives, forever misrecognised, in the imaginary realm of ideology.

It is clear that Althusser's conception of the subject as an effect of ideology performs an important theoretical manoeuvre by contesting the autonomy of the subject, drawing attention to the subjection of the subject and departing from it as the primary unit of theoretical analysis. Indeed, it is the virtue of Althusser's work to have theorised this system of dominance which was to have such analytic importance in cultural, gender and film studies, as well as social and political theory more generally. However, there are a number of shortcomings in Althusser's position, some of which may be encountered and reframed in the writings of Foucault, Lacan and Derrida below. The most repeated criticism levelled at this ideological formulation is that the constitution of the subject as subjected being is absolute. Whilst it is apparent that Althusser wishes to protect his analysis from the risks of subjectivism, this anti-humanist gesture stops short of an analysis of exactly how material practices constitute particular forms of subjectivity, that is, the degree to which ISAs *succeed* in their task of normalising and disciplining individuals (see Žížek, 1989). Is the subject a tabula rasa or could it be an unstable being who can never be fully brought under the sway of ideology? Althusser seems to presume rather than interrogate the sense in which the process of interpellation must be continuous if it is to produce and maintain a self-disciplining subject (see Hirst, 1976). This is precisely where Foucault's theorisation of the subject in relation to power may be of some assistance. Whereas Althusser pushes the problem of the internalisation of ideology to one side, preferring to consider the mechanism of interpellation as an imaginary form of recognition, Foucault continues the focus on the physical processes of subjection, the way in which the subject inscribes within itself the principle of subjection, and the body as a transmogrifying site of disciplinary power.

Michel Foucault: Discourse, Power and Subjection

In a response to the question of the centrality of the subject in his writings Foucault stated his concern to be with the relations and forces which constitute the subject rather than with an autonomous subject whose reason and agency constitutes knowledge and endows the world with meaning: 'one has to dispense with the constituent subject, to get rid of the subject itself ... in order to arrive at an analysis which can account for the constitution of the subject within an historical framework' (Foucault, 1980: 117). Foucault is interested in what engenders, shapes and modifies the subject. The objective of his writings is to trace the conditions which have given rise to the subject in the interrelated spheres of knowledge and politics.

Foucault's early works, particularly *The Order of Things* (1974) and *The Archaeology of Knowledge* (1972), reflect an interest in the discursive construction of the subject. Here, discourse is not reducible to speech, nor is it amenable to distinctions between theory and reality. Discourse does not just 'get to work' on the real. It constructs the real as a discursive entity. When Foucault writes of the discursive construction of the subject, he is concerned with the strategic, epistemological relations between language and the classification and representation of objects within knowledge. No longer the author or the origin of discourse, the subject is the object of discursive analysis. How is it, Foucault asks, that, at a particular juncture in time and space, the subject took itself as the object of knowledge? What epistemological transformations underscored the birth of the subject? *The Order of Things* isolates the conditions of possibility for the modern form of discourse which takes the human subject as its centre. It identifies those events in knowledge which push the structure of representation into crisis because they can no longer be fixed by relations of analogy and symmetry. As the possibility of deception emerges into the sphere of language, so too does the possibility of grounding and understanding human experience. As Foucault notes, 'representation has lost the power to provide a foundation – with its own being, its own deployment and its power of doubling over on itself – for the links that can join its various elements together' (Foucault, 1991: 238–9). It is this epistemological crisis which marks the promulgation of the modern age. Cut loose from its place within the order of things, the subject is engendered as a new, finite and uncertain being who must search the realm of knowledge for meaning and self-understanding. In the modern age the subject becomes both *subject* and *object* of knowledge but its contingent status causes the rational basis of knowledge to falter and implode. If it is this insecure entry on to the modern stage of knowledge that inspired the Kantian critical system, then, for Foucault, all of the human sciences are preoccupied with this problem of understanding and gaining meaning of the subject. From phenomenology to psychoanalysis, modern knowledge seeks to discover and name those realms of subjective existence (the unconscious, the un-thought, the body) which can elucidate and give meaning to the subject.

According to Foucault, it is discourse that offers the means to analyse the construction of the subject without seeking out a knowledge of the subject which draws on some plane of interiority. Like Althusser before him, Foucault's quest is to make knowledge autonomous of subjective experience. The subject is shorn of its a priori status as origin of knowledge. Rather, the concept of the subject can be broached only by exploring the pre-conceptual level of discursive rules which allow something *called* a subject to be gathered together as a speaking and thinking being. *The Archaeology of Knowledge* examines how the rules and statements governing discourse offer certain possibilities for concept-formation, for enunciation, for truth and, indeed, for certain *subject-positions* within discourse. Clearly, the subject does not simply *disappear* in Foucault's discursive analysis. Rather, its determinant status and epistemological power is put into question.

If the concern in Foucault's early work is with the difficult relation between subjectivity and knowledge, in his later writings, particularly *Discipline and Punish* (1977), he turns his attention to those relations of power which produce forms of subjectivity and seek to contain and tame the subject through techniques of normalisation. It is not that the study of discourse loses its importance, but that the bond between power, knowledge, truth and subjectivity, previously explored by Nietzsche, is brought into sharper focus. *The Archaeology of Knowledge* and *Discipline and Punish* complement each other because the modern technology of power is inseparable from the regime of modern knowledge, characterised by the practices and possibilities of discourse. The insidious contract of power with truth and knowledge institutes a domain in which the subject is situated and on which it is dependent. Foucault rejects every theory of power which begins with the state, reducing the multiplicity of ways in which the subject's subjugation is achieved. For Foucault, power is not a capacity or possession of subjects, as liberal political thought presupposes; it is a strategic relation. Mobile, fluid and continuous, power invests institutions and subjects with possibilities for action. It is never stationary, but 'always already there', caught up in a matrix of forces which create lines of division, relations of oppression and exclusion, codes of discipline and sites of subjection.

Drawing upon the human sciences, Foucault illustrates the ways in which power individualises, classifies and manipulates the body according to certain precepts of knowledge. He utilises Bentham's model of the panopticon as a figure of the political technology of power (see the discussions in Foucault, 1977, and Deleuze, 1988). The panopticon is a disciplinary space, a material construct of power, which offers up its functions as a means to create economy, efficiency and effectiveness and, more significantly, docility, on the part of those subjects who become its investment. The objectifying gaze of the

panopticon acts as a guise of continuous surveillance, leading the subject to
regulate behaviour automatically:

> He who is subjected to a field of visibility and who *knows* it, assumes a respon-
> sibility for the constraints of power; he makes them play spontaneously upon
> himself: he inscribes in himself the power-relation in which he simultaneously
> plays both roles: he becomes the principle of his own subjection. (Foucault, 1977:
> 203–4)

In this way, not only is the subject constructed by forces and relations of
power, it also participates in its own subjection. This analysis marks an
important development in the construction of the subject, which has an
important psychoanalytic resonance (see Butler, 1998). Nevertheless, the
philosopher of discourse does not probe some opaque interiority of subjectivity in the manner of the human sciences because the space of interiority
is something which is carved out of the subject by power. This is why, for
Foucault, psychoanalysis, as a human science, is doomed from the start.

If both the subject and the possibility of resistance and transgression (be
it conscious or unconscious) appear to inhere in power, is there a way of
understanding the subject as a site of struggle that may exceed or disrupt the
lines of power that seem to constitute it? Here we return to some of the
problems posed by Althusser's theory of the subject of ideology. Does
Foucault underestimate the extent to which power's investment of the body
itself requires psychic expenditure on the part of the subject? Is it such a
passive recipient of power or is it a source of volatility, an unfinished project
of social being that power can seek to master but never contain? These
questions will be considered briefly below. But, first, let us turn to Lacan's
construction of the subject.

Jacques Lacan: Imaginary Subjects and Symbolic Signifiers

Lacan's conception of the subject is particularly interesting for its attempt to
enjoin psychoanalysis with linguistics. For Lacan and Derrida too (see below),
language and subjectivity are intrinsically related; the subject is always inscribed within language and engenders itself through the grammatical
staging of the 'I'. However, language is not simply a capacity of subjects.
Rather, for Lacan, language is an autonomous a priori structure which envelops
reality, creates signs and meanings, and designates certain linguistic and
symbolic relations between subjects. Lacan claims to find the basis for his
linguistic construction of the subject in Freud, but it is also clear that he draws
heavily on phenomenology, surrealism, anthropology and, of course, structural linguistics (see Williams, 1999).

One of the early (and clearest) expressions of Lacan's construction of the
subject can be found in his essay on the 'mirror stage' which claims to

describe a phase in human development as well as offering several philosophical insights (see Lacan, 1977: 1–7). For Lacan this is the structural moment
that necessitates the birth of the subject and its primary identifications. The
event of the 'mirror stage', through which the subject perceives a self-image
which is other than the largely mute, discordant being that it is, offers the
subject its first apprehension of bodily unity. It allows the young, dependent,
fragmented being to become an 'I' and to identify with an imaginary image of
itself. In this way, the subject is harnessed to an ontological structure according
to which it may think, perceive and recognise itself as a permanent, coherent
structure. Lacan believes this experience of subject formation anticipates
every account of the subject and it is this moment of imaginary identification
to which Althusser alludes in his own account of the interpellation of the
subject presented above.

   This imaginary structure of subjectivity is given a socio-symbolic sense
through the structure of language. Drawing upon the linguistic theory of the
sign developed by Ferdinand de Saussure, Lacan claims that the structure of
language and the construction of meaning is the result of a constitutive
algorithm: the signifier as sound-image, the material attribute of language,
and the signified as the concept of a particular sign. Signifier and signified
exist in a relation of reciprocal difference and language is itself an arbitrary
system where meaning shifts endlessly between different referents. Signs,
then, are differential in form; they are created only through their interdependence and difference with other signs. Language does settle or fix its
terms of reference according to certain signs because signifier and signified
are 'indissolubly joined' (Culler, 1985: 120). Lacan's account of language takes
this Saussurean notion of the sign as its basis and it is this conception of
language which is the material support for the subject's speech. However,
Lacan introduces two significant changes to Saussurean linguistics. First, he
establishes 'the incessant sliding of the signified under the signifier' (Lacan,
1977: 154) destroying the representationalist function of the sign. As a result,
the signifier is polysemic and operates with a certain autonomy from the
signifying process. Second, in taking up its position within language, the
Lacanian subject (as *speaking* subject) must itself become a signifier. In short,
Lacan removes the bar which separates signifier and signified, introducing
fluidity and multiplicity into the structures of language and subjectivity.

   This account of language and signification has radical implications for
the concept of the subject which, as a consequence, is viewed not only as an
illusive, imaginary being but one which is also lost (or caught, depending on
one's reading) within the mobility of signifiers. It is here, however, that the
unconscious may be heard. The unconscious, from this psychoanalytic
perspective, is structured like a language and it is through the freedom of the
signifier that unconscious effects may be expressed in language. Of course,
the fixing of signification by symbolic conventions, laws and practices (what

Lacan calls the *symbolic order*) also attempts to place limits upon modes of enunciation and thus upon unconscious expression. An incessant dialectic thus appears to characterise symbolic and imaginary relations, as well as the dynamic exchange between the unconscious and the subject-as-signifier. Clearly, the subject is not simply abandoned here; it is relocated within three different registers: the imaginary, the symbolic and the real. It is this last concept which has been utilised by many political interpretations of Lacan. Lacan uses the concept of the real not to describe a conception of human reality or, indeed, a discursive construction of reality, but to draw attention to an aporetic structure of existence which forever occludes signification and symbolisation. It remains foreclosed in the experience of speech. For Lacan, there is a kernel to subjectivity which can never by represented by or expressed in language. Slavoj Žižek utilises this account of 'the real as impossible' in his post-Althusserian ideological analyses. Ideology will always try to create a fullness in social meaning, and a completeness to the subject's identity, by rationalising social contradictions and by reconfiguring the traumatic pro- duction of subjectivity within national, religious and cultural narratives. At the same time, this kernel of *real* meaning, present in its ideological effects (as contradiction, paradox, excess), indicates the failure of symbolisation and the impossibility of filling out ideology and the subject (see Žižek, 1989: 153– 99; 1990). Thus for Lacan, as for Žižek, the dimension of the real frustrates and undermines every presupposition of the autonomy, self-determination and agency of the subject and has important implications for the theorisation of the political.

Derrida: Deconstruction and Subjectivity

Derrida's project, like those of the preceding analyses, is one of rethinking the boundaries of subjectivity. However, Derrida takes as his focus the entire metaphysical tradition and his analysis has clear implications for the form of political critique. Deconstruction works to uncover the intersection and inseparability of language, thought and philosophy. All forms of knowledge – philosophy and political theory most obviously – operate under the con- straints of language. The possibilities for thinking, as Lacan has shown in a quite different way, are profoundly affected by the form and structure of language. Language is rarely considered as anything more than the commun- icative surface of human expression. When language is viewed, in contrast, as *delimiting what may be signified*, then, by critically exploring the limits of discourse and considering other possibilities for thinking, the form, structure and possibilities for *thinking differently* may be encountered.

Deconstruction seeks to undo forms of discourse that centre the subject in relation to knowledge, using the metaphysical qualifications of self-reflec- tion, self-consciousness, purposive speech and thought, in order to ascertain the mode of existence of objects and the production of ideas. It was this aspect of epistemology that Althusser, Foucault and Lacan were also critical of. Deconstruction scrutinises the conceptual formation of the subject and asks the following questions. What conceptual apparatus gives rise to the concept of the subject? How is the constitution of the subject achieved and how is self-certainty maintained? These questions are deeply political in that they expose the hidden assumptions, repressions and exclusions that are required in order to constitute the subject without remainder and aim to show how this structure of the subject is unsustainable and ultimately breaks down. To analyse this interrogation of the subject is to illustrate the act of decon-struction itself. As Derrida writes, 'deconstruction accomplishes itself through the deconstruction of consciousness' (Derrida, 1974: 70).

In his many readings of philosophical figures, Derrida deconstructs the primacy and stability of the subject as the origin of thought and represen-tation, that which he calls, in *Of Grammatology*, the '*self-presence*' of the subject. Here, some of the fundamental insights of deconstruction are presented through readings of writers such as Husserl, Saussure, Rousseau and Lévi-Strauss. Each is shown to privilege a primordial unity of speech and sub-jectivity, This metaphysical, 'logo-centric' gesture folds subjectivity in upon itself, securing and confirming its essence and self-identity. It also, simul-taneously, represses and silences the forces, the *difference* or *otherness*, which are prior to the subject and generate the subject's possibility.

Derrida calls this passing over or masking of difference and alterity the movement of *différance*, understood within deconstruction as the condition for the possibility, and function, of every sign and meaning, every subject and every movement of history. However, like Lacan's real, *différance* is difficult to define, not least because Derrida understands it as fluid, mobile and dynamic in form but not representable in discourse. It is the denial of the play of *différance* which authorises the plenitude and certainty of the subject and yet *différance* interrupts every self-identity and exposes the contingency of its metaphysical claims to transcendence. Thus 'the speaking or signifying sub-ject could not be present to itself as speaking or signifying, without the play of linguistic or semiological *différance*' (Derrida, 1982: 16). In this way, *différance* envelops the subject *before* itself, forever preventing and unsettling its attempts to become a subject. This ensures that the moment of constitution or closure of subjectivity, by whatever theoretical means, never quite arrives. This failure of constitution, moreover, cannot be isolated as an original fracture. Whilst this deconstruction of the subject clearly disrupts every theory of human nature, and of natural beginning, it cannot simply precede the subject. Rather, it co-exists with and accompanies the subject. There is no place for chronological or teleological reference in deconstruction.

What are the political implications of this deconstruction of the subject? Derrida has argued that there can be no subject of ideology in the sense

described by Althusser because the completion and containment of subjectivity are impossible. In this way, the conditions of possibility for the subject
are also its conditions of impossibility. Thus, the interpellation of the subject,
in the Althusserian sense, is underivable because the subject is interrupted
and inhabited by traces of difference (Derrida 1991: 103). For Derrida, every
political construction of the subject is an unfinished project and the subject is
a function which is ceaselessly modified by the form and structure of the
political. This theoretical insight not only draws attention to the interminable
aspect of political critique but also pushes deconstruction towards an analysis
of the political as that which offers the site for negotiating, contesting and
creating the socio-political and philosophical horizon for new modes of
subjectivity.

Conclusion: Post-structuralism and Political Theory

It remains for us, finally, to draw together these diverse reflections upon the
concept of the subject and assess their implications for politics and the
construction of the political. Althusser, Foucault, Lacan and Derrida each
question the status of the subject in philosophical and political discourse, and
each may be understood to have transformed, repositioned and reconstituted
the question of the subject. Indeed, the principle of methodological individualism, together with the idea of the subject as an a priori, self-contained being
who is the holder of all sense and meaning, is uprooted by post-structuralism
and the presuppositions informing this account of the subject are interrogated and rethought. The post-structuralist project of rethinking the subject
as a modification of power relations (Foucault), as a function of ideology
(Althusser), as an imaginary being caught up in a linguistic relation (Lacan)
and as being opened up by the play of *différance* (Derrida) together characterise the subject as a function which is ceaselessly modified and radically
incomplete. Thus, the theoretical gesture that summons the subject as a
principle of self-presence, coherence, certainty and individuality is also one
that establishes its radical dislocation. For post-structuralism, a central task of
political thought is that of understanding the mechanisms which produce this
open relation of subjectivity and this, in turn, requires a more dynamic
conception of the political.

Thus, it is an unstable and fluid conception of the subject which marks
post-structuralists' reflections upon politics. The political cannot be viewed as
a system or as an expressive totality of relations when the subject is understood as a determinate effect. Such a view produces a reductionist conception
of the subject and risks totalising the production of the subject without
remainder. There are no transparent, objective, political structures, for post-
structuralism, because the locus of subjectivity that supports them is forever
incomplete and hence contests such totalisation. Rather than signalling the

closure of the political by constructing a subject who can be determined by it, post-structuralist political theorists draw our attention to the shape of antagonism, and the mode of identification, between subjects, as well as the mechanisms by which subjection is achieved (see Laclau, 1990; Agamben, 1993; Butler, 1998). Indeed, every political theory, be it of community, state, or ideology more generally, must recognise the ways in which the question of the subject presses in on every political concept. When the fragile, contingent nature of the subject's constitution is emphasised, the groundwork of political thought is itself reopened. Thus, political thought can evade the question of the subject only at great cost to its formulations.

In the introduction to this chapter, we pointed to a paradox of subjectivity pervading the work of post-structuralist thinkers. This paradox arises because the subject is at once dislocated and displaced *and* still required as a principle of analysis. Thus references to the subject always seem to assume the existence of some form of subjectivity, even though this is precisely what is open to question. Judith Butler draws attention to this paradox in her account of the incomplete constitution of the subject by practices of power. Butler recognises a certain 'ambivalence of the subject' (Butler, 1998: 10) which, she argues, structures contemporary discussions. She views the subject *as the site of such ambivalence*: it is simultaneously a site of agency (albeit qualified), and a site of subordination and discipline. Subjection signals this ambivalence (whose linguistic play we observed above in Althusser). Subjection signifies, at one and the same time, the mechanism of becoming subordinated to power and the process of becoming a subject. It is this ambivalence, or paradox of the subject, which must be interrogated. Certainly it introduces a circle of referentiality because it appears that, in its desire to account for the emergence of the subject, post-structuralism resurrects that which it seeks to question. This epistemological slippage in the concept of the subject is inevitable. Indeed, all political theories which seek to constitute the subject must, it seems, presuppose that which is to be created. Perhaps the uniqueness, and critical sense, of post-structuralism can be seen in its efforts to interrogate perpetually the paradox of the subject and to imbue it with political significance.

2

The Theoretical Link Between Politics and the Subject

JEREMY VALENTINE

Introduction: The Paradox of the Subject

One of the effects of the influence of structuralism and post-structuralism on the study of politics has been the increased recognition of the political relevance of the category of the subject. Initially the political dimension of the subject arose in the study of the social, economic and political determinations of cultural forms and phenomena such as films, novels and the practices of everyday life. Cultural theorists used the category of the subject to explain the relation between cultural forms and the types of experiences with which they were associated. On this basis, cultural theorists made various attempts to establish an explanatory framework that would comprehend cultural form, meanings and material determination. The discipline of Cultural Studies arises from this project and its political perspective has expanded into hitherto traditional approaches to the study of politics and, arguably, the forms of political practice that characterise modern democratic societies. This has occurred as a consequence of the effects of the broader social, cultural, economic and political transformations that are usually categorised by the term post-modernity. The category of the subject itself has not been immune to these processes. Perhaps Judith Butler has done most amongst contemporary thinkers to locate the political relevance of the subject within these developments (Butler, 1997).

In this chapter, we will explain the political dimension of the subject by looking at how the category functions simultaneously as both a technical/ analytic term and a value to which more specific senses of politics have become attached. In particular, we will critically examine the dynamic of this attachment with reference to the theoretical contexts in which the political dimension of the subject is intelligible. As we shall see, this entails negotiating an overlap between the ordinary understanding of politics in terms of regimes, procedures and ethical values, and a more nuanced sense of politics which seeks to transform the ordinary understanding in both theory and practice. Thus, in numerous ways, the possibility of political transformation hinges on the manner in which the political subject is conceived and the types of evidence used to support such a conception.

The stakes of this negotiation are set by a paradox in which the subject 'necessarily *subjects himself to himself* or, if you like, performs his own subjection' (Balibar, 1994: 10, original emphasis). The political relevance of the subject is defined by this paradox in which the category of the subject refers simultaneously to a notion of agency, of subjection and subjectivity. A situation in which the same word is used to mean different things may suggest that a stiff dose of conceptual clarification is required. Unfortunately things are not that simple. Even if someone could put a brake on the use of words in order to repair their machinery, this would neither account for nor prevent their material effects and consequences. In other words, Balibar's paradox is not resolved by the hope that it can be defined out of existence. This is because the paradox enjoys a material existence coextensive with the scope of modernity. By modernity is meant the possibility that the present, the here and now, is a terrain of action that can be acted upon in order to effect radical transformation. The actor is not external to this terrain and is thus transformed by the effects of his or her actions. This situation arises because no independent criteria are available with which to determine or regulate action. For moderns, the appeal to past examples is no justification at all. Similarly, as the future cannot be known, then it has no bearing on the present. Modernity refers to both the creation of this situation and the various attempts to provide a rational account of it. To illustrate the relation between modernity and the subject we can consider two examples.

Modernity and the Subject

Firstly, we can recall that, since Descartes, modern philosophy has sought to ground subjective experience in something which is both objective and, at the same time, given by subjective experience itself. This is because, for Descartes, one could always doubt the objectivity of what one was experiencing even if one could not doubt that one was experiencing (Descartes, 1968). Subjective experience thus acquired the status of a reliable fact. As, according to Descartes, there is nothing from which subjectivity can be derived, then we might as well say that subjectivity is a property of a subject, in the same way that we might say that Godness is a property of God. Subjectivity is therefore identical with the subject in so far as subjectivity arises out of itself and not from some external cause. Subjectivity is the essence of the subject – what there must be for there to be a subject – and it is contained in the existence of the subject. Thus the subject is self-sufficient and identical with itself, in the sense that there is nothing alien or different within it. Consequently, the subject's experience is more objective than objects encountered in the world.

However, this cannot be true of all subjectivities simply because there is no way of knowing what they are. An experience will always be true for the subject that experiences it even if, for example, the experience takes the form of a dream. Yet equally any subjective experience could just as easily be false. Once the authority of subjectivity is accepted there is no way to establish criteria external to the subject through which the distinction could be determined. In which case, whatever is the case would simply be whatever subjects happen to think. At the same time, given the priority of subjectivity, such criteria have to emerge from the subject itself in order to respect the self-identity of the subject. As a solution to this problem, Descartes proposed a universal form of the subject that would guarantee the subject's objectivity through the famous formula 'I think, therefore I am'. The fact that a subject could confirm that it is thinking was taken as sufficient proof of its existence, irrespective of what it was thinking about. Experience is equated with thought and thought is equated with existence. So the subject came to be understood as essentially a thinking thing and this definition took priority over the things that it happened to be thinking about, whether this was a dream, the trajectory of a canon ball or a twig plunged into a stream. Hence subjectivity is essentially self-reflective. Subjectivity exists through an act of self-reflection (see Gasché, 1986).

In establishing the ground of the subject in the reflective experience of thought, Descartes left several matters unresolved. For example, what is the relation between thought and whatever is thought about? What is the relation between thought and the thing that thinks and where can this be located? These problems arose because Descartes does not so much establish criteria of validity and truth as establish the truth of the subject and thus the validity of subjective experience. Subsequent philosophers have addressed these problems and continue to do so. However, we cannot go into this matter here. Instead we can consider a second example to illustrate our thesis concerning the material effects of the paradox of the subject; namely Hobbes's political thought (Hobbes, 1991). Hobbes was a member of the same seventeenth-century European intellectual milieu as Descartes and they met on at least one occasion. However, whereas Descartes was an epistemologist, Hobbes was a political philosopher, although both writers imitated the style of geometrical proof in order to make their arguments look convincing. But Hobbes rarely used the word subject and, when he did so, he referred to the more familiar political sense of subjection. That said, Hobbes's philosophy exhibits all the characteristics of the paradox of the subject identified by Balibar. Indeed, somewhat controversially, Balibar has insisted that Descartes used the word subject in the political sense familiar to Hobbes to describe the position of the subject with respect to knowledge (Balibar, 1994: 8).

Hobbes's ambition was to show how essentially free individuals, individuals who could do whatever they liked, could wind up in a relation of subjection under a higher authority. Indeed, Hobbes saw that this was generally the case and recommended it for the good of the individuals concerned. For Hobbes, such a situation could not be the result of the imposition of a greater force. Under these circumstances social life would be an actual or potential war 'of all against all' as force could be resisted by an even greater force until no one was left standing. To use Hobbes's memorable phrase, life would be 'nasty, brutish and short'. Neither could anyone use an excuse such as 'God commands' as this would only apply to a community of belief. After all, if God is all-powerful then why does he not appear directly, instead of issuing orders through a representative? Indeed, *Leviathan*, the title of Hobbes's most famous book, is a joke at the expense of belief in God. It refers to an incident in the Bible where God appears to Job, one of his most devout but miserable followers, and explains that he has made his life miserable simply because he has the power to do so. To reinforce the point, God compares his power to that of Leviathan, a legendary sea-monster. Hobbes's point is that Job's life was disastrous because he accepted God's authority.

Therefore, any relation of authority, which Hobbes considered to be essential to social existence, had to be built on those self-same essentially free individuals themselves. If this condition was met, then subjection would be justified to the satisfaction of those subjected and authority would take the place of the random exercise of force. Authority would be legitimated by the freely given consent of those over which it was exercised. Indeed, for Hobbes, power, the ability to get something done through the actual or potential application of force, only exists once authority is established. At the same time, individuals possess power because they alone have authority over the actual or potential deployment of the force at their disposal. Therefore, Hobbes is faced with the problem of explaining how individuals accept the exercise of authority over them. In other words, how free individuals become subjected. Hobbes's solution to this contradiction, the Social Covenant, was a formula in which individuals would agree to create some higher power which would alienate their individual powers in order that they may be subjected to the power they had created. In other words, authority is transferred and the recipient of the authority is created in the act of exchange. In return, the donor is guaranteed security against the use of power by others. In theory, the fact that the relation was consensual would set limits to the authoritative exercise of power.

Of course, this is no solution at all. The outcome is presupposed in the form of the agreement necessary for the greater power to be established. It makes no difference if we think of the Social Covenant as a real event, a mythical narrative or a regulatory formula that should be applied every time political disputes become acute. Hobbes's solution is paradoxical. Yet this is only a consequence of the undeniable fact that individuals are free to do what they want unless some greater force prevents them. So Hobbes simply shows that there is no rational account of this greater force despite the fact that it coexists with individual freedom. After all, Hobbes lived in a society, admittedly considerably more violent than what we would experience now. In this respect Hobbes fails to account for the political relation of subjection. On the other hand, Hobbes does show that this relation is connected to individual agency, in the absence of any higher authority, and thus arises as a consequence of the self-sufficiency of the political subject's freedom, where freedom means absence of restraint.

Both Descartes and Hobbes can be read as responses to the same problem. Descartes, perhaps under the influence of the growth of scientific knowledge that conflicted with the authority of religion and those institutions dependent on it, accepted that individuals were free to think what they wanted. Hobbes, perhaps under the influence of popular revolution and violent religious disputes, accepted that individuals were free to do what they want. This does not mean that either thinker thought that individuals should be free. Freedom is something that only exists to the extent that it is exercised. Descartes accepted that individuals are free to doubt. Hobbes accepted that individuals are free to resist. In attempting to provide a rational account of freedom, Descartes and Hobbes thereby attempt to provide an account of how freedom is, and can be, limited. Although both thinkers reach their conclusions in very different ways, Hobbes's political subject shares certain properties with Descartes' self-sufficient epistemological subject. Both Descartes and Hobbes establish the authority of the subject as subjection and subjectivity. Descartes subjects thought to the authority of the self-reflective subject. Hobbes subjects politics to the authority of the Social Covenant. The subjection of subjectivity, the subject as such, is not something given, a natural fact, but has to be established.

It may be objected that this authority is not very well grounded. However, this is no objection at all. Rather, this is simply a property of the authority both Descartes and Hobbes established. Authority is not removed but becomes modern. It becomes a matter of what can be done in the here and now. In Descartes' case, any established epistemological authority has to be subjected to the authority of subjectivity. In Hobbes's case, any established political authority has to be subjected to the authority of the free individual. Or, rather, the existence of the subject entails the subjection of subjectivity. The paradox concerns the extent to which the manner in which this takes place is intelligible to the subject.

The logic of modernity gives rise to a process in which the grounds of authority are undermined, such that any relation of authority is always antagonistic. There is no independent ground available from which to decide the conflict. At the same time, the existence of the subject entails a relation of subjection to subjectivity. Thus the political dimension of the subject is always a question of the relation of politics to modernity, and thus to the historical, political, economic, social, scientific and metaphysical context in which modernity is sustained (see Kolb, 1986; Pippin, 1991). This is not because modernity can be characterised as the invention of a relation between subjectivity and subjection. Doubtless such a relation is present in forms of historical experience that would not be described as modern. Rather, modernity poses the question of how such a relation can be established. Hence the attempt to establish such a relation brings it into question, which can be confirmed by the fierce opposition Hobbes's arguments received from those established authorities that Hobbes had intended to serve (Mintz, 1962). By posing the question of the grounds of power, modernity brings all authority into question, even if that is not the intention (Bauman, 1989). In which case, the paradoxical nature of the political subject is hardly surprising. For modernity, to be free is to be a subject with the paradoxes that this necessarily entails, not least of which is the existence of other equally free subjects.

Hence, for modernity, the political dimension of the subject arises from its paradoxical nature. Structuralist and post-structuralist thinkers have attempted to clarify this political dimension by differently weighting the elements of the paradox. For some theorists, notably Althusser, the different senses of the subject are taken as equivalent within the description of the form and structure of ideology. Notoriously, the elimination of ideology entails the effacement of the subject, a position which attracted the criticism of 'anti-humanism' and which was, given Althusser's Marxist affiliation, curiously self-defeating. Althusser offered very little encouragement to the idea that political change might be accomplished by political actors (Althusser, 1971). Others, notably Foucault, would insist that the resources of agency cannot be reduced to subjection, even if these resources do not arise from a form of existence that is wholly different in kind. In other words, Foucault and those associated with his work argue that subjection is not a one-way affair. Power is a relation not a possession (Foucault, 1982). Similarly, Lacan and those associated with his work also insist that, in any relation of subjection, something else is left over that allows a space for agency, even though Lacan's explanatory framework is fundamentally opposed to Foucault's (see Copjec, 1994). In this chapter, we shall draw out the political dimension of Lacan's account of the subject as it relates to modernity. Firstly, we shall explain how the paradox of the subject is addressed within structuralism, the basis of Lacan's account.

Structuralism and the Subject

As an analytical and empirical theory, structuralism does not address the political dimension of the subject directly and even less the location of this dimension within modernity. That said, the analytical resources of structuralism have been applied to these questions by structuralist and post-structuralist thinkers, and many political thinkers have integrated these resources into normative and speculative discussions of political modernity (see, for example, Lefort, 1986). The basis of the relation between structuralist and political thought arises from the relation between the category of the subject and the structure of language. This relation is established by two important properties of language. Firstly, one of the functions of language is to refer to things. Everyone knows that in ordinary language the word 'subject' simply means what you are talking about – that is to say, what you are referring to. In this respect by referring to something language represents it. Secondly, language works by rules which enable speakers to evaluate whether language is working well. These rules are referred to as grammar. So, although perhaps less well known, the subject is also a grammatical category which every sentence has to possess in order to be a sentence. The subject is the formal name for the agent of the sentence which must agree with the verb, the doing that the agent does.

Although these two senses of the subject are not necessarily connected, structuralism seizes on a specific instance when both coincide. This is when the sentence is about the agent of the sentence and only occurs in the moment in which the sentence is enunciated or, less strictly, in the representation of this moment. The subject of the sentence is the grammatical subject that represents the subjectivity of the speaker, such that, whatever the subject claims to be doing, he or she is also speaking about doing it. The sign through which this coincidence takes place is the word 'I'. Put simply, whenever 'I' is said, 'I am speaking' is said as well. Hence the word 'I' designates a situation in which the speaker who utters the word is both the grammatical subject and also the subject of the utterance, what the utterance is about. Grammar and subjectivity coincide. As we saw above, Descartes relies on this coincidence in the formula 'I think, therefore I am'.

Applying Sausurre's notion of the sign to this situation, Benveniste concluded that, for the word 'I' to occur, an essential doubling takes place in any instance of the word 'I' of the 'I' that the 'I' refers to and the 'I' of the utterance through which this act of reference takes place. Benveniste summarises this as the simultaneity of 'the instance of *I* as referent and the instance of discourse containing *I* as the referee' (Benveniste, 1971: 218). So 'I' always refers to the instance of discourse in which it is enunciated as well as, and at the same time as, the subjectivity of the subject who enunciates it. Hence, any instance of 'I' is always qualified by its temporal location, for example, I am, I will, I was and so on, and which in each case is always a predicate of existence. In metaphysical terms, being precedes doing.

The consequences of Benveniste's argument are both far-reaching and unsettling for they strike at both what is so unique about speakers as subjects and at the subjective relation they have with language when they speak it. It is through this relation that the self-identity of the speaker is secured such that the subject coincides with subjectivity. Benveniste specifies these consequences as follows:

> It is by identifying himself as a unique person pronouncing *I* that each speaker sets himself up in turn as the 'subject'. The use thus has as a condition the situation of discourse and no other. If each speaker, in order to express the feeling he has of his irreducible subjectivity, made use of a distinct identifying signal (in the sense in which each radio transmitting station has its own call letters), there would be as many languages as individuals and communication would become absolutely impossible. Language wards off this danger by instituting a unique but mobile sign, *I*, which can be assumed by each speaker on the condition that he refers each time only to the instance of his own discourse. This sign is thus linked to the *exercise* of language and announces the speaker as speaker. It is this property that establishes the basis for individual discourse, in which each speaker takes over all the resources of language for his own behalf. (Benveniste, 1971: 220)

Thus, prior to any reference to an empirical individual, the first person singular refers to the act of speaking in which it is enunciated. Through this structure the speaker is designated as a moment in language; 'The reality to which it refers is the reality of the discourse' (Benveniste, 1971: 226). When I say 'I', I refer to myself as the 'I' that is speaking in the act of doing so, and not some other 'I' that could take my place. It is only through language that there is an 'I' that I can refer to so that, when a speaker says 'I', it is himself or herself that is meant and not someone else. On this basis, the alleged individuality or difference of the 'I' depends on the sameness and conventional status of the 'I' that is spoken. And, what applies to the first person singular applies to all its temporal modifications and to all collective forms of the pronoun and the proper names and categories through which they are specified. That is to say, to agency of and within language. Thus, to be a subject that is identical with its subjectivity requires a moment of subjection in the political sense to the word 'I' which is necessary for these two senses to coincide and for the proof of this coincidence to be demonstrated by the simple act of saying 'I'. For Benveniste, the direction of subjection flows from the speaker to language such that the speaker masters discourse through the production of well-formed sentences. The subject subjects himself or herself through the subjection of language in order to express his or her subjectivity. The subject is present to its own subjectivity in the moment of subjection.

In which case, since every speaker is an 'I', how is the specificity of the speaker and the act in which it is constituted established? Benveniste is very clear on this point. Any act of speech is addressed to someone and it is in contrast with this someone that the specificity of the subject and thus the agent is established. The position of someone has to be filled in, even if this only takes place in the mind of the speaker. Such an event is no less concrete for being an imaginative act. Here, Benveniste is consistent with the Saussurean principle that signs have no positive value but acquire signification on the basis of a negative differential relation. 'I' am 'I' because 'I' am not 'you'. Although this relation is reciprocal as the other is also an 'I', it is not one of equality or symmetry *in the actual moment of speech*. Within the simultaneity of the structure of its enunciation, the relation between 'I' and 'you' is hierarchical, with the first term dominant. In short, individual identity, the discursive subject of 'I', requires otherness as a principle of structural necessity.

On the surface, Benveniste's technical account of the linguistic subject appears to mirror and confirm the position of the subject established by modernity. The word 'I' simply confirms that what I say is an expression of what I think and, therefore, who or what I am. I choose and, therefore, consent to the words I use to do this and, thus, confirm my control of, or mastery over, language. In short, Benveniste confirms the self-identity of the subject, present to itself in the moment that it speaks. Moreover, Benveniste appears to have removed the dimension of arbitrariness that Saussure established as a property of language such that the relation between signifiers and ideas, and thus between ideas and objects, seems necessary to the speaker.

The Discourse of the Subject

However, this does not remove the paradox. In Benveniste's account, what takes place in the moment in which the word 'I' is enunciated is impossible. All at once and at the same time, the speaker must master language through the detour of another in order to satisfy the structural requirement of the sign. That is, the coincidence of the signifier of the subject, the sign 'I', and the signified of subjectivity, the I that speaks. The distinctiveness of Lacan's contribution to this problem is that it shows how such an impossible event can take place. Or, rather, Lacan shows how the speaker exists with the consequences of its impossibility if it does take place. For Lacan, who trained as a psychoanalyst in the Freudian tradition, these consequences can be summarised by the concept of the unconscious. Thus: 'What the psychoanalytic experience discovers in the unconscious is the whole structure of language' (Lacan, 1977: 147). In this respect, Lacan's contribution can be understood as a synthesis of psychoanalysis and structuralism. As he once remarked to an audience of psychoanalysts: 'if you want to know more, read Saussure' (Lacan, 1977: 125).

Whereas Benveniste's theory sought to rescue the reference to subjectivity from the priority of signification, Lacan reversed this move by returning to the question of the word 'I' as a sign which exists prior to self-reference. Lacan is concerned with the presence of the arbitrary nature of the relation between the signifier of the subject and the signified of subjectivity within the act of enunciation itself. The significance of the arbitrariness of the word 'I' derives from the fact that access to the bar that marks the attachment of the signifier and the signified is, under normal circumstances, prohibited to the speaker in the act of speech or, as by definition, there is no instance in which the speaker is external to language, to the speaker as such. This relation cannot be signified yet it is necessary for enunciation to take place. Hence the relation is represented mathematically, thus: S/s. Lacan equates the presence of the distinction between the signifier and the signified with the unconscious, insisting that: 'The unconscious is neither primordial nor instinctual; what it knows about the elementary is no more than the elements of the signifier' (Lacan, 1977: 170).

Through this move, Lacan goes beyond the arbitrariness of the sign established by Saussure or, indeed, the classical problem of accounting for the relation between a word and a thing, by analysing the agency of something that cannot be represented within speech or discourse itself, despite the fact that it is its condition; namely, the bar separating S/s. Without arbitrariness there would be no 'I' to speak of and no 'I' to speak it. Speakers would resemble Benveniste's radio stations. Yet, precisely because arbitrariness has no meaning, the relation appears as necessary to the speaker. Hence arbitrariness constitutes both a limit of self-reflection and mastery and the necessary illusion that these things are possible.

In which case, how is subjectivity maintained in the speech of the subject? How is it that when a speaker says 'I' it is himself or herself that is meant? To solve this problem, Lacan provides an account of the entry of the speaker into language. As a psychoanalyst, Lacan argued that the motor capacity of the human is insufficient with respect to its intellectual capacities such that humans are born prematurely. The experience of the human body is disordered by comparison with its intellectual abilities and a human life is organised around the discovery of ways of coming to terms with these unfortunate circumstances. Lacan updated this theory with the thesis that an infant becomes a subject, an agent capable of action, by identifying with an image of itself like a reflection in a mirror that is more perfect than its actual experience of itself. This 'mirror stage' corresponds to the moment when the infant enters into language such that self-consciousness is given by the acquisition of the ability to use the word 'I' correctly, thus reinforcing the illusion of perfection or the illusion that the perfection that is experienced through reflection corresponds to the thing that one is. In reality, the idea of what one is derives from the reflection. (Lacan, 1977: 1–8).

Hence, subjectivity derives from an identification with something that one is not, something other that is misrecognised as the same. In this case, an image of one's body. The relation between the subject and subjectivity is imaginary, derived from a specular act of mimicry with something that is not thought and which is other than what one is. In short, the self-sufficiency of the subject is established through a detour via the other. So the theory of identification accounts for the presence of otherness in the relation through which the subject is constituted. Yet it is important to note that Lacan's notion of otherness is not singular. In the same way that the 'I' is doubled in the moment of enunciation, so too is otherness. Firstly, the image of perfection is other than the subject that identifies with it. Secondly, the entity through which the identity of the subject is confirmed through an act of speech is other to the subject as well; namely, language. Indeed, Lacanian terminology codifies this distinction as one that exists between the other, in the lower case, and the Other, in the upper case, where the latter represents the arbitrariness of language itself, and thus the conventional and contingent status of the identity of the subject that takes its place within it. The presence of the Other is more damaging to the self-identity of the subject than the presence of the other. Moreover, any concrete other, any 'you', is always mediated by the imaginary other. This places a limit on what we can know of others.

To put it concisely, the subject is never present to itself or is 'de-centred'. A speaker is never where or what he or she thinks he or she is in the moment of speech, or in the moment of thought as such. In other words, the subject is *split*. As Lacan stated the position: 'It is not a question of knowing whether I speak of myself in a way that conforms to what I am, but rather of knowing whether I am the same as that of which I speak' (Lacan, 1977: 165). This does not mean that the subject has no centre, but that the centre of the subject is elsewhere in the structural determinants of language of which the subject is an effect not a cause.

Lacan provides a very specific account of the nature of the structural determination of the subject. The unconscious cannot be reduced to either structure or subject because it is what there has to be in order for the distinction to be made. By the same token, in order for the distinction to persist, arbitrariness prevents their correspondence. Indeed, for Lacan, it makes no difference if one were to approach the question in terms of the omnipotence of structure. This would just be a reversal of the equally illusory belief in the omnipotence of the subject. For psychoanalysis, this opposition simply expresses the difference between paranoia and narcissism. A subject can only experience this opposition as an effect of the unconscious. Consequently, because the relation between the structural element of the signifier 'I' and the subjective element of the signified 'I' is not one of correspondence or repetition, it does not follow that there is no relation at all. Clearly, some kind of relation has to exist for the notion of illusion to be meaningful. The presence of the unconscious, or the presence of the unrepresentable dimension of arbitrariness, entails that the relation is one of displacement.

The notion of displacement is understood as an unstable relation between the signifier and the signified. It is confirmed by the existence of the cases that psychoanalysts treat where, typically, patients believe themselves to be an animal or some famous person. So displacement explains how this happens. It does not explain how it does not. That is to say, it does not explain what Lacan understood as the tautological nature of language in which the world corresponds to the subject's experience of it, such that when a subject speaks everything is necessarily so, 'it being an effect of its existence as a language (*langue*) that it necessarily answers all needs' (Lacan, 1977: 150). To provide an answer to this problem Lacan considers the gap between the moment of enunciation and the content of the enunciation. For Lacan, as a speaker:

> I identify myself in language, but only by losing myself in it like an object. What is realized in my history is not the past definite of what was, since it is no more, or even the present perfect of what has been in what I am, but the future anterior of what I shall have been for what I am in the process of becoming. (Lacan, 1977: 86)

For Lacan, arbitrariness is fundamentally a temporal phenomena in that all speech is belated. And this is true of the speech one enters into with oneself, one's self-consciousness or capacity to reflect on oneself. By the time the words come out, you are something else. Your words are a trace of what you were and this trace is what you will identify with in order to become what you are. In this way, I overcome my necessary alienation in something other than myself which allows me to be myself – namely, language. By means of the retroactive constitution of the 'I', it appears that I always intended to be who 'I' am and to mean what 'I' say, thus adding the gloss of consistency to my account of myself. The situation is, therefore, one 'in which the subject appears fundamentally in the position of being determinant or instrumental of action' (Lacan, 1977: 23).

Symbolic Politics

Lacan's work is notoriously difficult to understand. An enormous secondary literature exists that tries to clarify his argument, but even this is characterised by the dominance of dispute over agreement and this characteristic can also be used to describe work that seeks to apply Lacan to politics more broadly. Doubtless even the crude and simplified account of Lacan's position presented above will not satisfy both adherents of Lacan and those who are and probably remain sceptical. Indeed, the style of Lacan's expression suggests that it can only be understood in the way that one may be said to understand a poem, rather than a manual that explains how to analyse statistics on voting behaviour, for example.

That said, we can at least consider the extent to which Lacan helps us to understand the paradox of the subject. Here we might observe that the consequences of Lacan's argument for the modern notion of the subject are ambiguous. On the one hand, the modern notion of the subject as a point of intervention on a terrain fully present to itself is undermined. Yet, on the other hand, this modern notion is not destroyed. If anything, Lacan shows how the subject necessarily persists in its illusion. This ambiguity has some bearing on the extent to which Lacan pushes the question of the subject on to the terrain of post-structuralism. This arises because Lacan introduces a certain elasticity into the concept of structure itself by accommodating the impossible dimension of mastery and alterity to a principle of structural simultaneity. In other words, the notion of arbitrariness as the presence of a temporal dimension within the subject suggests that structures may not be as structured as Lacan initially assumed and that, therefore, the account of the subject on which it is based is unsafe.

Hence an examination of Lacan's relation to modernity may also shed light on the status of his work in relation to post-structuralism. To do this we can begin by examining the importance of identification in Lacan's theory. It is not just that, through identification, the subject overcomes the power of instinctual forces, ceases playing with its own faeces and becomes grammatical. The subject does more than learn to speak. Identification is also, and at the same time, a moment of entry into the symbolic order, a concept that ultimately derives from Durkheim. Importantly, Durkheim located the normative obligatory dimension of social existence within the symbolic realm through which social relations are represented. Hence the notion of the symbolic order provides a link or continuity between language and action or the social organisation and distribution of practices. Like language, this order exists prior to the individual and has the status of a social fact that determines individual behaviour, from outward ritual to internal reflection. Hence Durkheim's famous claim that 'social life, in all its aspects and in every period of its history, is made possible only by a vast symbolism' (Durkheim, 1976, 231). Through this symbolic order individuals know who they are and what they are supposed to do.

It is on the basis of the necessity of the symbolic order that Lacan confronts modernity. For Lacan defines modernity, the historical present that his discourse addresses, in terms of the annihilation of the symbolic order itself. Thus:

> What we are faced with, to employ the jargon that corresponds to our approaches to man's subjective needs, is the increasing absence of all those saturations of the superego and ego ideal that are realized in all kinds of organic forms in traditional societies, forms that extend from the rituals of everyday intimacy to the periodical festivals in which the community manifests itself. We no longer know them except in their most degraded aspects. Furthermore, in abolishing the cosmic polarity of male and female principles, our society undergoes all the psychological effects proper to the modern phenomenon known as the 'battle between the sexes' – a vast community of such effects, at the limit between the 'democratic' anarchy of the passions and their desperate levelling down by the 'great winged hornet' of narcissistic tyranny. It is clear that the promotion of the ego today culminates, in conformity with the utilitarian conception of man that reinforces it, in an ever more advanced realization of man as individual, that is to say, in an isolation of the soul ever more akin to its originary dereliction. (Lacan, 1977: 26–7).

Whereas modernity is opposed to the organisation of the symbolic order, Lacan insists on the necessity of maintaining it. This is because modernity presents the possibility that subjectivity is no longer rule governed. It is not so much that modern subjects are totally in control of their actions, or even that their belief that they are is true and not illusory. Rather, the problem is that nothing bad will happen to them if they are not. As Lacan put it: 'the Oedipus complex cannot run indefinitely in forms of society that are more and more losing the sense of tragedy' (Lacan, 1977: 310).

Indeed, it is no accident that Lacan is particularly observant of developments in the field of sexual affairs which are supposed to have caused the decline of group-belonging and the rise of individual freedom. This is because Lacan thought that the symbolic order was organised around the symbolic phallus. Yet, in doing so, Lacan imported some rather amateurish anthropological baggage into his account of the symbolic, as the following purplish passage makes clear.

> The phallus is the privileged signifier of that mark in which the role of the logos ['word' in Greek, J. V.] is joined with the advent of desire. It can be said that this signifier is chosen because it is the most tangible element in the real of sexual copulation, and also the most symbolic in the literal (typographical) sense of the term, since it is equivalent there to the (logical) copula ['connection' in Greek, J. V.]. It might also be said, by virtue of its turgidity, it is the image of the vital flow as it is transmitted in generation. (Lacan, 1977: 287)

Within Lacan's description of modernity, the phallus would be just one sign amongst others. It would lose its privileged position and acquire the status of a contingent particular and not the universal role of anchor of the symbolic order that Lacan wishes for it. Whether the phallus has ever played such a role is a moot point. But even more unsettling for Lacan's perspective is the fact that, for the phallus to enjoy this role, it must have a signified content built into it. There is no arbitrariness in the signification of the phallus and, thus, no temporal gap through which signification could arise. Indeed, Lacan's argument is predicated on the idea that this signification arises from nature.

Lacan's critique of modernity is, thus, motivated by the fear that the form of social existence mediated by the symbolic, in which Lacan's account of the subject would hold good, no longer exists. In this connection, it is worth noting a similarity with Habermas's unfortunate faux pas when confronted by the possibility that, due to the advent of postmodernity, modernity was no longer organised around an authoritative centre. Habermas could only find such a state of affairs confirmed in pre-modern societies, although the consequences of this inconvenience were rigorously ignored by Habermas in a defence of centred modern authority that will *create its normativity out of itself* (Habermas, 1987: 7, emphasis original). That is to say, both Habermas and Lacan would like to provide modernity with a centre, in Lacan's case if only to announce that there is not one. Enigmatically, one could suggest that

Lacan's nostalgia for a pre-modern social existence is a typically modern type of anti-modernity. Hence we can say that Lacan's account of retroactivity is an account of what you would have to be in order to take your place in the symbolic order *if that order existed*. Thus, at the same time as retroactively constituting the identity of the subject, Lacan also retroactively constitutes the ground of the explanation of what the subject is supposed to be. Lacan's notion of the 'mirror stage' is as fanciful as Hobbes's notion of the Social Covenant. That is to say, a very modern version of non-modernity as structure.

Post-symbolic Political Subjects

By seeking to reinvent the symbolic as a ground of explanation within conditions that will not support it, Lacan installs a social-political limit beyond which his work will not go. Essentially, this is an arbitrary decision. In Lacanian terms, it constitutes a retreat from the big Other within his work, from a confrontation with its own contingency. Whether or not the project of reinventing the symbolic links up with wider social and political projects is an interesting point.

Here we can consider Laclau's Lacan-influenced diagnosis of the structural conditions of postmodernity which are described in terms of the high degree of complexity which they exhibit. For Laclau postmodernity is caused by a plurality of dislocations 'that increasingly dominate the terrain of an absent structural determination' (Laclau, 1990: 62) with no place available from which to designate a negative other. For Laclau, under these conditions the fate of the subject is to become *mythic*, as a reaction to the insufficiency of structure that would otherwise determine it. Thus: 'The mythical space is constituted as a critique of the lack of structuration accompanying the dominant order' (Laclau, 1990: 62). In other words, the political space of postmodernity is constituted as a reaction to the absence of structure, or to post-structuralism as such. Hence political agency is an expression of the ruin that the subject has become, desperate for something to identify with. As Martin Amis once remarked: 'Once people stop believing in God they do not stop believing. They believe in anything'.

Fortunately, this does not, and need not exhaust the political space of postmodernity. It only describes the behaviour of popular political movements organised around a desire for certainty and, thus, the idea that bad subjectivity has bad consequences. In some cases, this takes the form of the labour to reconstruct traditional symbolic structures. In others, the endeavour is directed towards establishing a closed symbolic universe of one's own, organised around some contingent feature of one's existence to which is attributed a universal significance. Both cases mimic a form that no longer exists.

Yet there is another more sophisticated approach to the question of the subject that preserves the paradox of the subject. This derives from Foucault's use of the notion of discourse, a term for the historically specific and contingent ways in which talk about an object or field of objects emerges and the practices that sustain this talk. In this respect, Foucault shifted from the reflective notion of the subject as a process of identification to the production of the subject within discourse, or subject-position. Importantly, for Foucault, the subject in the modern era is characterised by an essential freedom or indeterminacy. Discourse does not exhaust its subjects. Instead, discourses are sites of contestation and conflict in which subjects sometimes support discursive strategies and sometimes resist them. This notion of the subject is sustained by a concept of power as a relation and not a property or possession of subjects. Although some subjects may have greater advantages with respect to the deployment of power, no subject is external to games of power. Yet the possibility of such games rests on the modern freedom of subjects (Foucault, 1982, Balibar, 1991).

Therefore, to conclude, we might say that the persistence of politics depends on the persistence of the commitment to the paradox of the subject, to the games of freedom that modernity enables. This commitment has no guarantees. Undertaking it is neither a good thing nor a bad thing. Whether we do so is an indication of the extent to which we would prefer to ventriloquise our desires through symbols that we can destroy if our demands are not met. However, all the signs are that such symbols will no longer be around to do this job for us. This is not surprising if we can no loner satisfy ourselves with our accounts of their existence. In which case, the political relevance of the subject does not disappear. Rather, the scope of the subject is expanded as a terrain of power and, thus, intervention. In other words, it is not relations between subjects but relations within subjects that become a terrain of contestation. In which case, the paradox of the subject – subjectivity, agency, subjection – is expanded. This requires nothing less than a new grammar of politics to comprehend the 'de-alignment' of the subject, the various ways in which speech, identity and power are constituted as a political relation. It would be a shame if the study of politics was left behind by this process, but not a disaster.

3

The State and Sovereign Subjectivity

JAMES MARTIN

Introduction

The state is unquestionably the principal theme of political studies. It is understood as the sole agent of legitimate violence, the authoritative source of law and, in democratic societies, the executor of the will of the people. Consequently, modern politics, it is presumed, must, like political studies, be fundamentally concerned with the business of the state.

However, it is not always the state per se that is placed under examination by political analysts. More often it is the actors who operate in it or who seek to enter, control and even abolish it and the wider social forces shaping and constraining the state that form the subject matter of political analysis. Nevertheless, whether the topic in question is elections or civil servants, industrial policy or social revolution, the state has an implicit presence in modern political analysis – it is the apparatus to be utilised or a source of coercion with which to be reckoned.

Yet we never really confront the state as a unified and discrete object of enquiry. What we call the state is a diverse ensemble of institutions and agencies which gather information, formulate laws and issue edicts. It is simultaneously an employer of personnel, a supplier of goods and services, a place of political representation and an agency of repression. Because its remit extends far beyond its own apparatus into wider realms of social life, it is not easy to establish a clear boundary between what is 'state' and what is 'non-state'. For instance, we might assume that the family and the workplace are independent of the state, yet these are two areas of social life greatly affected by public legislation. They are not independent of the state. But they are not really 'inside' the state either.

Establishing boundaries is not the only difficulty encountered in analysing the state. To add to our difficulty, it never appears as one single organisation. The various branches of the state (administrative, parliamentary, judicial, military, policing and so on) are formally separate and autonomous in their day-to-day activities. For all the simplicity of its appellation, 'the state' is a complex and fluid social organisation. Yet, despite this complexity, we are accustomed to thinking of it as a unified entity, a singular identity.

In this chapter we will examine how post-structuralists approach this peculiar institution, how they have drawn critical attention to the disjuncture between the unity the state is claimed to symbolise and the fragmented system and contradictory purposes that gather under its name. The attempt to subsume complexity and difference under a single ordering principle is one of the key legacies of Enlightenment that post-structuralists vigorously contest. Whilst we cannot say there is a distinctive post-structuralist theory *of* the state, something we can say about other political theories such as liberalism and Marxism, we can see how post-structuralist analyses have drawn attention to the way the state is itself *politically constituted*. There are three basic points that characterise this approach.

Firstly, post-structuralists commonly dispute the very idea that political power can be monopolised, concentrated and rationally controlled within 'legitimate' boundaries. The assumption that it can diverts attention from the multiplicity of sites of power that extend throughout society and organise people according to a variety of designs (religious organisations, factories, medical institutions, for example). The state, in democratic societies, is in a kind of permanent contestation with these other centres of power which it seeks to domesticate. The existence of a single centre of power is not axiomatic. Rather, there is an ongoing effort to constitute the authority of the state.

Secondly, the notion that power is necessarily repressive is also rejected by post-structuralists for whom power is also a 'positive' force in as much as it operates to position subjects as particular kinds of agents with certain kinds of capacities. Thus the powers of the state must be viewed not simply as negative (as prohibitions or coercively enforced laws) but also as productive, enabling certain kinds of subjectivity. For instance, law courts are not purely repressive; they 'produce' legal subjects with 'rights' that may be exercised to secure certain rewards (to fair employment, for example).

Thirdly, post-structuralists typically focus on the 'discursive' nature of social practices, that is, the organising principles, vocabularies and symbolic frameworks that make human activity both intelligible and possible. These are mechanisms of power just as much as organised violence; it is the way the state functions in and through symbolic practices that has been to the fore in post-structuralist analyses. The state is constituted politically because its very existence depends upon struggles against other centres of power and the successful production of subjectivity through certain discursive practices.

These three general claims or attitudes do not add up to a wholesale theory of the state. On the contrary, post-structuralists are typically critical of the very notion of the state as an independent agency that can be theorised separately from other social practices and operations of power. Nevertheless, they do constitute characteristic elements of post-structuralist approaches *to* the state. Inevitably, however, in different analyses there are different aspects of the state under consideration and consequently different emphases. In this chapter we shall consider some of the main analyses of the state undertaken by post-structuralists. These include 'deconstructive' approaches to the idea and practice of state sovereignty; 'genealogical' analyses of the state as an organisation charged with governing society; and studies of 'hegemonic' strategies that operate in and through the state. Although these approaches overlap in many respects, they remain sufficiently distinctive to warrant separate attention.

Deconstructing State Sovereignty

The idea of the state as a singular space of political authority over a given territory and its population is one of the defining features of modern thought. Since the rise of absolutist monarchs in seventeenth-century Europe, the state has come to represent the principle of order in society – that is, a coherent, unified and absolute source of authoritative commands. According to this discourse of sovereignty, the state is a hierarchically organised space of decision-making that is self-supporting – that is, it is distinct from both the persons who act in its name and the persons over and for whom it acts (Skinner, 1989). What is 'modern' about the modern state is its 'abstract' nature, its conceptual difference from any actual person or persons; it is a 'legal fiction' in James Joyce's phrase or, as Hobbes put it, 'an artificial person' (see Skinner, 1999). This abstraction permits us to ascribe to it 'absolute' qualities that cannot be mistaken for those of an ordinary human being; thus Hobbes described the state as a 'mortal God'.

Hobbes's description points to the major claim of modern sovereignty – the superior rationality that is expressed through the state. After an age of religious war, and in light of the claims made by the Enlightenment, the state was afforded the status of a rational calculating subject charged with the task of ordering and legislating in the name of its own truth and reason, rather than biblical authority or monarchical fiat (Viroli, 1992; Bauman, 1992). To say that a state is sovereign is to say that there is no other source of legitimate authority outside of its space. The state, according to this discourse of sovereignty, is the limit of legality, outside of which there is only anarchy. Sovereignty, therefore, marks a limit; it is a claim that defines the ensemble of institutions, agencies and practices of the state both 'internally' and 'externally'. Internally, the state is co-extensive with the territory over which it exercises supreme command; externally, the state exists as an autonomous and independent agency in an international environment or system of states (Held, 1989: 215–16). In the first instance, sovereign commands in the form of law are taken to be final and absolute; in the second, there is an assertion of the sovereign's autonomy to determine its own policy free from external interference. The notion of state sovereignty, therefore, mirrors the Enlightenment conception of the subject as a rational individual who exercises control over 'his' own internal needs and values but who enters an insecure world of other individuals with whom 'he' must either conflict or cooperate.

It should come as no surprise to find that sovereignty has been a central topic of certain post-structuralist readings of the state. As with the notion of the rational calculating subject, deconstructive approaches to sovereignty have taken to task the notion of the state as a stable, essentially coherent identity with an a priori claim to supremacy over its domain. Like so many other dichotomised, hierarchical spaces, the 'presence' and conceptual coherence of state sovereignty is premised on marking off other categories as secondary and inferior. Deconstruction, by contrast, explores these exclusions and reveals their function in constituting an identity. Such readings are growing in critical approaches to conceptions of sovereignty within the disciplines of international relations and legal studies where the conceptualisation of the state as a unified formation has hitherto been a central theoretical prop. States can only be conceived as 'actors' on the world stage, 'calculating' their strategic interests and making 'autonomous' decisions if we understand them as essentially unified agents with control over their own territories. Thus the idea of the sovereign state as a fully-constituted agent capable of decision-making within an otherwise anarchic international environment has been central to 'Realist' and 'Neo-realist' approaches to IR. In recent years, however, the concept has been under sustained attack (see, for example, Hoffman, 1998), not least from post-structuralists (see Der Derian and Shapiro, 1989).

In his deconstructive reading of what he calls the 'anarchy *problematique*', Richard Ashley (1988) examines the dichotomy of sovereignty/anarchy in which the latter functions as the supplement to the former. Sovereign states with authority over their domestic societies are taken as foundational, whilst the world 'outside' states is essentially anarchic, an unregulated space within which a multiplicity of sovereign states compete or cooperate. In the absence of a central agency, the question constantly invoked in this discourse is 'how is order possible?'. How, for example, can policy be coordinated? Self-identical, rational and self-interested state agents form the basis of this reasoning, whilst ambiguous, uncoordinated anarchy is the problem. The state, according to this discourse, is 'an unproblematic rational presence already there, a sovereign identity that is the self-sufficient source of international history's meaning' (Ashley, 1988: 231).

Yet, in Ashley's view, it is the uncritical acceptance of a rigid dichotomy between sovereignty and anarchy that itself creates the conditions for the very environment it claims to describe (see Ashley, 1988: 243). Taken as the objective condition of international politics, this 'monological' reading downgrades and even eliminates from view those ambiguous practices that subvert the notion of the sovereign state as the stable identity that seeks to master an unstable environment. In particular, non-state actors and agencies that compete with states, even the distinct branches of the state bureaucracy itself,

often work against unitary policies. The state coexists alongside other organisations such as transnational corporations, political movements, and non-
governmental organisations that often transcend and problematise its own
boundaries. For example, the migration of populations or refugees problematise the question of state responsibility for citizens.

The notion of the state as a bounded identity is brought into question if
these 'others' are properly examined. Its 'interests' can only be clearly defined
if the state's identity can be demarcated between a domestic 'inside' and an
international 'outside'. Yet, if the boundary between the two is contested by
competing agents, then the identity of the state is itself in question. The
distinction between inside and outside stops being an objective condition and
becomes, in Derrida's terms, 'undecidable'. That is, it is not an essential or
natural condition but a distinction specified though struggle and conflict both
within states and between them (see Bartelson, 1995).

Furthermore, critics of the notion of sovereignty have drawn attention to
the various ways in which inside/outside distinctions are *socially* constructed,
through, for example, the mutual recognition by other states of national
identity, territorial integrity or, indeed, assumptions concerning trade in
capitalist markets (see Biersteker and Weber, 1996). Such constructions are
designed to fix and stabilise an essentially arbitrary division in a constantly
shifting terrain. But, in attaching its claim to authority to notions such as
national purity or economic success, the state continually confronts resistance
to these efforts (often as a consequence of its own intervention) which expose
the partiality and historical contingency of its claims. As Ashley puts it, the
'figure' of the sovereign state

> is nothing more and nothing less than an arbitrary political representation always
> in the process of being inscribed within history, through practice, and in the face of
> all manner of resistant interpretations that must be excluded if the representation
> is to be counted as a self-evident reality. (Ashley, 1988: 252)

This is not to say that the state does not really exist or is a mere charade.
Rather, its existence as a sovereign entity in an international environment is
predicated upon an ongoing process that determines the nature of its 'inside'
and 'outside' through arbitrary practices of exclusion.

This sort of 'deconstructive' approach has also been employed to expose
the 'internal' functioning of state sovereignty. The modern democratic state is
a state of law in the sense that it is both regulated *by* law and makes claim to
represent the supreme authoritative source *of* law. Clearly law is a fundamental element of the state's function as an ordering agency and hence as a
monopolist of power. For the state to claim domestic authority, its law must
be viewed as formally unified and distinct from other sources of social control
(Goodrich, 1986: 4). This formality expresses the unambiguous and absolute
authority that the state represents, whether this authority be defined as the

'will of the people', of Parliament or even of God. The source of law is regarded as a unity; but it is a unity that is always deferred, invoked but never fully present. The authority of the sovereign is never immediate but instead must be interpreted through the text of the law. This absence distances the source of legal authority from its day-to-day administration; the courts are merely the 'mouthpiece' of the law and the police forces its 'arms'. These agencies do not constitute power relations in themselves, it is claimed by their defenders, they merely supplement that of the state.

Deconstructive readings of the law have turned on the purported unity and formality of legal institutions, and hence the claim to universality that underlies these characteristics. Legal critics – some of which are to be found in the Critical Legal Studies Schools in the UK and US (see Fitzpatrick and Hunt, 1987; Cornell, 1992) – have foregrounded the 'politics of interpretation' within jurisprudence, the rhetorical play that underlies all legal decisions, and the way the internal unity of law is repeatedly subverted by appeal to 'external' sources, such as 'common sense' (see Fish, 1994). For instance, gender and racial prejudices can often inform judicial decisions when conceived as 'normal' assumptions about women's duties to their children or the 'threat' posed by black youths. Such examples operate inside the fiction of the law as a formal unity and the decisions they inform are deemed to be merely secondary to a pre-existing body of universal principles, rather than active interpretations within an 'open' textuality. Yet it is this very assumption of formal closure that erases practices of power from view and gives the legal institution (such as law schools, courts and the legal profession) an aura of expertise and supreme civility. As Peter Goodrich remarks:

> The legal institution is everywhere concerned to inculcate values, to teach modes of living and belonging, to authorise texts and interpretations as the written embodiment of the reason underlying the law. As a totality of discourses and practices the legal institution continuously strives to present the legal code as the symbolic representation of an ideal sociality, as a way of life and as the fundamental morality of belonging to the social whole. (Goodrich 1989: 217–18)

Deconstructive readings of the law do not reduce it to the instrument of some external power infiltrating the formally neutral agencies of the state (such as a cultural elite or the structural power of capital to determine the entirety of a social formation). Rather, the implication is that the state is a fictive unity invoked within the text of the law as the ultimate, incontestable source of its pronouncements. The law's 'amazing trick', according to Stanley Fish, is precisely the rhetorical distance it establishes between its source and its decisions. This enables judicial decisions to vary from case to case without appearing to be purely arbitrary. The law, he claims, is 'in the business of producing the very authority it retroactively invokes' (Fish, 1994: 179).

Deconstructions of the state's sovereign identity in the discourses of both

international relations and legal theory seek to critically dismantle the
symbolic unity and coherence invoked by the claim to represent absolute
authority. They expose the arbitrary, shifting boundaries that underscore the
supposed stability of the state as a principle of order in society. Sovereignty is
revealed to be something of a rhetorical device, a technique of persuasion that
bypasses logic; it is a way of inscribing a complex series of decisions and
judgements within a stable frame whose unity is presupposed and therefore
not open to debate and contestation. However, and this is crucial, state
sovereignty is no less real for being 'rhetorical'. Important decisions that
affect the lives of millions of people may be at stake in judicial decisions or in
the negotiations between states on an international level. To deconstruct state
sovereignty is not to deny the actuality of state actions but to try to examine
the way in which such acts are staged and so take place.

Genealogies of the State

Political debates concerning the control of state power or the legitimacy of its
use have diverted attention from the multitude of mechanisms and techniques through which state power is realised. As Foucault argues, 'political
theory has never ceased to be obsessed with the person of the sovereign'
(1980: 121). The notion of sovereignty must be disputed, not merely to problematise its conceptual status, but to open the way to a closer examination of
the peculiar strategies and practices that comprise the contemporary
operation of power (see Foucault, 1980 and 1981). His 'genealogical' approach
to discursive practices has provided the basis for a critical understanding of
the state that displaces its claim to be the unique and exclusive site of power.
For Foucault, the reduction of power to a state construed as a rational,
calculating subject obscures the organisational continuity between state and
non-state agencies that work throughout society to administer 'disciplinary'
and 'normalising' techniques of governance.

For Foucault, the idea of the state as a unified expression of legitimate
authority is not a natural presupposition of analysis but an *effect* of a more
complex series of processes and activities that are fairly recent in their
emergence. The organisational structure of the state is not a unified will but a
diverse variety of agencies, apparatuses and practices with different mechanisms of control. Behind the unitary authority of the state lies an ensemble of
authorities in the form of knowledge and expertise to whom individual
subjects are encouraged to defer (for example, doctors, academics and
economists). Conceived as a sovereign authority, the state is a part of the myth
of power that characterises modernity – namely, a repressive instrument
emanating from a single, coherent source (see Rouse, 1994: 99–109).
Foucault, by contrast, is interested in the operation of power as a positive force
which is dispersed *throughout* society: 'the state, for all the omnipotence of its

apparatuses, is far from being able to occupy the whole field of actual power relations, and further because the State can only operate on the basis of other, already existing power relations'. It is a derivation from 'a whole series of power networks that invest the body, sexuality, the family, kinship, knowledge, technology and so forth' (Foucault, 1980: 122).

Foucault's historical studies trace the emergence of these networks of power in relation to techniques of control, surveillance and discipline that were gradually adopted within a number of institutional settings in the eighteenth century. These practices made possible new kinds of knowledge about human behaviour. The codification of procedures to monitor and observe subjects, to interview them, to gather information, document and tabulate the results and so forth enabled techniques of constraint that would mould behaviour and produce new kinds of person: useful, obedient and self-monitoring subjects (see Rouse, 1994: 96–7). These practices – increasingly utilised in prisons, hospitals, clinics, the army, schools and factories – permitted a form of social control more subtle than brute force and they have become increasingly generalised in contemporary society. They correspond to what Foucault called a 'microphysics of power' in which the human body becomes the object of a variety of knowledges that categorise, problematise, discipline and normalise subjects (Foucault, 1977: 24–31). Power is not opposed to truth but, on the contrary, truth and power are interlinked, for it is through 'neutral' and 'disinterested' forms of knowledge-acquisition and dissemination that power is exercised. This kind of power cannot be referred back to some prior agency that 'wields' it because its agents are also effects of the practices and knowledge in question (Foucault, 1977: 27–8).

Foucault's approach can be utilised to examine the way state practices overlap with more widely deployed techniques of control. Of particular importance here are the later writings on 'governmentality' where he is concerned, not so much with the disciplinary practices of specific institutions, but with techniques for administering to whole populations, emphasising the attempt to shape and guide the behaviour of subjects who, in a modern liberal society, are formally free (see Foucault, 1991; Gordon, 1991). Liberalism is not just an abstract ideology but also a distinctive 'rationality of government'.

A 'rationality of government' is 'a system of thinking about the nature and practice of government ... capable of making some form of that activity thinkable and practicable both to its practitioners and to those upon whom it is practised' (Gordon 1991: 3). It constitutes the objects of government as questions to be solved or failures to be rectified. Such problematisation invites the formulation of 'programmes' which then justify the utilisation of 'technologies' (such as financial measures, legal controls, bargaining procedures, policies of criminalisation and so forth), turning an unruly reality into a form that is amenable to the application of instrumental calculation (see Rose and Miller, 1992: 181–7). Liberal forms of government, where the population consists of legally autonomous individuals, demand that the practice of ruling operates at an objective distance from the subjects of rule so that individuals are given space to govern themselves. Government does not mean repressive techniques of control and command but, rather, indirect mechanisms designed to administer to independent subjects such that they internalise a disciplinary code. The very idea of state action, often invoked in demands for effective policies and global remedies to generalised problems, is premised on the effectiveness of these practices and discourses of government.

Foucault's work on governmentality has inspired a variety of investigations into the problematics of government within liberal and neo-liberal discourses (see Burchell, et al., 1991; Gane and Johnson, 1993; Barry, et al., 1996). These have focused on such concerns as the government of the economy, social policies concerning the family, poverty, the uses of statistics and the nature of welfare and expertise (see Miller and Rose, 1993; Rose, 1996b; Hacking, 1991; Donzelot, 1980). The technologies employed in these areas, for instance the use of 'experts' in post-war planning or the deployment of incentives to encourage businesses to render themselves more 'competitive', are attempts to alter the behaviour of subjects. The needs and interests, even the physical bodies of citizens (think of housing relocation schemes or hygiene and vaccination programmes) are incorporated within discourses of 'improvement' and 'efficiency', thereby redefining what those needs, interests and bodies are like. Such technologies and policies do not simply order and command but positively construct types of subjects who thus become more governable.

These studies show how the state is one of a number of settings within which the operations of governance are exercised. Its specificity lies not in any essential grand function (such as to maintain capitalism or represent the public) but in its capacity to discursively codify governmental practices, separating them off into the spheres over which it must rule. In so doing, it grants technologies 'a temporary institutional durability'. The state, or more particularly the discourses that shape that state, are, as Rose and Miller put it, 'an historically variable linguistic device for conceptualising and articulating ways of ruling' (1992: 177).

Genealogical analyses highlight the complex and irreducibly plural nature of the state's practices; indeed, the state begins to look like a multiplicity of mini-authorities, utilising knowledge to categorise and shape the subjects under their command. Attention to this complexity has been important in qualifying accounts of the state that tend to treat it as a neutral instrument of power. The Marxist political theorist Nicos Poulantzas, for example, was especially influenced by Foucault's work in as much as it pointed to the role of state power (the courts, the police, army and so on) in producing the subjects through and over which it ruled (see Poulantzas,

1978). These, he argued, ultimately supported capitalist relations of production. Likewise, some feminists have used Foucault's work to argue that patriarchy is not simply a matter of men occupying positions of power but is inscribed in the very practices of the state apparatus. Welfare agencies, for example, actively construct and institutionalise unequal gender roles in their categorisation of 'legitimate' work or their regulation of the family and adult responsibilities to it (see Pringle and Watson, 1992).

What is absent (though not logically excluded) in Foucauldian approaches, however, is any sense of the state as a relatively unified whole with a functional specificity distinct from other social practices. Even if we reject the view that the state has objective boundaries and a stable identity, efforts to utilise the state as though it did represent a unified purpose are frequently made by social and political forces. Despite its organisational diversity, the symbolic unity of the state is often invoked to justify the use of organised force against 'enemies' within and without its boundaries (Poulantzas, 1978: 76–86). At key moments, such as in the event of war or during social and political disorder, the state is invested with a unity of purpose that legitimates its distinctive repressive functions and articulates its diverse elements around a relatively coherent project. The deployment of both force and consent in the restructuring of the state has been the basis of analyses of 'hegemony'. It is to these that we now turn.

Hegemony and the State

The concept of 'hegemony' was developed in the 1930s by the Italian Marxist Antonio Gramsci (1891–1937) to theorise the complex interaction of state, economy and civil society. Instead of reducing the realm of the 'superstructures' – state and civil society, ideology, culture and so on – to a reflection of the interests of the dominant class, Gramsci argued that the state functioned as a relatively autonomous site of class compromise. In his conception, the term 'state' was coextensive with the diverse socio-cultural practices of civil society, too, in so far as these (including the Church, newspapers, intellectuals and the like) contributed to maintaining social order by disseminating certain values (Gramsci, 1971: 242–7, 261–3). A class could be said to exercise hegemony when it succeeded in making its domination a matter of 'common sense' throughout civil society. This reduced the need for coercion to enforce obedience amongst subordinate groups and classes. Hegemony involved the forging of class alliances and linkages such that different social groups and classes would see themselves not as opposed interests but as part of an inclusive 'collective will'. In Gramsci's conception, the state is the site in which this complex unity is formed.

Gramsci's analyses have been immensely fruitful in challenging reductionist aspects of Marxism; in particular, the notion that societal unity is an automatic reflex of economic structures. Instead, the form taken by 'society' is understood as the outcome of open-ended struggles to achieve a balance of forces between distinct and, in various ways, opposed social groups and classes (see Jessop, 1990; Poulantzas, 1978; Martin, 1998a). In their critique of economic reductionism, Laclau and Mouffe (1985) sought to develop Gramsci's concepts in a direction that moves beyond the Marxist frame of reference. This meant dropping the foundational claim that society must ultimately cohere around endogenous economic laws and the concomitant assumption that economic classes are the primary agents of social and political change (see Howarth, 1998). While rejecting Gramsci's assumption that classes were its fundamental agents, Laclau and Mouffe continue to employ the concept of hegemony to denote the constitution of collective identities. However, in their use, hegemony is not necessarily led by an economic class. The values and identities that might fill out the content of hegemony often take a number of forms: such as nationalist, populist, ethnic, racial and gendered. Class interests do not always function as the unifying principle, especially in societies without strong class traditions.

For Laclau and Mouffe, hegemony denotes the contingent, discursive unity that temporarily ties together (or 'articulates') a variety of distinct identities. These identities are conceived as essentially polyvalent and, therefore, open to a variety of articulations. The state apparatuses themselves are not necessarily the place in which this discursive unity is forged. Following Foucault, they argue that the state is a complex ensemble of institutions that exhibits no essential unity of purpose; it is 'an uneven set of branches and functions, only relatively integrated by the hegemonic practices which take place within it' (Laclau and Mouffe, 1985: 180). While they do not develop a comprehensive theory of the state, Laclau and Mouffe's analyses follow the 'extended' conception developed by Gramsci (see Mouffe, 1981). The state is conceived broadly, as the whole gamut of agencies and techniques that serve to institutionalise a hegemonic system; this may at times differ from or extend beyond the institutions of the state proper. Unlike Gramsci, however, they are more attentive to the plurality of both class and non-class identities that may fill out the content of hegemony.

Laclau and Mouffe's interpretation of hegemony has been focused principally on the formation of identities, forms of subjectivity and concepts in political theory and not on institutions and organisations such as the state (see Laclau, 1990, 1994 and 1996; Mouffe 1995). Their lack of attention to political structures has brought some criticism, even from relative sympathisers (for example, Mouzelis, 1990). Whilst there is some validity in these criticisms, there is also a misconception in play: for Laclau and Mouffe, social and political structures are discursively constituted, that is, their objectivity is a social construction. This does not mean they are unreal or arbitrarily conjured up (as some critics mistakenly suggest when they accuse them of abandoning the idea of an 'extra-discursive' reality); on the contrary, social constructions are real and have an existence external to human conscious-ness. The family is real in as much as it exists externally to individual consciousness but it is no less a social construction. To stress the social character of such structures and practices is to point to the *symbolic* form they take. Social, economic and political structures are social relationships and not independent physical objects. They require social and symbolic validation as part of their very existence; they are principles of organisation that must be continually reproduced via subjects who 'support' them. For Laclau and Mouffe, this is an ongoing, open-ended process of inscribing social experi-ence into discursive frameworks by marking out and privileging certain kinds of meaning and identity and excluding others. This process underscores all social and political institutions, even the seemingly most enduring. Thus their attention to identities and subjectivity is not a failure to understand the wider, structured conditions in which agents must act. Rather, social and political structures are present only as efforts to produce stable forms of identity and subjectivity.

Laclau and Mouffe's understanding of hegemony as the effort to stabilise social and political identities alerts us to a logic that cannot, in their view, be the exclusive claim of any distinct institution or organisation. *All* social relations are constituted through the 'hegemonisation' of identities and thus there can be no privileged space, such as the state, that can monopolise this activity. Nevertheless, in so far as the secular political tradition of the West identifies the nation-state as the highest principle of social and political unity and has laid down structures to fulfil this role, the struggle for hegemony will find its fullest expression in and through the terrain of the state. There is nothing inevitable about this, as the debate concerning the possible eclipse of the nation-state in a 'global' era suggests (see Dunn, 1994).

The advantage of Laclau and Mouffe's approach is that it allows us to think of the state's form and function as part of an ongoing contest to discursively position subjects. This process is ongoing because hegemony is always exceeded by the plurality of the social identities that it seeks to fix. The contest will, therefore, involve the mobilisation of concepts and categories which invoke certain kinds of social difference as 'natural' and, therefore, immutable, and it will typically involve an attempt to identify symbolic enemies and absolute antagonists (such as crime, unemployment or foreigners) that threaten social order in general.

Often such efforts to redefine subjects according to different notions of collective identity will seek to restructure the state apparatus itself. These structures will become part of the effort to cultivate certain forms of subjectivity, to discipline (in Foucault's sense) sectors of the public to accept certain kinds of norms and values as 'common sense'. Examples of this kind of analysis can be found in Stuart Hall's (1988) interpretation of Thatcherism,

Aletta Norval's (1996) analysis of apartheid discourse in South Africa or Jacob
Torfing's (1998) theorisation of the restructuring of the welfare state in light
of the exhaustion of the 'Fordist' model of capitalist development (see also
Bertramsen et al., 1991; Martin, 1998b). Whilst post-structuralist uses of
hegemony converge in certain respects with neo-Marxist analyses, they
diverge from these by looking beyond the logic of capitalist reproduction to
explain the formation and transformation of political orders by reference
across the social field.

Conclusion

At the start of this chapter I noted the peculiarity of the modern state's claim
to function as a unity despite its organisational complexity and unevenness. It
is the disjuncture between symbolic unity and concrete complexity that has
been at the root of many post-structuralist approaches to the state, rather than
questions of its overall function or proper limits. For post-structuralists, what
is at issue is not how to define the state and its role in society but to determine
under what conditions the state comes to be regarded as a unifying principle
and the discursive or ideological effects that may flow from this.

The complexity and unevenness of its apparatuses, their different modes
of intervention and the variety of domains in which they operate serve as a
reminder that the modern state's claim to supreme power and unified
authority cannot be presupposed; it is a political achievement in itself, one not
guaranteed by the mere existence of a state, because it is based on strategies of
power and persuasion. The approaches to the state that we have examined
above have underscored its political constitution. Deconstruction has opened
up the arbitrary conceptual divisions that support the state's claim to
sovereignty over a given territory; genealogical approaches have examined
how practices of government discursively codify rules and principles that
shape the subjects in whose name the state governs; and the theory of
hegemony points to the role of conflict and antagonism in unifying subjects
around specific 'public' goals that the state comes to represent. We might say,
then, that the state has no essential identity prior to these efforts; its unity is
not a function of the will of the people who 'contract' to generate it (as liberals
believe) or the needs of capitalism (as Marxists believe) but an ongoing
process. It is a process in which we are constantly invited to identify with the
principles and values that the state claims to defend, such as 'freedom',
'justice', 'national autonomy' and so on. Our common endorsement of these
values, as if they were the very foundation of society and could be fully
expressed through institutions, implicates us all in the fictive unity of the
state.

Yet to engage in any effort to organise the social world under some
principle of unity, as the state seeks to do, is to attempt to fix or stabilise it,

despite society's irregularity, excess of meaning and constant evolution. Paradoxically, then, this most supreme political institution must, in order to function at all, set limits to social differences, shared meanings and the direction of change. In this sense, the state is a profoundly *anti-political* formation. Its successful operation demands that choices be shaped and controlled through codified laws and procedural rules, that individuals are encouraged (and often coerced) to behave in certain ways, as both agents and subjects of authority, and that the range of acceptable differences amongst individuals and social groups be regulated. In short, to secure political governance of society, the state must suppress certain directions for change and opportunities to act. It must specify what is and is not subject to regulation, what is and is not available for political contestation and by what rules.

Political theory and analysis continues to frame enquiries into the political in terms of the state. Despite portentous claims concerning its demise in an era of globalisation, the state, as R. B. J. Walker suggests, still 'offers an extraordinarily powerful answer to questions about the political' (1995: 23). Post-structuralist analyses of the state, in various ways, have sought to denaturalise its form and its functions and to remind us that the unity of 'its' will is itself politically constituted through discourses and institutionalised practices that ultimately are based on contingent decisions made in specific circumstances. As long as the state continues to demand that we become subjects of its rule and citizens within its space, these analyses will continue to work against the naturalisation of the political.

4

After the Subject of International Security

JENNY EDKINS

Introduction

> Security is about survival. It is when an issue is presented as posing an existential
> threat to a designated referent object. (Buzan, Waever and de Wilde, 1998: 21)

International politics as an academic discipline often sees itself as concerned
with relationships between political entities such as nation-states. But
increasingly the discipline accepts constructivist or post-positivist positions
which acknowledge the importance of discourse. It is no longer simply the
number of weapons that is believed to determine power relations between
states – the way they interpret each other's actions is also seen as significant.
However, this constructivist or post-positivist thinking tends to fall short of
making the best use of the insights of post-structuralism. In this respect two
areas in particular can be highlighted.

First, much constructivist or post-positivist theory does not have an
account of how political communities, groups or individuals in the West are
constituted. It is concerned only with the system level: international not
domestic processes. Paradigmatically, these are treated as interactions between states, although increasingly other entities such as non-governmental
organisations, transnational corporations, international organisations, ethnic
groups, individual people and so on are included. Even so, in order to sustain
an analysis limited to this level, theorists have to assume that states exist
before there is any interaction between them. That is to say, they think as if
states are first formed and only afterwards interact with each other on the
international stage and acquire identities. Thus, although it may be accepted
that identity is constructed intersubjectively, this process is thought to happen
to an already existing, somehow neutral, entity or subject. This applies in a
similar way when the subject is a person, not a state. People are regarded as
existing as individuals before they interact intersubjectively. In this view,
identity is something states or people possess – it is an add-on. There is no
account of how modern subjects (political communities, organisations,
people) are produced in the first place. But, for post-structuralists, becoming a
subject always already involves a naming and an identity (see Chapter 1).

The second area where such theory does not pursue post-structuralist insights is in its failure to explore certain assumptions about the modern Western subject. The notion of the subject in post-positivist or constructivist international relations might be called, following Stuart Hall, the sociological subject (Hall, 1992). Hall traces the 'decentring' of the subject through several stages. The move from the Cartesian conscious, rational, pre-social individual and his search for certainty to the sociological subject is the first of these. The sociological subject is first born and then socialised. Through socialisation he (or, by now, she) acquires his or her identity, gender, nationality and so forth. Interactions with others in the social field produce the fully social individual. This notion of the subject retains a number of important limitations: socialisation takes place between pre-existing subjects and a completely socialised individual is possible; conscious processes are emphasised; identity is something that persons possess – it is seen as a quality or a characteristic that can be attached to subjects.

The notion of the sociological subject ignores Freud's questioning of the role of conscious thought and positing of the unconscious; it does not accept the implications of Marxist claims about the social nature of being, the priority of social being over conscious thought and the role of the ideological; it denies the claims of feminist theorising that subjectivity is constituted as gendered and that this includes notions suggesting that the body itself is constituted and not natural; and it ignores Foucault's work that shows how power/knowledge is productive of subjects and how, simultaneously, disciplinary practices constitute subjects and the knowledge about them. It also ignores issues of fragmentation, hybridity and diaspora and questions of coloniser and colonised. When we come to theories of international security, these blind spots are disastrous.

Contemporary continental philosophy and psychoanalytic work sees modern Western subjects as produced in the face of the limits to human existence. These reflections are largely neglected in studies of international relations. There are of course problems with psychoanalytic approaches. It might be thought that a psychoanalytic approach must involve reducing analysis to the level of the individual. But, on the contrary, it is precisely the psychoanalytic approach that subverts the distinction between the individual and the social and denies any notion of a settled, separate individual as such.

This chapter focuses on just one area of international theory where there are obvious parallels between the concerns of Western philosophy, post-structuralism and psychoanalysis – international security. After all, security is 'about survival' and about issues that are 'presented as posing an existential threat' (Buzan, Waever and de Wilde, 1998: 21). Michael Dillon has argued that security is a 'point of entry' that is fundamental both to philosophy and international relations, although, paradoxically, the literature of security in international relations 'does not ask the question of security as such'

(Dillon, 1996: 19). Within contemporary Western security studies, the socio-logical subject seems to be widely accepted.

There are a number of debates in this literature. Theories of international security based solely on the state and military power are no longer as persu-asive as they were. Recent work is widely seen as having made two moves away from what are taken as traditional approaches – a deepening and a broadening of security. Traditional security studies are centred around the study of state or national security and what is regarded as the prime threat to that security – military action by other states in the international system. The first move of contemporary developments in security studies, a deepening of notions of security, claims to extend the study of security to other so-called referent objects beside the state. This would typically include, for example, moving upwards to regional and international levels of security and moving downwards to substate levels, which might include examination of ethnic or national groups, or even individuals. The move from the state to alternative referent objects, such as society (see Buzan, 1991; Lipschutz, 1995), empha-sises identity as the key goal of security, replacing state survival or sovereignty (see Waever et al., 1993). Bill McSweeney has argued that these approaches retain an unproblematised notion of identity and see society as static and non-conflictual (McSweeney, 1996; see also Bloom, 1990). The second move, the broadening of security, entails the inclusion of issue areas other than military security: environmental, economic, and societal security, for example. There are those who contend that alternative, emancipatory approaches to security can be found through notions of human security within a global community (see Booth, 1991, 1995). But, insofar as this work is based on an analysis of states or statism and the state-system, it retains a state-centric view (see Latham, 1996). Moreover, the question of *whose* emancipation is at stake returns us to the question of identity (see Wyn Jones, 1995; Krause and Williams, 1996).

All these new approaches have been grouped together under the name of constructivist security studies (see Buzan, Waever and de Wilde, 1998: 205). The term critical security studies is also used, sometimes to embrace con-structivist *and* post-structuralist work (see Krause and Williams, 1998) and sometimes in an attempt to delineate a more specific new orthodoxy. They all share a view of the subject that more or less approximates to Hall's socio-logical subject – it is rational and individualistic, despite being constrained, and constructed and socialised in the course of intersubjective interactions. There are disagreements about whether we should be looking at the state or the individual as the subject of security, but there is agreement that the social world is constructed by these agents. The phrase 'the world is what we make it' encapsulates this position.

As R. B. J. Walker has pointed out, a rethinking of security involves much more than critical or constructivist security studies has yet attempted. Taking seriously the insights from post-structuralist thought would involve a re-examination of the political, a scepticism towards modern Western views of the autonomous subject, an involvement in debates on identity in feminism and postcolonialism, and the inclusion of discourse and ideology as material practices in social analysis (see Walker, 1997: 69). Thus, in this chapter, we will look at the contribution psychoanalytic notions of the subject might make to the rethinking of international security. This inevitably brings in the other factors that Walker identifies, since all are thought of differently in post-structuralism.

Rather than examine the contrast between post-structuralist approaches and constructivist or critical security studies in general (which would be impossible since this work does not add up to a single critical approach), I have chosen to focus on the work of Barry Buzan and, in particular, on the recent book by Buzan, Waever and de Wilde *Security: A New Framework for Analysis* (1998). This work follows and extends Buzan's earlier book (1991) which was itself a response in some sense to Kenneth Waltz's *Man, the State and War* (1959). As well as being seen as important in the discipline and widely included in undergraduate courses in security, Buzan's work, with his various collaborators of the Copenhagen School of security studies, is useful for my purposes because it seeks to elaborate a coherent new approach while holding on to what I have called the sociological subject. The book aims to set out a comprehensive framework for the wider agenda of security studies. It looks at five sectors of security: military, political, economic, environmental and societal. The argument is that security studies should not be restricted to the military sector. Rather than being appropriate for a particular issue area, security is a particular type of politics. The present chapter offers an altern-ative analysis of what type of politics that might be and takes issue with Buzan, Waever and de Wilde's conclusions about securitisation and politicization.

The (In)Secure Subject

In the Lacanian approaches to subjectivity elaborated by Slavoj Žižek, sub-jectivity is inextricably bound up with the social or symbolic order. It is through interpellation into the symbolic order that the subject is constituted (see Žižek, 1992, 1991, 1989; Edkins, 1999). However, the symbolic order itself does not exist before the subject. It only *comes into being* when it is posited by the subject as *already existing*. In other words, the subject brings the social order into being by acting as if it were already there. This act of positing constitutes the subject and simultaneously constitutes the symbolic order. It is an act without ground; there is nothing to which an appeal for legitimacy or foundations can be addressed. However, and most important, this process produces the illusion that both subject and social order are always already in being. This illusion includes an appearance of groundedness – subject and social appear to be rooted in pre-existing foundations.

It is through the supposing of the existence of the symbolic order that the symbolic order comes to exist and comes to appear to have always already existed. We enter a time warp, a peculiar space/time where things only ever *will have been*. Lacan describes this with reference to language, which for him is the social or symbolic order in embodied form:

> What constitutes me as subject is my question. In order to be recognised by the other, I utter what was only in view of what *will be*. In order to find him, I call him by a name he must assume or refuse in order to reply to me ... I identify myself in language, but only by losing myself in it like an object. What is realised in my history is not the past definite of what *was*, since it is no more, or even the present perfect of what *has been* in what I am, but the future anterior of what I *shall have been* for what I am in the process of becoming. (Lacan, 1977: 86 (my emphasis))

We inhabit a fantasy of the always already (and of linear time). But we also inhabit a fantasy of another sort, associated with the image of completeness. Both the subject and the social or symbolic order are inevitably incomplete or impossible. They are structured around a lack or an antagonism. This lack is constitutive or, in other words, it is the lack which enables the subject (or the social order) to constitute itself at all. In part this is what Ferdinand de Saussure identified in language: the endless play of associations and signi-fications which resist and destabilise meaning but at the same time produce it (Saussure, 1966). At the risk of over-simplification, this can perhaps be clarified in terms of self and other, using these terms very loosely. The other is put to one side or excluded for the subject to constitute itself as self. However, this other is necessary for the self to be constituted: it is the constitutive out-side (Staten, 1984). If there were no other, the self could not be distinguished. Moreover, the self is necessarily inhabited by a trace of the other or, what Julia Kristeva calls, 'the stranger within' (Kristeva, 1991). The self can only be produced with reference to the other or the not-self. However, this means that the self remains impure. It contains a trace or remainder of the other. It is incomplete. Moreover this trace is necessary for the self to come into being at all (see also Chapter 1).

In the Lacanian account, the subject is interpellated into the symbolic order through fantasy and constituted through desire. As Žižek puts it: 'The original question of desire is not directly "What do I want?" but "what do *others* want from me? What do they see in me? What am I to others?"' (Žižek, 1997: 9). The subject becomes what the other, the symbolic order, is assumed to want by taking on a certain symbolic position or mandate. But this position is always incomplete or unsafe because there is always something left over, something that cannot be symbolised. In Lacanian terminology, this leftover is the real. The real is that which cannot fit neatly into symbolic space. People are not just the subject positions that they hold – there is always an excess. The subject, once constituted, still has to face the question of why he or she has taken on a particular mandate. But, since there are no foundations for the social order outside it, there is no reassuring answer to this. Taking on a mandate is always arbitrary.

Simon Critchley has argued that subjectivity is constituted in the face of trauma (Critchley, 1996). In simple terms, trauma is an experience of overwhelming shock, terror or brutality – as in violent events, such as a car accident, shell shock in wartime, a natural disaster – when human beings are confronted with the limits to their existence as subjects. It involves 'the recognition of realities that most of us have not begun to face' (Caruth, 1995). It is an encounter with the real – that which cannot be symbolised. In the normal circumstances of everyday life, the social order provides the possibility of concealing or forgetting the real in favour of the fantasy we call social reality – it provides security. In the face of trauma the inadequacy of the social or symbolic order becomes horribly apparent. The lack appears and trauma is experienced as a betrayal by the social order.

If the social and the subject are not only mutually constituted but constituted through trauma, then what is at stake in issues of security is not identity, either of the group or the individual, but, rather, the simultaneous production of the social or symbolic order and the subject in the face of the traumatic real (Žižek, 1989; Critchley, 1992). The social is constituted by excluding the real, that which cannot be symbolised. Trauma is an encounter with the real.

So, to summarise, what we have in a Lacanian approach to subjectivity and the social order is, firstly, a view of the two as mutually constituted. The coming-into-being of the subject and of the social order are interlinked. Secondly, we have a view of both as constituted only in a temporary, incomplete and unsafe way around a lack or antagonism. It is only because of that lack and through an economy of desire that either subject or symbolic order is constituted in the first place. Neither subject nor social order *exists* at a particular point in time. Both are only ever in a process of *becoming*. Space/time is distorted and accounts of intersubjective interactions have to be rethought. Thirdly, we have a notion of subjectivity and the symbolic order as constituted in the face of the real, where the real is that which cannot be symbolised. The real has to be excluded for (what we call) social reality to come into being.

Psychoanalytic approaches raise and acknowledge the issue of security. Although the constitution of the social order and the subject is inevitably incomplete and insecure, the subject is, nevertheless, driven by a compelling desire for completeness. Despite its impossibility, this desire is fundamental. Discourses that construct certain subjects as threats or enemies function as fantasies concealing the impossibility of security. By producing security as an issue that could be solved by the defence of the state, for example, the need to raise the question of the limit to security itself is successfully averted.

What does this mean for security studies? How can we rethink approaches to security in international relations in the light of these psychoanalytic notions of subjectivity and the real? As we have seen, the deepeners and wideners of constructivist security studies see themselves as engaged in a debate about two extensions of security: first, to different referent objects and, second, to a variety of issue areas (Buzan, 1991). Each issue area will have different referent objects (Buzan, Waever and de Wilde, 1998). However, this split arises because the notion of construction sees areas and referent objects as distinct. A post-structuralist view of subjectivity, such as the one I have outlined, would stress how the constitution of a specific issue area involves the constitution of corresponding referent objects. These then become, in Foucauldian terms, subjects of power/knowledge – securitisation both produces and controls them.

As Dillon points out, security is 'the progenitor of a proliferating array of discourses of danger within whose brutal and brutalising networks of power-knowledge modern human being is increasingly ensnared and, ironically, radically endangered' (Dillon, 1996: 16). In order to elaborate further how and for what reason security has begun to proliferate in this way, it is first necessary to consider in more detail the psychoanalytic account of the formation of subjectivity in relation to the symbolic order and, in particular, in relation to what Lacan calls the master signifier.

Security and the Master Signifier

We have seen in the discussion so far that the incompleteness or insecurity of the social or symbolic order has to be concealed in order for social reality to appear. This process of concealment takes place though the operation of a master signifier. It is a double-edged process, at once both productive and controlling. The master signifier (its masculinity reflecting the patriarchal structure of societies such as that of the modern West) is the so-called quilting point or *point de capiton* around which the shifting of signifiers is temporarily halted and meaning installed. This quilting produces the particular social order and constitutes subjectivities by concealing the lack around which the social order is constituted, the antagonism at its heart. The master signifier is that which takes up the place in the structure that conceals the antagonism. It might be, for example, divine providence, the invisible hand of the market, the monarch, the Jew, the objective logic of history, patriarchy (see Žižek, 1992) – in a sense any master signifier will do, and any individual or object can occupy that position.

In the political communities of Western modernity, paradigmatically, the modern nation-state, one of the signifiers that performs this function is sovereignty (see Edkins and Pin-Fat, 1999). It is around sovereignty that the social order is constituted and this is reflected in that signifier's centrality to modern discourses of politics and international relations. Political acts are legitimised in relation to sovereignty and inaction or non-intervention in the internal affairs of states is legitimised in the same way. Force and violence are tools that the sovereign state lays claim to and its right to do so is not one that can be disputed (or even raised as an issue) within the symbolic order of sovereignty. Of course, this constitution of the state or political community demands a sovereign individual. The state is formed and derives its sovereignty through the apparent consent and agreement of individuals that constitute it. As Michael Williams reminds us, the modern Western notion of security takes as its referent object the political community of the state, a community which is constituted around the individualistic subject (Williams, 1998).

In the social or symbolic order centred around a particular master signifier, and the political community or symbolic order which it embraces, security occupies the place of the constitutive outside or supplement. In Jacques Derrida's work, the notion of the supplement is one example of the logic of the undecidable (Derrida, 1992a and 1992b). Literally in the case of a book, the supplement is both something which has been added in order to complete the book or to fill a lack in the original publication *and* something which is inessential, not needed, outside the main publication. The supplement is external and internal at the same time, both necessary and unnecessary, essential and inessential. The supplement is the constitutive outside we met above, as discussed by Staten (1984). The role of the supplement is to produce the original or, rather, the *appearance* of an original – the presumption that an original must have existed. As Derrida argues:

> Through this sequence of supplements a necessity is announced: that of an infinite chain, ineluctably multiplying the supplementary mediations that produce the sense of the very thing they defer: the mirage of the thing itself, of immediate presence, of originary perception. (Derrida, 1974: 157)

For Derrida, presence is not originary but constituted by an absence (a lack) or, in other words, by difference. In Western modernity, political community is constituted in reference to sovereignty; sovereignty conceals the lack around which the (nation-)state is constituted. Security is guaranteed by the sovereign; insecurity is concealed. More than that – security is the supplement, that which produces the semblance of reality in sovereignty, that which assures us that the master signifier, the sovereign state, is present and that we are safe. Our subjectivity, constituted in reference to the sovereign state's guarantee of the symbolic order, is secured. The legitimacy and, hence, the power and political authority of the sovereign nation-state are assured (see also Chapter 3).

We can extend this discussion to examine how, in what we call the post-cold-war era in the West, other referent objects are being brought into being. As we have seen, Buzan, Waever and de Wilde argue that there are a number of sectors that constitute the wider agenda of security. In addition to the traditional military sector, there are now the political, economic, societal and environmental sectors. These sectors are 'distinctive areas of discourse in which a variety of different values (sovereignty, wealth, identity, sustainability, and so on) can be the focus of power struggles' (Buzan, Waever and de Wilde, 1998: 196). In each sector, Buzan, Waever and de Wilde seek to locate specific referent objects. In the military and political sectors the referent object is the state or, in the case of the latter, also the international community, while in the societal sector it is 'large-scale collective identities ... such as nations and religions' (Buzan, Waever and de Wilde, 1998: 22–3) and, in the environmental sector, species, habitat and climate are all contenders.

So a series of master signifiers (sovereignty, wealth, identity, sustainability) produce corresponding subjects (state, economy, ethnic group, environment) whose survival is seen as at stake. In an important sense, however, the referent objects of security are not the state, economy, ethnic group or environment but, rather, 'state sovereignty', 'economic wealth', 'ethnic group identity' or 'environmental sustainability' and it is these that have to be securitised. Sovereignty, identity and so on represent what is worth preserving about the subjects themselves. There is no ethnic group without identity, no state without sovereignty. These signifiers have a crucial structural part in the constitution of the subjects they appear merely to describe.

The implication is that the extension of the discourse of security, or the process that Buzan, Waever and de Wilde describe as 'securitization', should not be regarded merely as the extension of a new way of dealing with issues to areas previously dealt with in other ways. To the advocates of increasing securitisation, this process seems to be a way of bringing to prominence issues or subjects previously ignored by agents in positions of power. However, there are dangers as well as advantages in securitisation. It is a process that leads not only towards emancipation (were that possible) but also towards totalitarian closure. The problem comes with the claim that the antagonism around which a particular social reality is (temporarily) constituted can be resolved and that this would then resolve antagonism per se (if only we could secure the environment, all would be fine, all social antagonisms of other sorts would disappear). This is the totalising impulse that can be so dangerous and that works alongside and hand in hand with the technologised, securitised and depoliticised culture of Western modernity.

To argue this through, let us return to the state and the preservation of state sovereignty. Lacanian approaches teach us that the state is, like every other subject, incomplete or structured around a lack or antagonism. As such, it is, in its very character, insecure. However, this lack of completeness has to be concealed in order for the social order centred on the state to come into being and for the fantasy of sovereignty to be effective. This is why the state has to be securitised. Now, securitising is normally seen as a question of making threats obvious. Threats to the environment are made clear, for example, when the environment is securitised. But, in fact, it is something quite different that is taking place. Securitising involves concealing the inherent insecurity in any referent object, in other words, concealing the *impossibility* of security. If something is impossible we conceal that impossibility by shifting the blame somewhere else. For example, during the cold war, state insecurity in the West is blamed on the Soviet threat. We can then say that the state *would be* secure but for the Soviet threat. The impossibility of security appears contingent. It is well known that an external threat is manipulated by regimes whose internal control is threatened. This account explains how that works.

Subjects, then, are produced by the very discourse of security and are always produced as subjects of security. Security is impossible, of course, since the subject can never be fully complete or secure. In contrast, for Buzan, Waever and de Wilde, 'it is a choice to phrase things in security (or desecurity) terms'. Issues exist before they are securitised. Referent objects like the environment exist prior to their discursive construction as security concerns. However, this does not reflect the complexity of the processes involved. The very being of a subject is a question of (in)security. However, that can be concealed. Indeed, that is what normally happens. If the question of security is hidden, subjects appear to exist unproblematically until they are made into referent objects of security.

The process of securitisation is related to the source of value that any symbolic or social order takes as fundamental. We can see, for example, how 'God' as master signifier gives meaning to religious wars and crusades; how the economic threat increases in significance when so much of our identity as subjects is tied up with questions of economic value; and how the security of the nation-state embodies the value given to contractarian principles of citizenship in modern, liberal democratic states with their sovereign individuals. In the so-called third-world, traditional approaches to security linked to the state might not be appropriate, not just because the state is in effect a threat to its population, but because it does not perform the same ideological function as master signifier in this context as it does in liberal democracies (see Ayoob, 1995).

The question of the referent object of security in contemporary humanitarian crises is an interesting one. Buzan, Waever and de Wilde claim that the use of military force in humanitarian intervention is not an instance of security: 'routine world order activities, such as peacekeeping and humanitarian intervention ... cannot be viewed as concerning existential threats to their states, or even as emergency action in the sense of suspending normal rules' (Buzan, Waever and de Wilde, 1998: 22). However, in humanitarian crises in the 1990s, we have seen a threat to the constitution of subjects as 'human beings'. I am not referring here to the physical threats to those in whose name interventions were mounted but to the way observers, those whose desires were apparently instrumental in bringing about interventions, were constituted as subjects. Intervention secures the humanitarianism of the bystander and constitutes an international (humanitarian) community. International humanitarianism replaces state sovereignty as the ultimate value around which the international community is constituted. To 'state sovereignty', 'economic wealth', 'ethnic group identity' and 'environmental sustainability' we can add 'international humanitarianism'. Through humanitarianism the international is defined and secured in the image of the West.

Intervention calls on international security, producing the international community in the place of the state as referent object and humanitarianism in place of sovereignty as master signifier. This, then, internalises the external, producing military action by nation-states as police or enforcement action. The security threat is a threat to the survival of the international community in the image of the West and humanitarianism becomes the master signifier around which a social order, sceptical of alternative master narratives, can constitute itself. Whether a master signifier that internalises the external by claiming humanity as its source will work is doubtful. In recent episodes, there has been a move away from humanitarian intervention by the international community to action which, while still in the name of humanitarianism, is linked more closely with a specific power grouping (Edkins, 2000).

The Politics of Securitisation

In a political order constituted around a master signifier, security occupies the place of the undecidable or the supplement. Subjects and political communities are constituted as referent objects through the setting to one side or excluding of (in)security. This can lead us to a politics of security – a political account of processes of securitisation or of discourses of security. I will explore, in a preliminary way, what some elements of such a politics might be.

The logic of the supplement in Derrida's work is related to the logic of the undecidable (Derrida, 1987: 43, 101; Edkins, 1996, 2000). Undecidables mark the gap between the overturning of the hierarchy of opposites and the emergence of a new term. Undecidables are terms which embody *différance* within themselves – they resist specification and incorporate opposites. Undecidability is emphatically not, however, to be confused with any move to a relativistic position. On the contrary, although in a very specific sense we cannot know that a decision has been taken and ethico-political responsibility exercised, what is called for is a continuous process of ethico-political decisioning. This process would be based on the specifics of particular cases and would replace attempts to formulate generalisable rules or to resolve, once and for all, the debate between those who wish to extend security to an increasing range of issues and those who wish to limit it.

Buzan, Waever and de Wilde (see also Waever, 1995) explain how they see securitisation.

> 'Security' is the move that takes politics beyond the established rules of the game and frames the issue either as a special kind of politics or as above politics. Securitization can thus be seen as a more extreme version of politicisation. In theory any public issue can be located on the spectrum ranging from nonpoliticised (meaning the state does not deal with it and it is not in any other way made an issue of public debate and decision) through politicised (meaning the issue is part of public policy, requiring government decision and resource allocations or, more rarely, some other form of communal governance) to securitized (meaning the issue is presented as an existential threat, requiring emergency measures and justifying actions outside the normal bounds of political procedure). (Buzan, Waever and de Wilde, 1998: 23–4)

What is at stake here is the choice between the 'wideners', who want to securitise issues such as the environment, politics and the economy, and those who claim that this extension of securitisation is not desirable. Claims to treat a particular issue as a security threat or a security crisis are made in various areas. Military activities are most readily cast in this light but any issue can be the subject of a claim to securitisation. But if, as has been argued here, security is undecidable, then securitisation is sometimes to be promoted, sometimes not. We must pay attention to the exact political decision in a specific historical situation. Ethico-political decisioning has to take place *each time* the question of securitisation arises. Any general formula would depoliticise, leading to what David Campbell describes as 'no ethics, politics, or responsibility, only a programme, technology, and its irresponsible application' (Campbell, 1994). However, it is crucial to stress, yet again, that there is no question of indeterminacy or of relativism. As Derrida insists: 'There would be no indecision or double bind were it not between determined (semantic, ethical, political) poles, which are upon occasion terribly necessary and always irreplaceably singular' (Derrida, 1988: 148). This most emphatically *does not* mean that we do nothing. What it means is that we *must* act responsibly. Indeed, it is only in these situations that we *can* act responsibly. The fact that there is no generalisable rule or universal principle that we can follow means precisely that:

> Not only *must* we ... negotiate the relation between the calculable and the incalculable ... but we *must* take it as far as possible, beyond the place we find ourselves and beyond the already identifiable zones of morality or politics or law, beyond the distinction between national and international, public and private, and so on. (Derrida, 1992: 28)

An example of the double bind is the way the state (or any other political community) may be a source of security or insecurity for individuals within its jurisdiction. As we have seen, the constitution of the person as subject relies on the constitution of a social or symbolic order, so the relation of the person to the threatening state will, in any case, be ambiguous. This is, of course, especially visible when citizens are conscripted to fight. To deny the validity of the state's claim on one's life in those circumstances may be to repudiate the very support of one's existence as subject in the symbolic order. To accept it would, quite clearly, be life threatening in another way, were it not the case that, in contemporary warfare, civilians are more at risk than soldiers. Even given physical survival of combat, the veteran can suffer trauma which might conceivably be related to his or her almost untenable position within the symbolic order.

Putting forward a claim to treat a particular issue as a question of security – the attempt at securitisation – is a political act. Buzan, Waever and de Wilde argue that their approach

> points to the responsibility involved in talking about security (or desecuritization) for policy makers, analysts, campaigners and lobbyists. It is a choice to phrase things in security (or desecurity) terms, not an objective feature of the issue or the relationship itself. That choice has to be justified by the appropriateness and the consequences of successfully securitizing (or desecuritizing) the issue at hand. (Buzon, Waever and de Wilde, 1998: 211)

In this regard, my conclusion is much the same. However, the approach developed in this chapter highlights what is at stake in what Buzan, Waever and de Wilde call a choice and enables us to analyse how it may play out in different instances. Drawing on psychoanalytic perspectives gives us an indication of *why* there is an impulse to securitise in the first place, and *how* this is connected to the constitution of subjects.

There is another side to this coin. A securitising act is a political act. It is, however, also an act that depoliticises. Securitisation makes a distinction between the extreme and the merely political. 'The special nature of security threats justifies extraordinary measures to handle them ... By saying "security", a state representative declares an emergency condition, thus claiming a right to use whatever means are necessary' (Buzan, Waever and de Wilde, 1998: 21). The normal or merely political (the everyday social order, what we call social reality) is, in Derridean terms, the constitutive outside of security. The agenda that seeks to widen or broaden security by securitising an ever increasing range of issues is one that is putting the political outside and removing issues from both decisioning and responsibility. It is producing subjects of power/knowledge and the means of controlling them and extending the realm of the technical.

Buzan, Waever and de Wilde's use of the term political is distinct from mine, of course. They suggest a spectrum of ways of framing issues, ranging from the non-political, through the political (where issues are 'merely politicized'), to the point where they are 'also securitized'. If I had to suggest a spectrum, I would suggest a rather different one: from the political, through the depoliticised or technologised (where issues are rendered non-political), to the securitised. Technologisation is the term I use for what happens when the political is depoliticised by the appeal to expert knowledge which relies on the (irresponsible) application of a programme or technology (Edkins, 1999). To see the starting point of social life as non-political (as Buzan, Waever and de Wilde appear to do) assumes consensus and condones (or renders invisible) legitimised force within the state. I would want to argue that securitisation parallels technologisation, but takes place in different instances. It is a similarly disciplining, depoliticising process that legitimises what we call political control, usually by the state.

Conclusion

I have argued that security is not just 'about survival', as Buzan, Waever and de Wilde argue in the quotation at the beginning of this chapter, but about the production of referent objects and their constituent (and threatening) outsides. Security is not only concerned with how referent objects survive, it is also about how they come into being in the first place. I have argued that, although a social order is, of necessity, incomplete and insecure, it is a requirement for the constitution of the subject or subjectivity at all. This process relies on fantasy and on the role of the master signifier that conceals the insecurity or lack and sustains the fantasy.

This examination of psychoanalytical approaches to subjectivity has shown that what notions of security do is put to the outside or externalise (in the form of a threat) something which inhabits the centre of existence or subjectivity itself (as the inevitable accompaniment of any form of existence as subject). The way Lacanian approaches see subjectivity and social order as mutually constituted around a lack or an antagonism is closely connected with notions of security in that the constitution of both subject and symbolic order is incomplete, unsafe, insecure. Current analysis in security studies tends to treat threat as something that can be added to a pre-existing object or subject. Lacanian approaches produce a move away from an externalised view of security as residing in relations of self/other that take place *after* the subjects are constituted *as* self and other (a notion of security as to do with the outside of the political community and its identity in relation to others) and towards a notion of security as implicated within the constitution of the subject, self and social order. Psychoanalytical approaches enable us to give a politicised account of the constitution of referent objects of security as well as of the constitution of threat. They indicate, as we have seen, where a more critical analysis of the role of state or other political community might be possible.

The subject and the social order are both constituted around a lack and are, as a result, incomplete or impossible. The subject is always inescapably enmeshed in a security problem. The desire for certainty or security leads to the temptation to securitise but this, paradoxically, can lead to personal insecurity. Psychoanalytic approaches emphasise the subject as never fully existing as such, but always in process or becoming. As Buzan, Waever and de Wilde argue, security is about the future (1998: 32). As they claim, security is concerned with an existential threat. From a Lacanian view, existence only ever *will have been* and this leads to the paradox of security to come.

Where does this leave the subject? Is it in any sense possible to have a subject without a master signifier? I argued in the final section of the chapter that what we have to put to the outside, to exclude in order to securitise, is the political. Perhaps the key to retaining the political is living with insecurity or traversing the fantasy. Žižek argues that, though this may not be possible, the duty of the intellectual is to make visible the constructed, arbitrary nature of the master signifier – to denaturalise it. He calls this 'tarrying with the negative'. In the introduction to his book of that name, Žižek describes the image of the rebels in Romania in 1989 waving the national flag with the red star, the Communist symbol, cut out from its centre, leaving nothing but a hole (Žižek, 1993). This epitomised the brief period of openness – a state of passage – where the old apparatus had been cast off and a new one had not yet appeared. For this brief interim, the hole in the symbolic order was visible. It could be seen in this symbol of the flag. Žižek sees the role of the intellectual as being to offer this type of scepticism all the time:

> The duty of the critical intellectual – if, in today's 'postmodern' universe, this syntagm has any meaning left – is precisely to occupy all the time, even when the new order ... stabilises itself and again renders invisible the hole as such, the place of this hole, i.e., to maintain a distance toward every reigning Master Signifier ... The aim is precisely to 'produce' the Master Signifier, that is to say, to render visible its 'produced', artificial, contingent character (Žižek, 1993: 2).

As we have seen, social reality as such requires an organising master signifier. The critique of ideology tries to make it impossible to conceal this – to naturalise the social structure. The discourse of security, in contrast, works to hide the incompleteness or arbitrariness of the social order and the master signifier around which it is produced. Usually it is a conservative discourse, in the sense that it supports the pretence around which the social order is secured and perpetuates existing structures of power. It can be an emancipatory discourse, when it is in the business of producing a master signifier that will usurp the reigning order. However, emancipation, like security, is always *to come*. Once the usurper is in power, securitising in the name of the new master again conceals the impossibility of security itself.

PART TWO

Doing Political Analysis

5

Ideology and Social Movements: the case of the FN

STEVE BASTOW

Introduction

A key area of inquiry for political studies is the analysis and characterisation of political ideologies and social movements. Such analysis can potentially proceed in a number of directions. We may, for example, characterise ideologies according to their class basis – as bourgeois or proletarian, perhaps. In this case, analysis consists of determining the social constituency of a particular ideology and from this inferring something about its character. This presumes that these constituencies are relatively unambiguous and that, in some sense, they exist independently of the movements and ideologies that seek to animate them.

A second form of analysis might proceed by examining a particular social or political movement in order to establish the ideological forms to which it is most similar. This kind of approach would hold in mind a priori examples of these ideologies, say liberalism, socialism or nationalism, in order to make comparison with real-world case-studies. This form of analysis may allow for various subcategories and even hybrids but it proceeds by imagining certain 'ideal types' against which concrete cases can be measured. Here, the task of the political scientist is to develop a set of conceptual referents, ensuring that they are adequate to their function while altering categories as new findings arise.

Post-structuralist analysis rejects these sorts of approach. It regards them as attempts to impose order on to a political field that is intrinsically disordered. How can ideological discourses be understood in terms of the extent to which they match up to a conceptual schema invented by analysts? The unity or coherence that characterises an ideological discourse does not consist of its resemblance to other versions of other ideologies. Listing the policies or opinions of a social movement and mapping them on to supposedly preexisting doctrinal configurations neglects the strategic contexts within which ideological discourses are formed.

This chapter examines some of the ways in which those motivated by post-structuralism have sought to understand social movements and ideologies in a different way. Here emphasis is placed, firstly, on how these may be understood as contingent and strategic phenomena that must be related to the contexts of their emergence and, secondly, on how ideologies and social movements are themselves responsible for shaping, defining and producing the sorts of constituency or subject they represent.

We will explore this through a case-study of the *Front Nationale* in France. We will see how different analysts have employed different concepts and methodological tools in order to characterise the movement and we will see the advantages of adopting a post-structuralist approach based on the discourse theory of Ernesto Laclau and Chantal Mouffe. But, before turning in detail to this case study, we will briefly consider, in greater depth, the approach to ideology developed within such discourse theory.

Post-structuralist Approaches to Ideology and Social Movements

Post-structuralist analysis views political ideologies as context-based attempts to bind together different moments or aspects of social identity, re-articulating them into new political forms. The theoretical basis of such an approach can be found, in part, in the analysis of ideology derived from the Marxist philosopher Louis Althusser. Althusser characterised ideological discourse in terms of the 'subject' or identity it produces. Ideologies define individuals (they 'interpellate', or 'hail' them), inserting them into structurally defined subject positions. Individuals (mis)recognise themselves in ideology as particular sorts of social actors and it is in this way that, for Althusser, capitalism is able to continue reproducing itself as a social system.

Thus, ideology is not held to be derived from a pre-given social or political identity though it is unified around particular subject-positions. But the open-endedness to identity that this theory may imply is limited since, for Althusser, the class structure of capitalist society is still ultimately determining and, in the last instance, all ideological operations are held to be unified around class interpellations.

The determining power of class is something with which post-structuralists break. A good example of this development is Laclau's analysis of Fascism and Populism that builds on Althusserian foundations only to break with them (Laclau, 1978). Laclau argues that the ideologies of Fascism and Populism involve an ambiguous condensation of class-based and popular-democratic interpellations. Social agents are not defined solely in terms of class but also as 'a people'. Every class 'struggles at the ideological level simultaneously as a class and as the people'. It 'tries to give coherence to its ideological discourse by presenting its class objectives as the consummation of popular objectives' (Laclau, 1978: 109). In distinction to the Marxist theorist Nicos Poulantzas, whose analysis of Fascism Laclau criticises for reducing 'every contradiction to a class contradiction' and assigning 'a class belonging to every ideological element', he argues that non-class ideological elements are involved in the integration of popular-democratic themes into Fascist ideological configurations that are, as a result, not reducible to class ideologies (Laclau, 1978: 133).

Laclau has since developed this revision of orthodox Marxist perspectives into a 'post-Marxism' based on the insights of post-structuralist conceptions. He breaks with the notion that the structure of society can be reduced to that of class opposition and instead argues that society must be thought of as a network of relations with no ultimate foundation. He and Chantal Mouffe (1985) focus on 'discourses', by which they mean sets of statements and social practices that construct the objects about which they speak. Discourses are historically contingent and politically constructed; the subject positions which they construct have no a priori necessary basis such as class or gender and so forth, and they do not represent an 'objective' reality, but produce it by attempting to 'fix' meaning in a particular way. This does not entail a denial of the existence of objects externally to our thinking about them but rather the more phenomenological statement that objects cannot be constituted outside of the discursive (historical and political) conditions of their emergence (see Laclau and Mouffe, 1987: 82).

For Laclau and Mouffe, it is impossible to finally, once and for all, fix meaning in an absolute sense. Hence discourses need to create a frontier or boundary of difference in order to establish their own self-identity. The production of a discursive ensemble requires the constitution of an 'enemy', or 'other', whose antagonistic threat to the existence of a fixed discourse is paradoxically what enables it to be constructed in the first place. The agents and groups produced by a discourse are incapable of acquiring a full and positive identity, as 'the presence of the "enemy" in an antagonistic relationship prevents the attainment of identity by the "friend"' (Howarth, 1995: 122). Therefore, a fundamental tenet of Laclau and Mouffe's concept of discourse is the argument that discursive articulations are always pierced by contingency, that there is always an 'outside' to any referential totality, which escapes its grasp, prevents its full closure and renders its structuring of identity and difference unstable (see Laclau and Mouffe, 1985: 125). Political discourses attempt to 'fix' meaning, as a closed system of differential identities with a necessary or given character; to arrest the 'floating' character of discursive elements, even if they are only partially successful in so doing, through the institution of 'nodal points' (see Žižek, 1989: 87–8). These are key points within a discourse that act so as to anchor it and draw in other elements within a seemingly more unified structure. For example, one might think of the way in which concepts and practices built around terms such as 'nation' or 'family' function within conservative discourses. These terms help to tie together and ground such a political discourse, but Laclau and Mouffe's work seeks to show the ultimately unsutured character of discursive formations and the different ways in which they, nonetheless, attempt to fix the meaning of their signifying elements.

This represents a different way of understanding and analysing social and political movements. Instead of looking for singular defining features to mark off on our check-list of ideal types, we examine the constant attempt to bind together and stabilise an ensemble of elements and to broaden them out in such a way that they can be articulated together in an attempt to establish a wider unity. It is this process that Laclau and Mouffe designate as 'hegemony'.

With this theoretical background in mind, we can now see how such a post-structuralist position varies from other approaches to the analysis of ideology and political movements by turning to our example of the Front National (FN). Mainstream political science approaches to the analysis of the FN have generally attempted to interpret the party through positing varying (and variously defined) categories such as Fascism, extremism of the right and Populism. Such categorisation has also informed the strategies or analyses of mainstream French political parties and the media where the FN has generally been represented as an extreme-right party threatening French democracy. This approach increased following the pronouncements of Jean-Marie Le Pen (the FN party leader), in August 1996, favouring white supremacy and racial inequality (Chombeau, 1996a; 1996b).

However, such analysis has been both an academic and political failure. The orthodox analysis of the FN understands the political discourse of the party in an ahistorical, essentialist manner. The meaning of Frontist discourse is assessed by reference to hypothetical universal categories that blind us to the social and political context within which the party operates, making it harder to understand the dynamics within the party, between the party and the electorate and between the party and the political system. But it is this very dynamic which frontist political discourse aims to mediate. This failure to understand the dynamic of frontist discourse, to understand how the attitudes and practices of FN discourse act as means of interpellating both internal and external party supporters, led to a strategic inability to combat the rise of the FN (see Samson, 1998).

Rather than begin by asking whether the FN is a 'Fascist' or 'extremist' party, in order to fit it into a pre-existing analytical category, we should focus on the way in which it identifies and defines particular social or political problems and then advocates solutions. Thus we can build up an understanding of its ideological character based on an analysis of its mode of discursive articulation. We will see that the key mode is that of a Populism distinguished by the deployment of particular elements. These elements have a 'floating' character, which is to say that their meaning is not unambiguous or fixed in advance of their deployment within political discourse. In political discourse key terms (such as 'democracy', 'nation', 'people' or 'freedom') have contested meanings and the particular understanding of a term derives from the way in which it is articulated within a wider framework (see Howarth, 1995: 122). As we shall see, this lack of fixity enabled the FN to mobilise diverse strands of opinion and to occupy an ambiguous position with respect to the political system.

An analysis proceeding on this basis is not merely a case of more or less entertaining politico-philosophical interrogation. It has implications both for an understanding of why FN militants and voters are mobilised by the FN and for the kind of strategy which must be adopted in order to combat it. We will now turn to an examination of the problems produced by various other attempts to make sense of the FN before returning to an outline of the ways in which a post-structuralist approach characterises such a movement.

Analysing the Front National

In the 1980s, the FN seemed very similar in ideology to British Thatcherism. It echoed that ideology in combining notions of 'the free economy and the strong state' (Gamble, 1988) presenting itself as a party of the orthodox right (see Le Pen, 1984: 70). In economic policy it supported tax-cuts and privatisation. It recommended the sale of council housing, the opening of the public sector to the market and curbs on union power. Also advocated were an increased role for the state with regard to law and order, a toughening of the penal code, a 'family' policy aimed at reversing decline in the birth rate and a harsh immigration policy specifically targeted against non-white North Africans. Immigration, it claimed, weakened French moral fibre (see Front National, 1993: 36, 60–5, 294–7).

Simultaneously, neo-liberal economic policy was linked with Populist nationalism. For example, privatisation was regarded as a means of handing ownership back to French families (see Mégret, 1990: 282) and the sale of council houses was intended to benefit French families alone. The party called for greater popular input into the political decision-making process, arguing that the main parties were part of a corrupt, oligarchical system (Mégret, 1990: 102). Presenting itself as the champion of 'the people', the FN called for greater use of referenda (see Lefranc, 1989), and fiercely criticised the European Union for calling French sovereignty into question (see Front National, 1993: 366–72).

It thus claimed that economic, social and political problems could all be overcome by a focus on the French nation (see Peltier, 1997) that was compatible with elements of neo-liberalism. More recently, these elements have been progressively undermined within the FN discourse and a 'Third Way' has been introduced (see Mégret, 1997; Bastow, 1998). Economically it has adopted protectionist measures (Front National, 1993: 137–8, 144–8; Bastow, 1997) while, in social policy, the party moved away from neo-liberalism to a more interventionist approach, urging a policy of 'national preference' (see Front National, 1993: 221; National-Hebdo, 1997). It has begun to form its own trade unions and supported the wave of strikes held in

the public sector in the Autumn of 1996 (Duval, 1996), arguing that a number of services should be provided by the public sector (Chombeau, 1996c).

While analysts have responded to this apparent variability or mobility
within the ideology and policy of the FN in a number of ways, these attempts
are linked by a common attempt to relate Frontist discourse to universal
categories composed of a core of ideological elements common to all of them.
The attempt is to establish an essence by which the FN can be defined and
understood. This is the case with analyses which claim the essence to be that
of Fascism, extremism or Populism. We shall examine each of these, and
their shortcomings, in turn.

Analyses premised on the view that the FN can best be understood as a
Fascist party have drawn on studies that have attempted to define a fixed core
of Fascist ideology, such as Payne's (1983) typological description of Fascism,
Nolte's (1966) six point 'Fascist minimum' or Griffin's assertion that Fascism
is 'a genus of political ideology whose mythic core in its various permutations
is a palingenetic form of populist ultra-nationalism' (1991: 26). Each of these
analyses attempts to specify the key or core features that make up the Fascist
character of a political movement. By finding these features present within
the claims of the FN, several analyses have consequently explained it as a
form of Fascism or 'neo-fascism' (Fysh and Wolfreys, 1992: 325; Husbands,
1992: 267; Eatwell, 1995: 258).

But a number of analyses specifically deny this Fascist character, arguing
that the discourse of the FN in the 1980s was not assimilable 'to any of the
Fascist experiences undergone by Europe' (Rollat, 1985: 139). This was
characteristic of analyses of the FN in the 1980s, claiming that elements of its
programme did not correspond with Fascism, whatever the definition. For
example, the call for a strong state was tempered by the limitation of this
demand to its 'regalian functions' and calls for the rolling back of the state
from both the economy and the educational system (though others noted that
this deviated only from 1930s Fascism (see Milza, 1987: 429–30)). Other
factors cited as evidence of the problematic character of FN Fascism included:
the fact that it was not a mass party or 'party-army'; its self-designation as a
party of the right; its acceptance of political pluralism and parliamentary
democracy; its emphasis on a humanist, Christian tradition and the absence
of a discourse of war (Milza, 1987: 431–3).

Thus, debates over the Fascist character of the FN came to turn on
empirical disputes over whether or not certain elements of the party's policy
could be properly fitted into prior notions of what counts as a Fascist ideology.
But it has proved almost impossible to come up with a definition of a Fascist
minimum which can say anything meaningful about any specific party
discourse, rather than merely produce a descriptive generality in which no
single movement can be found whose programme or self-description exactly
matches the abstract definition. This is the fundamental difficulty behind an

approach to ideological analysis that seeks to reveal the 'ideal type' or essential core underpinning a political discourse. This problem is exacerbated when faced by a movement such as the FN that has demonstrated marked shifts in policy and rhetoric. While developing a 'Third Way' the party still claimed to stand for political pluralism, albeit within a more authoritarian Republic. It still lacked any paramilitary structure and elements of neo-liberalism remained party policy.

Thus, analysis based on ideal types was unable to explicate the particularity of the discourse of frontism as shaped through its policies, institutional practices and ideals. Concerned to explain and identify the party in terms of academic definitions of Fascism, this approach ended up suggesting that the party was 'pre-fascist' (see Rollat, 1985: 139; Monzat, 1996), a perspective dependent on analogies with pre-war Fascism, teleologically projected into the future.

Similar problems emerged with attempts to label the party as belonging to the extreme right. Here analyses have focused on the diversity of the FN's internal components which are made up of elements from a number of different extreme-right heritages, including the integral nationalism of the turn of the century, neo-Fascism, aspects of the French 'new right' and elements stemming from the experiences of the resistance to Algerian independence in the 1950s and 1960s (see Camus, 1996; Algazy, 1989: 257–62). Here the disparate strands of FN ideology are understood as united by a common basis in the broader ideology of the extreme right in France. This explains similarities between the discourse of the FN and those of the counter-revolution, boulangism, the inter-war Leagues, Vichy and poujadisme (see Rollat, 1985; Chebel d'Appollonia, 1990; Safran, 1993; Bréchon and Mitra, 1992; Buzzi, 1991).

However, the ideological composition of FN members extends beyond the boundaries of those normally labelled as extreme right. Elements within the party are closer to the traditional right. These cannot be ignored as they have played a prominent role in the party since their entry and were largely responsible for the neo-liberal economic policy of the 1980s (Buzzi, 1991). In analysing the movement, one needs to be sensitive to the diversity of its supporting constituencies both within the party and within the wider electorate (see Perrineau, 1997 and 1998). But this is hampered by analyses concerned to base themselves on a universal category of extreme right discourse into which one can fit the FN. As Mudde (1996) has shown, like analysts of Fascism, those of the extreme right are unable to agree on any shared minimum definition. The search for such a category results in the construction of abstract discourses whose components do not always bear comparison with actual political movements. The problem is not that the correct universal definition remains to be found, but that the very search for such a definition is a false start. Even if one could identify an ideal-type extreme right ideology and show that FN discourse was in conformity with it, the meaning of its individual ideological elements would vary according to the ideological tradition within which each member of the FN and of the electorate at large was inscribed. What needs to be shown is how the ideological practices of the FN have managed to do this.

The heterogeneous character of FN discourse is perhaps best captured by analyses which focus on the 'Populism' of the party. Populist discourse, reaching out to all those who are defined as members of the nation, tends to have a mélange of support, cutting across social cleavages such as class. Understanding FN discourse as a form of Populism might enable us to explain both how it unifies its many internal currents and how it has reached out to a mass electorate. Given that Populist discourses are compatible with a wide variety of ideological perspectives, such an approach has to reveal what is specific to this form of Populism and how it relates to its various bases of support. But, as with those of the FN as Fascist or far-right, such analyses utilise abstract models of Populism which fail to show the specific ways in which FN discourse mobilises diverse supporters.

For example, Pierre-André Taguieff has characterised the party as a specific variant of 'national-populism', which he labels 'national-liberalism'. This is 'more or less a crossbreed of complete economic liberalism and catholic integralism, as opposed to a "nationalisme révolutionnaire"'. It is based on 'an imperialist Europeanism, rejecting "liberalism" as much as (and sometimes more than) "social-communism"'. Its centre was the leading 'new right' movement, the *Groupement de Recherche et d'Etudes pour la Civilisation Européenne* (GRECE), which acted as a pole of attraction for smaller movements (see Taguieff, 1985: 1841). Such a conceptualisation is similar to that of Taggart (1995) who argued that the resurgence of the extreme-right across western Europe in the 1980s represented the emergence of a 'New Populism'. Ideologically, Taggart maintains, such parties 'are on the right, anti-system in orientation, and claim to be speaking for the "mainstream" of society' (Taggart, 1995: 43). They are anti-statist, promoting the freedom of the individual, practice exclusionism and are also 'characterised by strongly centralised structures with charismatic and personalised leadership as an integral component of their institutional development' (Taggart, 1995: 38, 44).

Certainly the 'Populist' approach is illuminating, but characterising the discourse of the FN in the 1980s as 'national-liberal' populism ignores the fact that there were elements in the party, even in the 1980s, who were not in favour of a liberal and pro-American stance. Moreover, such arguments are more difficult to make since the abandonment of many elements of that strategy in the 1990s. They fail to show the mobilising effects of FN discourse or ask who it was acting to interpellate in specific political, social and economic contexts.

An attempt to engage with more recent changes in FN discourse from a Populist perspective is the work of Hans-Georg Betz. Again, however, one finds that the Populism in question is articulated around a reference to two abstract ideal types. Betz breaks radical right party programmes into national and neo-liberal Populisms. Neo-liberal populists place 'particular emphasis on the economic aspects of immigration, while occasionally reminding their voters that immigrants not only cause economic problems but also represent a threat to their hosts' culture and identity' (Betz, 1994: 126). National Populists, on the other hand, are more aggressively anti-immigrant and xenophobic (Betz, 1994: 126). Generally, he argues, since the end of the 1980s, the latter elements 'have increasingly come to predominate over neo-liberal ones', as a response 'to the new opportunities engendered by growing public anxiety over economic globalisation', which saw a number of parties 'embrace a new, much more protectionist program' (Betz, 1994: 108). For Betz, however, the difference between 'national Populism' and 'neo-liberal Populism' in the FN was never that great, as the ultra-liberal economic and social doctrines of the FN in the 1980s were 'fundamentally different' to those of neo-liberal radical right parties in subordinating 'purely economic goals to the safeguarding of French national identity' (Betz, 1994: 128). Thus, he seems to suggest that the discourse of the FN was always, at root, 'national Populist'.

However, significant ideological splits could still be found within the party in the 1990s, the most notable of which resulted from the rise of Mégret whose alliance around a 'Third Way' discourse (mirroring the strategy of the *Allienza Nazionale* in Italy) sought to hegemonise the right. This was opposed by supporters of the FN general secretary, Bruno Gollnisch (see Chombeau, 1997a), and later by elements united around Le Pen himself, as he came into conflict with Mégret (see Chombeau, 1998b; Le Monde, 1998; Dely, 1998).

The essentialism underpinning Betz's analysis means that, again, it is unable to show how the heterogeneity of ideological positions in the FN finds expression in the political discourse of the FN. He argues that all of them 'have at one point or another adopted elements of both' of the types outlined above (Betz, 1994: 108) and envisages the construction of some middle ground position between the twin poles of 'national' and 'neo-liberal Populism', bringing elements of both poles together into the same discourse. But the abstract nature of the analysis means that these elements have their meaning fixed independently of their position within FN discourse, by reference to ideal types of radical right Populism. Thus, the discourse of the 1980s might be portrayed as 'national-Populist', but with some neo-liberal elements 'added in', whilst that of the 1990s is more akin to the ideal-type 'national-Populism'.

The FN: a Post-structuralist Perspective

What we see in these varying attempts to analyse and characterise the FN is a constant kind of taxonomical excess. The desire to establish fixed, perhaps scientifically verifiable, categories of ideology or party type becomes subject to a kind of endless proliferation as the elements it is intended to contain continually elude the strictures imposed by the varying typologies. What is lost in this is perhaps exactly an appreciation of the political character of ideological discourses which consists in their efforts to construct and define coalitions of support in a way that redefines them in order to make them the subjects of a new political discourse. Ideology is not a static body of doctrine but rather a process which, in Stuart Hall's terms, articulates 'into a configuration, different subjects, different identities, different aspirations. It does not reflect, it constructs a "unity" out of difference' (Hall, 1987: 19).

How may we begin to apply this sort of approach to the FN? Let us begin with Populism. Laclau argues that the wide variety of Populisms which can be identified all share a common motif of acting to mobilise 'the people' as 'an antagonistic option against the ideology of the dominant bloc' (Laclau, 1978: 173). Frontist discourse, organised around the category of 'the nation' and mobilised against what it calls the 'Establishment', clearly falls into this category. But this is not sufficient explanation. We have to show the specific ways in which this Populist discourse is articulated.

A first aspect we can consider is the specific context in which the FN seeks to mobilise individuals around a 'popular' subject position. 'Popular' subject positions, those mobilised around an identity as 'the people', seek to create a logic of equivalence between social actors, such that the specificity of their social position is dissolved into a generalised expression of something identical underlying them all, namely their 'popular' identity. For example, in colonised countries, differences of dress, skin colour, language and customs, insofar as they are a manifestation of a common differentiation from the coloniser, may be rendered equivalent through this opposition (see Laclau and Mouffe, 1985: 127). In a country such as France, however, the potential for mobilisation around popular subject positions is diminished because of the complexity of cross-cutting divisions. Early-modern forms of society, and those currently on the capitalist periphery, may possess relatively simple social formations in which 'imperialist exploitation and the predominance of brutal and centralised forms of domination tend, from the beginning, to endow the popular struggle with a centre, with a single and clearly defined "enemy", such that a logic of equivalence between different points of antagonism, dividing the political space into two fields and reducing the diversity of democratic struggles, is possible (Laclau and Mouffe, 1985: 131). This is clearly the aim of the FN, which seeks to divide the social space along the lines of French ethnicity but the complexity of the society runs counter to this attempt. The advent of advanced capitalism in the mid-nineteenth century was accompanied by 'the multiplication and "uneven development" of democratic positions' which 'increasingly diluted' any 'simple and automatic unity around a popular pole' (Laclau and Mouffe, 1985: 133). An advanced industrial society like France thus contains a proliferation of points of antagonism permitting the multiplication of struggles, but these are so diverse as to make it extremely difficult to articulate some form of equivalence between them around the term 'the people', disabling their unification and the division of the political space into two antagonistic fields.

As a result, in order to interpellate social actors as 'the people', Frontist discourse must deal with French social complexity, articulating elements in such a way as to transform democratic subject positions into 'popular' ones. It does this by utilising 'floating signifiers', elements marked by an ambiguity which prevents them from being fully fixed (see Laclau, 1996: 36). This ambiguity becomes productive for organisations such as the FN since it means the discourse can be 'read' in a number of different, even contradictory, ways. The introduction of such ambiguity enables the interpellation of diverse social groups around a 'popular' identity.

A few examples can illustrate this process. A concept or term such as 'popular capitalism' can ease the 'tensions around the economic programme of the party, which divides party officials' (Birenbaum, 1992: 200). That this concept does not always succeed in interpellating all the elements of its internal audience – precisely because of the relatively open character of the discourse of the FN – can be seen in the argument of Michel Schneider. Leader of the national-revolutionary group, *Nationalisme et République*, Schneider argued that there was an irreducible opposition in terms of economic policy between defenders of the national-Populist line and liberals (see Birenbaum, 1992: 202).

A second area where the mobile character of the discourse of the FN can be seen concerns the whole relationship of the FN to democracy, the Enlightenment tradition and the French Revolution. The FN embraces the French Revolutionary heritage by claiming it as an expression of the more profound development of the rights of national peoples, rather than universal human rights (see Mégret, 1990: 26–7). Hence the FN can advocate that liberal democracy be reinforced through the establishment of a strong executive, renewing the nation through the pursuit of strong measures aimed at control of the immigrant population, crime prevention, protection of the family and social morality, and refusing further European integration in order to protect the rights of the French people. In this manner, the FN attempts to reconcile the reactionary, Maurrassian elements in the party with those more individualist elements that stem from organisations such as the *Club de l'Horloge* or the *Comité d'Action Républicain* (CAR) (formed by the right in the aftermath of the 1981 socialist election and led by Mégret and other former RPR/ UDF members) as well as the self-proclaimed 'revolutionary' neo-Fascist elements in the party (see Rossi, 1995: 127).

We can consider here, in more detail, the stance of the FN towards the European Union as it relates to notions of pan-European identity. Whilst the party is against the EU, it supports the idea of a European identity, suggesting that the European nations 'must unite in order to preserve their identity and regain power' (Front National, 1985: 115). The articulation of such a vision is, however, riddled with conceptual ambiguities, bringing together a variety of conflictual elements: the notion of western Christendom, the values of the Enlightenment and biological racism. The FN's discussion of European identity constantly switches between two modes of identification, the cultural and the biological. Thus, one can find Le Pen, on some occasions, locating European identity in the Hellenic-Christian cultural tradition (Le Pen, 1994), whilst, on others, he proposes a vision of 'the white man of Europe', which is based more on biological claims (Le Pen, 1989). In FN discourse 'Europe' is a signifier which can be read in different ways, making an appeal to both biological racists (such as those hailing from GRECE) and cultural racists (such as those linked to the Maurrassian tradition), as well as enabling a wider ideological appeal by the party to the electorate.

A final example of this discursive ambiguity can be found in the officially non-confessional nature of the party, used so as to be able to reach out to both pagan and Catholic groups alike. But, once again, this can only go so far. Birenbaum notes that 'there exist different logics of action' between traditional, non-schismatic, Catholic organisations and the FN's non-confessional character (Birenbaum, 1992: 221).

The fact that the discourse of the FN is not intended to act as a fully sutured discursive totality, the meaning of whose elements is fixed, is further reflected in the institutional framework of the party which has no 'official' institutional linkages with tendencies within the party. This enables opposition to appear between one or more 'sub-societies' without overall party unity being called into question. The leaders of these subsections can thus adopt positions which are more extreme than those officially pronounced by the party.

This strategy of ambiguity does, however, make the assertion of the Populist character of FN discourse problematic. The fact that the political horizon of the FN mirrors the 'floating' character of the signifying elements of FN discourse means that its position vis-à-vis the system, the extent to which it represents an absolute assault on the system or merely its revision, becomes difficult to discern. With the FN one finds that a plurality of different readings are possible.

One should note, however, that such a strategy has its limits, as the recent split in the party reveals. As number two in the party, Mégret sought to rearticulate FN discourse, leading to the abandonment of several of their neo-liberal economic policies and the move towards a 'Third Way'. This represented a move 'left' in terms of appeal, attempting to address those elements of the working class, the unemployed, small business owners and so on who felt let down or abandoned by the neo-liberal programmes of the governments of the 1980s (see also Bastow, 1997: 69–70).

This proved impossible, however, Mégret becoming more vocal in his attempts to take control of the party from Le Pen. This led to a split in the party, with Mégret forming his own movement, initially labelled the Front National-Mouvement National (FN-MN), now called the Mouvement National Républicain (MNR). Each claimed to represent the true heritage of the FN. The split suggests that the strategy of ambiguity, which proved so successful electorally, was itself premised on the acceptance by all the different groupings within the party of the status quo. As long as everybody accepted their position within the party hierarchy, this strategy could be maintained. Mégret's attempt to depose Le Pen and form a new leadership around a new, 'Third Way', strategy has blown this internal harmony apart.

This has not undermined the ambiguous nature of Frontist discourse. With both sides keen to recruit members of the formerly unified party and to maintain electoral success, the strategy of discursive ambiguity which was developed by the FN has been continued by both parties. After the split, Le Pen outlined fifty policies which were in continuity with the old FN (see Altier, 1999). The initial policy pronouncements by the MNR, which focused on the threat to French people posed by immigrants (see Chombeau, 1999b; Le Monde, 1999c) and a policy of 'zero tolerance' on crime (see Besset, 1999), were largely drawn from the FN manifesto, *300 Mesures*. Indeed, Mégret declared that the policies of the MNR would be in continuity with those developed whilst he was in the FN. As I argue elsewhere (Bastow, 2000), the strategy of the MNR has been to articulate a discourse which would interpellate orthodox right-wing voters, former FN voters and those social elements mobilising on the far right, precisely the kind of ambiguity which this chapter has documented.

Notwithstanding this attempt at maintaining ambiguity, in the longer term and especially since the poor European elections results in July 1999 (for both parties, though most particularly for the MNR, which failed to cross the five per cent threshold to have MEPs elected and thus failed to get any state funding), both FN and MNR have begun to fragment. The FN has suffered a number of fractures since the summer of 1999, when conflicts emerged with Catholic integrists at the FN Congress over whether France was a 'multi-confessional' country, as Samuel Maréchal, Le Pen's son-in-law, claimed in June 1999 (Chombeau, 1999c). These conflicts have been ongoing and led to Maréchal quitting his party post (Chombeau, 1999d).

Since disputes over the name and strategy in October 1999 (see Chombeau, 1999e), the MNR has seemed torn between more moderate and more extreme elements, unable to articulate a discourse uniting them. Several of the more moderate elements have departed to join the right wing party, Rassemblement pour la France (RPF), or have formed their own independent groups (see Chombeau, 1999f, 2000) but, at the same time, conflicts have emerged with the more Fascist elements within the movement (see Grosz, 2000). The longer term consequences of this process of fragmentation for the discourse of the mainstream extreme right in France remain to be seen.

Conclusion

The general tendency of political science orthodoxy has been to try to define FN discourse in relation to a number of different, universal ideal-types. This has been problematic for two reasons. Firstly, they have led to a failure to explain the dynamic underpinning FN discourse, the social categories interpellated by the discursive configuration of frontism. An analysis based on discourse theory which, rather than imposing a priori universal categories on FN discourse, seeks to show what the basic features of this discourse are and how they address social actors in the French polity manages to do this. Such an analysis shows how the different elements of FN discourse are capable of being read in a number of different, often highly contradictory, ways, in order to achieve some degree of unity of a far-right which historically has been very fragmented. This enabled the FN to break out of the extremist electoral ghetto to which the extreme-right was confined in the post-war period in France. The discursive fluidity of the FN has enabled it to articulate a plethora of highly Populist anti-government sentiments, reflected in the diverse social background of its electoral support. The fluidity of FN discourse must be accommodated by analyses of the FN. It is not that the analyses of the political discourse of the FN which link it to Fascism are wrong but that they are partial, failing to deal with its inherently ambiguous character, such that they ignore the ways in which non-Fascist militants and voters are mobilised by FN discourse.

Secondly, the attempt at fitting FN discourse into taxonomic categories hinders the solution to the practical political problem of combatting the ways in which people are mobilised by the FN. The question should not be 'Is the FN Fascist?' but 'with what social imaginary does FN discourse interpellate actors and how can this be undermined?'. Thus, rather than asking whether the FN is a 'Fascist' or 'extremist' party, opposition to the FN needs to focus on unpacking the particular solutions proposed by the party to concerns shown by the electorate, revealing their practical inefficacy as well as their conflict with other elements of the FN programme. One could go further and suggest that the essentialist approach to an understanding of FN discourse actually has negative consequences for the struggle against the FN, as the attempt to pin labels on the party like 'Fascist', 'neo-Fascist' or 'extreme-right', often provides a unity within the FN that is not found in the party programme itself (see, for example, Camus, 1996: 83). Ultimately, a discursive analysis is not simply an academic one – it is also a political one that has a place in the formation of radical political strategies and in opposition to the right.

6

The Work of Ideas and Interests in Public Policy

STEVEN GRIGGS AND DAVID HOWARTH

Introduction

Numerous political scientists have suggested that, while post-structuralist theory may be useful in explaining marginal practices and identities or issues of abstract political theory, it has little to say about mainstream topics of analysis, such as the formation and implementation of public policy or the political decision-making process in general. Nevertheless, a number of contemporary debates and discussions pertaining to the relative importance of ideas and interests in the policy process, the relationship between social structures and individual agents, and the process of policy change, may fruitfully be addressed from a post-structuralist perspective. It is our contention that the theories and methods of discourse analysis, elaborated by writers such as Jacques Derrida, Michel Foucault and Ernesto Laclau and Chantal Mouffe, provide an important set of conceptual resources to investigate these issues.

Take, for instance, the current debate about the role of ideas in explanations of policy change. Standard explanations of the complex, and often contradictory, processes of policy change are intertwined with the game of interests and the instrumental calculations of individuals and groups. More recently, some policy analysts have contested the primacy of interests and emphasised the transmission of ideas and advocacy as key determinants of policy decisions. While such ideational accounts raise new challenges for models of policy-making, it is not sufficient to substitute the primacy of ideas for that of interests. Instead, as Peter John argues, ideational accounts must 'propose a theory which can both take account of the complexity of the political world and explain why an idea can suddenly take hold and become implemented as a policy choice' (John, 1999: 40). Such a theory requires an understanding of the relationship between ideas and interests, and their impact on questions of social agency. This chapter responds to such challenges.

The first half of this chapter presents a novel articulation of the role of ideas and interests in the policy process by drawing upon discourse theory. It offers a middle path between the primacy of interests and the primacy of ideas by emphasising their discursive construction in conditions of contingency and undecidability. The second half examines mainstream accounts of policy change and suggests how discursive accounts might improve or supplement our understanding of policy-making. We conclude by drawing out the implications of these reflections for the overall study of public policy.

Discourse Theory and the Policy Process

Policy-making is not a strategic or rational process in which politicians or bureaucrats, possessing all the qualities of perfect information and foresight, engage in an objective search to find an optimal solution to emergent policy difficulties. Recent attempts to restructure welfare services, combat unemployment or ameliorate the plight of the inner cities reveal just how much policy-makers face seemingly insurmountable and persistent problems. They are armed with insufficient knowledge and administrative resources, encounter entrenched veto groups, work within overbearing socio-economic constraints, and suffer the vagaries of contingent and unpredictable events. Such policy environments often lead politicians and state agencies into haphazard, almost trial and error, negotiations with changing coalitions of interest groups, as they seek incrementally to push through marginal changes from the status quo while maximising levels of agreement.

Equally, it is possible to discern, behind these policy vacillations and often partly failed innovations, longer-run dynamics of more coherent and consistent policy change. Institutional constraints, the policy inheritance of past governments, and broader shifts in the external political economy can lock politicians and state agencies into path-dependent policy choices. Such complex and often contradictory processes of policy change raise important questions about how we understand the actions of social actors in the policy process. In this respect, much depends on which of the many complex processes of policy-making we choose to emphasise.

To begin with, if we were to privilege the importance of the haphazard negotiations between chaotic and ever-shifting coalitions of actors, we might endorse explanations which build upon the short-term calculations of individual political entrepreneurs intent on 'playing off' different actors in order to maximise their own set of interests. By contrast, if we were to privilege the trial-and-error character of much of the policy-making process, we might be led to question the primacy attributed to interests in explanations of the policy process. From this perspective, it could be argued that preferences are often compatible with more than one policy choice and that ideas, rather than interests, provide the 'map' which leads actors to choose one policy over another. Finally, if we were to privilege the powerful socio-economic forces that structure the choices of policy-makers, we might dismiss the role of social actors altogether. In this approach, policy outcomes would be explained in terms of the functional demands of the social and economic systems into which social actors are socialised.

In short, these distinct interpretations of political action raise two important questions about the nature of human agency in the policy process. Firstly, to what extent do ideas or interests determine and drive the behaviour of social actors in the policy process? Secondly, how far is the recognition of external pressures by social actors and their subsequent interventions mediated by their own construction of events? In other words, to what extent are social actors 'bearers of structures' as opposed to free and rational choosers?

Interests, Ideas and Signifiers

It is important to begin by clarifying the terms and concepts that dominate existing debates on the policy process. What do we mean by concepts such as ideas, interests and agency, and how are they to be understood from a post-structuralist perspective? Beginning with the former, it is already clear that the concept of an idea has been used in a variety of ways for different purposes. Let us begin by considering two classical, though strongly divergent, accounts of the relationship between ideas and interests. According to John Maynard Keynes:

> the ideas of economists and political philosophers, both when they are right and wrong, are more powerful than is commonly understood. Indeed, the world is ruled by very little else. Practical men, who believe themselves to be quite exempt from any intellectual influence, are usually the slaves of some defunct economist. Madmen in authority, who hear voices in the air, are distilling their frenzy from some academic scribbler of a few years back ... Soon or late, it is ideas, and not vested interests, which are dangerous, for good or evil. (Keynes, 1936: 383–4)

Against this idealist stance, Marxists deny the autonomy of ideas in favour of underlying material conditions and economic processes. As Marx and Engels put it, the materialist conception of history 'does not explain practice from the idea but explains the formation of ideas from material practice' (Marx and Engels, 1970: 58). From these premises, Eric Hobsbawm concludes that a concern with the impact of ideas is 'extremely misleading and confusing', especially 'when vested interest, practical politics or other untheoretical matters are involved'. Moreover, reminding us of Marx's famous dictum that it is not men's consciousness that determines their material existence, but social existence that determines consciousness, Hobsbawm argues that it 'was not the intellectual merits of Keynes' *General Theory* which defeated Treasury orthodoxy, but the great depression and its practical consequences' (Hobsbawm, 1973: 130). Even Max Weber, Marx's great intellectual adversary, claimed that it is 'not ideas, but material and ideal interests' that 'directly govern men's conduct' (although, of course, Weber immediately qualified this assertion with the proviso that 'very frequently the "world images" that have been created by "ideas" have, like switchmen, determined the tracks along which action has been pushed by the dynamic of interest' (see John, 1998: 144)).

Not only do these conceptions of the relationship between ideas and interests present us with an unsustainable binary opposition, in which Keynes argues for the completely autonomous role of ideas and Marx for their reduction to underlying material processes, we are no clearer about the concept of ideas itself. Hence, it is necessary to articulate a 'third way' between an autonomous and free-floating conception of ideas and a reductionist and deterministic approach as well as to clarify and deconstruct the very concept of an idea from a post-structuralist perspective. We will begin with the conceptual task and then, having outlined a discursive approach to the analysis of ideas, we will show how it transcends the opposition between ideas and interests.

Without attempting to construct a genealogy of the concept of 'ideas' in Western thought, which would stretch back inter alia to Plato, Descartes, Hegel and Husserl, suffice it to note the essentialist and idealist connotations of this dominant understanding. In this tradition, ideas are understood as unchanging expressions of the mind or the direct products of thinking, which then represent or even constitute a world of externally existing objects. In this conception, language is viewed as the transparent means of representing and communicating ideas. For instance, Ludwig Wittgenstein's early 'picture theory of language', as elaborated in his *Tractatus Logico-Philosophicus* (1961) postulates a clear correlation between ideas as expressions of thought, language as an uncontaminated means of representation, and the world as a logically distinct set of objects. This representational model of language and the stark division of science and non-science propounded by Wittgenstein's early philosophy provided a strong justification for logical positivism and the behaviouralist movement which has dominated much of political science in the twentieth century.

On the other hand, this overall conception of ideas has often been connected to a particular analysis of ideologies. As is well known, the French Enlightenment thinker Destutt de Tracy coined the term *idéologie* to refer to 'a science of ideas', which he believed would provide the foundation for all other sciences, and he outlined a programme of inquiry into the way in which our thoughts are constituted. It was, in part, against this conception of ideas that Marx and sociologists, such as Karl Mannheim, developed a materialist conception of ideology to stress the particular social and historical context in which ideas emerged and flourished. In more social and political terms, the positivist conception of ideologies defines them as systems of ideas that structure the social and political world, and are drawn upon by social actors to explain and justify their organised social action.

This particular picture of ideas is problematic when extended to social and political analysis. Substantively, as we have already suggested, it leads to the idealist view that ideas determine social processes such as policy-making, interest formation and so forth. On a methodological level, it raises questions about how ideas can become legitimate objects of political analysis and a number of writers have shown how ideas can only be encountered and analysed when manifested in linguistic forms such as words, phrases and sentences. For example, Quentin Skinner borrows from the philosophy of the later Wittgenstein to show that ideas expressed in linguistic terms only acquire meaning within a specific 'language game' and, ultimately, an entire 'form of life'. As he puts it, 'the project of studying histories of "ideas", *tout court*, must rest on a fundamental philosophical mistake'. Instead, 'the meaning of an idea must be its uses to refer in various ways', and this must take into consideration 'the nature of all the occasions and activities "the language games" within which it might appear' (Skinner, 1988: 55).

In a similar vein, although arguing from a post-structuralist perspective, Jacques Derrida shows how the articulation of ideas always presupposes a system of language consisting of available and repeatable signs. In this sense, language is not a neutral medium of signs and symbols, which simply represents ideas and objects, but a fund of possible meanings that structures the way the world is, thus enabling us to experience and think about it in certain ways (see Derrida, 1974). In sum, what we might broadly call a post-structuralist perspective substitutes the analysis of language as an already existing system of signs and meanings for the role of ideas as autonomous and determining aspects of social life. In this view, ideas are to be understood as 'signifiers' whose meanings and identities depend on systems of significant differences or discourses. Hence a concept such as the 'Third Way', associated with the Labour Party under Tony Blair, only becomes meaningful when contrasted with signifiers such as the 'New Right' or 'Old Labour'. Similarly, a policy of 'privatisation' only makes sense in relation to other policies such as 'nationalisation', 'public-private partnerships' or 'the issuing of bonds' to raise public money.

Discourse theory

Within this post-structuralist approach, we need to say a little more about our discursive approach to social and political analysis. At the outset, how does it escape the problems of idealism and reductionism? While it has been claimed that discourse theory reduces the social world to texts and ideas (see Geras, 1990; Osborne, 1991; Wood, 1998), it is important to stress that our conception of discourse is not restricted to language narrowly construed. Instead, discourses are relational worlds of meaningful practices that systematically form the identities of subjects and objects (see Foucault, 1972: 49). From this perspective, they are meaningful systems that are intrinsically political, as their formation involves acts of radical institution via the construction of antagonisms and the drawing of political frontiers between 'insiders' and 'outsiders'. This always includes the exercise of power, as the constitution of discursive systems involves the exclusion of certain possibilities and a consequent structuring of the relations between different social agents (see Dyrberg, 1997). This means that discourses are contingent and historical constructions, which are always vulnerable to those political forces excluded in their production, as well as the dislocatory effects of events beyond their control (Laclau, 1990: 31–6).

It is important to stress that this conception of discourse does not reduce ideas and human actions to closed systems of discursive practices. Just as Derrida argues that there can be no 'saturated contexts' of meaning, as every sign can be 'grafted' on to an infinite number of linguistic chains, so Laclau and Mouffe argue that social structures are never closed and homogeneous systems of practice. Rather, they are incomplete and undecidable orders containing a plurality of 'repressed' meanings and practices which, in times of crisis and dislocation, can be reactivated and actualised in different ways. This makes possible a rethinking of the character of human agency. As against the voluntarist connotations of rational choice models of agency, in which individual actors make decisions on the basis of rational calculations, and the determinism of structuralist accounts, in which social actors are little more than 'bearers of structures', the discursive model argues that agency is only possible when contingent social structures fail to confer identities to social actors. In other words, it is only in conditions in which actors are unable to identify in the 'normal' ways that agents take decisions to reconstruct the discourses and rules of social life. This occurs in situations when social structures are in crisis or are dislocated by events beyond their control.

This model of agency means that we have to think about decisions and actions in at least two ways, namely, as decisions taken *within* existing rules of the social structure and decisions taken *about* the structures themselves (see Howarth, 1996). That is to say, when social structures are relatively stable, social actors draw upon 'normal' decision-making procedures, and these may include strategic calculations à la rational choice theory. On the other hand, in times of political and social crisis, a more radical conception of human agency emerges because social actors literally have to reconstitute the social orders that constitute their identities by making decisions about the structures themselves.

This reformulation of the concept of ideas and agency from a discursive point of view still begs the question about how we are to understand the role of interests in the policy process. Our approach endeavours to find a tertium quid between interests as the subjective preferences of social agents (à la rational choice and mainstream pluralist models) and radical views (such as Marxism) which stipulate the existence of real interests that are systematically distorted (or even erased) by the exercise of power (see Lukes, 1974). Drawing on discourse theory, we view interests as discursive constructs, which are always *relative* to historically positioned agents with an identity. In other words, interests are never simply given by history or experience, or imputed on to agents by the researcher, as they are historical and contingent constructions specific to a particular time and place (Laclau and Mouffe, 1990). This means that the definition and constitution of interests is a political project in two senses. On the one hand, interests cannot be assumed to pre-exist agents, as they are constructed politically and discursively via hegemonic projects. On the other hand, as we have suggested, social actors are themselves historical and political products whose identities are contingent upon their relation to other identities. It may seem obvious, but interests are always the interests of particular agents. Moreover, both the identities and the interests which are relative to them can never be assumed, but are *strategic* outcomes (see Griggs and Howarth, 1998).

One final question concerns the way in which we are to understand how and why certain ideas come to predominate in the policy process and not others. In the language of discourse theory, this question centres on the way in which certain signifiers emerge and are taken up by social actors such as politicians and key decision-makers, and how they come to hegemonise a field of meaning at a particular point in time. We have already suggested that ideas conceived as signifiers are never fixed in any final sense, but take on different meanings depending on the various contexts in which they function. This intrinsic contingency and indeterminacy is particularly marked in contexts of crisis and dislocation when signifiers are, by definition, more difficult to stabilise. In these situations, they acquire what might be termed a 'floating' status and are 'up for grabs' by different groups and projects pursuing their interests. This process by which different groups endeavour to fix the meaning of particular signifiers – their attempts to convert 'floating signifiers' into 'empty signifiers' that temporarily fix meaning by representing what Laclau calls the 'absent fullness' of a particular group or policy community (Laclau, 1995: 171) – is a central aspect of the logic of hegemony. That is to say, the achievement of hegemony by a group pursuing its interests involves the construction of empty signifiers that enables the group to cover over its internal differences and show the dependence of its own group identity upon the opposition of other groups (see Howarth, 1995). Such empty signifiers are logically required for the completion of any system of signification.

Three important theoretical conditions have to be satisfied for the emergence and functioning of empty signifiers. These are the *availability* of potential signifiers that can be articulated by competing hegemonic projects; their *credibility* as means of representation and interpellation; and the presence of *strategically placed agents* who can transform these floating ideas into empty signifiers (Laclau, 1990: 66; see also Howarth, 2000). Careful empirical investigation is needed to determine *how* and *why* any particular signifier can and does perform this role.

Take, for instance, the way in which New Right ideas on the market economy, the role of the state and the function of special interest groups such as trade unions emerged and came to structure debates about economic policy during the late 1970s and 1980s. At the outset, it is clear that key signifiers such as 'the free market', 'inflation', 'entrepreneurship', 'monetarism' and 'anti-collectivism' were made available by writers such as Friederich von Hayek, Milton Friedman and Samuel Brittan at various points in the twentieth century (see Gamble, 1988: 27–60). However, it was only in the conditions of the 1970s and 1980s that these ideas became credible ways of explaining the crisis of social democracy and of constituting the means of representation for an alternative to welfare capitalism. The task of reactivating and reiterating these ideas and of transforming their abstract character into viable and con-crete policies, of making them 'speak' to the new situation, fell to the organic intellectuals and politicians who rose to power in the Conservative Party during the 1970s. After the victory of the Tories in the 1979 election, they began implementing these ideas in the country at large. Strategically placed actors in and around the Conservative Party, in the crisis of social democracy in the 1970s, were liberated from the existing structural and organisational constraints of the post-war consensus and begin to construct radical possi-bilities.

We can only fully understand the dynamics of policy-making if we are able to conceptualise this relationship between ideas and interests. Attributing primacy to ideas or interests helps us little but discourse theory offers a middle path between the primacy of interests and the primacy of ideas. It emphasises the role of agents through the conception of dislocation and crisis of structures, and it provides a series of conditions that govern the emergence of ideas in the policy process. We need now to establish how such a post-structuralist approach might improve upon existing mainstream accounts of the policy process.

Mainstream Accounts of Policy-making Revisited

Each interpretation within mainstream accounts of policy-making offers a distinctive understanding of human agency and of the role of interests and ideas in explanations of policy change and political action generally. Three broad categories of explanations may be discerned: those that privilege interests; those that emphasise the role of ideas; and those that recognise the role of interests and ideas in the policy process. In what follows, we will examine how discourse theory can inform and advance these three broad accounts of policy change. Firstly, we examine rational choice theory which combines an agency-centred account of policy change with the primacy of interests. Secondly, we investigate ideational or social constructivist approaches which, in contrast to rational choice, emphasise the importance of ideas, policy frames and paradigms, thus privileging structural explanations of policy-making in that social actors are socialised within systems of beliefs and values. Finally, we examine synthetic accounts (John, 1998: Chapter 8) of policy-making such as policy streams (Kingdon, 1995), punctuated equilibria models (Baumgartner and Jones, 1993) and evolutionary theory (John, 1998; Ward, 1997). These accounts recognise the constant interaction of interests and ideas in the policy process, and stress how the coupling of interests and ideas leads to rapid shifts in policies. We begin with the first approach.

Rational Choice and Interest-based Accounts

Most mainstream accounts of the policy process maintain the split between ideas and interests and respond to questions of policy change by emphasising the primacy of interests, and by recourse to a positivist epistemology. For example, classical rational choice explains policy change as the result of the instrumental calculations of self-interested social actors. Social actors are seen to possess a fixed set of preferences, which pre-exist the exigencies and contingencies of the social world. This given set of preferences enables actors to evaluate and choose courses of action that best satisfy their preferences, thereby maximising their interests. Thus, individuals will only join groups and engage in collective action if there is a selective incentive that is dependent upon group membership. In the absence of such selective incentives, rational individuals will tend to free-ride because the costs of membership are likely to exceed the benefits they obtain, regardless of their involvement (see Olson, 1965).

Such rational choice accounts problematise the crucial concept of 'interests' and how they may be conceived. To return to the issue of collective action, such a problematisation of interests raises key questions concerning the relationship between individuals and groups, as well as the internal dynamics of groups. However, the inherent primacy of interests fails to conceptualise the relationship between ideas and interests. Ideas are simply tools or resources at the disposal of instrumental social actors. At best, they are 'focal points' that facilitate coordinated action such that the concept of 'ideas' could be replaced by that of 'information' (Blyth, 1997). Moreover, as besets its positivist epistemology, there is no place for the social construction of interests or the role of social actors in defining complex policy issues and external pressures. The identity of social actors is assumed to be that of self-interested 'utility maximisers' in which case the subjects of such analyses 'are without a history' (Hirschman, 1982: 79). In other words, key questions pertaining to the *identities* of agents, as well as their *agency* in relation to social structures, are not addressed and analysed. In a famous footnote, Olson explicitly rules out explanations based on non-material incentives, arguing that these other motivations can be explained by recourse to selective incentives of a material nature (Olson, 1965: 61, note 17). There is, here, a failure to recognise that interests are discursive constructions specific to a particular time and place. Such failings produce a logical fallacy, inherent in mainstream interest approaches, which is to read off preferences from observed behaviour and then use these very same preferences to account for the pattern of behaviour observed in the first place (Blyth, 1997: 233).

Policy Frames and Ideational Accounts

Ideational accounts increasingly recognise that social actors work under conditions of ambiguity whereby policy-making is less concerned with problem-solving than with the setting of norms and the definition of policy issues (see Majone, 1989: 23) More often than not, actors cannot even agree upon the nature of the actual problem that confronts them, let alone engage in an interest-maximising strategy that hinges upon an informed assessment of the costs of unpredictable policy alternatives (Zahariadas, 2000). This very ambiguity means that social actors are unable to resolve policy differences through recourse to further evidence or information. Rather, they are obliged to fall back upon interpretative frameworks to make sense of their external world. They work within a policy frame or paradigm which establishes a hierarchy of norms and codes for interpreting problems and guiding behaviour within the policy process (see Jobert, 1992; Hall, 1993; Rein and Schön, 1991; Kuhn, 1970). These policy frames determine what counts as evidence, how contradictory information is interpreted, and how problems are ultimately defined. As such, they guide actors down certain paths rather than others. Thus, it is the flow or transmission of ideas and *not* interests which ultimately determines policy decisions.

This recognition, by ideational accounts, of the significance of interpretative frameworks goes some way to acknowledging the underlying assumptions of post-structuralist theory. In contrast to rational choice accounts, the concept of policy frames appears to recognise the complex questions relating to the identities of agents and the discursive construction of interests. It accepts that our very interpretation of the world depends upon the meanings and interpretations that social actors give to events (see Howarth, 2000). In conditions of ambiguity, interests cannot be defined without recourse to interpretative frameworks as they are 'a dynamic "dependent" variable, framed by knowledge' (see Radaelli, 1995: 165; Radaelli, 1997). In brief, as befits a discursive approach to policy-making, the empirical world is given meaning and constructed by ideas. Interests are historical and contingent constructions specific to a particular time and place.

But what such accounts fail to grasp entirely is the importance of dislocation, the radical agency that is possible during periods of dislocation, and the antagonistic nature of all political identities. In policy frame accounts, social actors are born into pre-existing systems of ideas, which are embedded in particular institutional settings, thus giving meaning and content to the preferences of social actors. Certain policy frames will 'nest' in institutions and become institutionalised over time, depending on the nature of institutional designs. As such, frames continue to impact upon the distribution of costs and benefits of policies between social actors after 'the social power relations that gave rise to this distributional pattern have changed' (Coleman, 1998: 634). By contrast, discourse theory interprets policy frames as contingent and historical constructions that are always vulnerable to dislocatory events and the antagonistic constructions of opponents. They are neither closed nor homogenous, but incomplete and undecidable orders of meaning. As such, they contain 'repressed' meanings that can be reactivated in times of crisis and dislocation when agency becomes possible. This absence of closure implies a degree of instability which is not only necessary for explanations of policy change, but is notably missing from policy frame accounts. Thus, whilst discourses are recognised as contingent and historical constructions, policy frames border on closed paradigms embedded within institutions.

Their inherent stability means that shifts in policy frames will necessarily be associated with periods of policy failure, social learning and the success of trial and error experiments which undermine existing paradigms and the 'normal' ways that agents take decisions. In policy frame accounts, when faced with stubborn policy controversies, policy actors become enquirers who reflect on existing tensions and their potential resolutions. They do so through a 'conversation with their situation' (Rein and Schön, 1991: 267) in which they 'put themselves in the shoes of other actors in the policy environment' (Dudley, 1999: 54). Such stubborn policy controversy and frame reflexive discourse imply the dislocation of existing frames and the radical agency that becomes possible when social structures *fail* to confer identities on social actors. However, there is not an adequate explanation of the actions necessary for the emergence of new frames in periods of dislocation. Indeed, such accounts suggest a rationality in decision making that is incompatible with the ambiguity of the policy process. In practice, social actors do not necessarily learn from experience; social learning is nothing if not haphazard (Dudley and Richardson, 1999: 246). In addition, these accounts tend to privilege the mechanisms of debate and the entrepreneurial skills of actors and fail to recognise how ideas, as distinct from their advocates, 'can be persuasive in themselves' (Hall, 1997: 185).

In fact, during periods of dislocation, radical agency only becomes possible because the breakdown of 'normal' rules means that decisions can be taken about the nature of structures themselves. Social structures fail to confer identities to social agents, and agents, who are unable to draw upon 'normal' decision-making procedures, are able to reconstruct the discourses and rules of social life. Strategically placed entrepreneurs will, indeed, act as policy brokers, sustaining collective action and facilitating alliances between different groups in the construction of empty signifiers. However, it is not simply a question of the entrepreneurial skills of such actors. Not all frames or ideas are possible. Only certain signifiers will emerge and hegemonise a field of meaning at a particular point in time; certain signifiers will, thus, be more 'persuasive'. This logic of hegemony – the process by which groups convert 'floating signifiers' into 'empty signifiers' that temporarily fix meaning – has to be explained. The conditions surrounding the availability of empty signifiers, especially the need for dislocations which disrupt sedimented systems of meaning, cannot be ignored. Ideational accounts cannot simply argue that policy change occurs when 'a new idea stands in opposition to an existing idea and so forces a reconsideration' (Bevir and Rhodes, 1999: 225). Rather, for new ideas to emerge and temporarily fix meaning, potential and credible signifiers have to be transformed into empty signifiers by the actions of strategically placed agents. The adequate explanation of this logic of hegemony is absent in policy frame and ideational accounts.

Coupling and Synthetic Accounts

Synthetic accounts of policy change reject the split between ideas and interests. Instead, they stress the importance of the constant interactions of interests and ideas in the policy process. Pivotal to this explanation of policy change is the way in which ideas are coupled with interests, thus offering solutions to the difficulties facing social actors. Typically, Kingdon identifies three separate 'streams' which influence the processes of policy change: problems, policies and politics (Kingdon, 1995). Policies are the ideas or proposals for change which are promoted by political entrepreneurs in response to the ebb and flow of the stream of policy problems. Politics is the stream of political processes, such as changes in government, that can alter existing interpretations, not only of problems but also the range of solutions facing social actors. It is the coming together or articulation of these streams that explains radical shifts in policy. Ideas 'take off' when windows of opportunity, such as new ministerial appointments or technological change, bring streams together and enable social actors to introduce new agendas. At such times, bandwagons towards issue expansion can begin as more and more actors take up the issue. The serial processing of organisations (the inability of organisations to deal with any more than one issue at a time) facilitates the promotion of the 'new' idea on to the top of the political agenda (see Baumgartner and Jones, 1983).

Ideas are said to float in some sort of 'policy primeval soup' as actors learn over time and changes in the external environment undermine or reinforce various policy alternatives. As John argues:

in one time period an outlandish idea appears to lack sense, but through the failure of previous policies and changes in the media and public opinion, in a subsequent time-period policy-makers shift their preferences to the newly accepted policy choice. (John, 1998: 185)

Social actors constantly test ideas and policy proposals, engaging in trial-and-error experiments and borrowing successful policies from other sectors. The random mutation of ideas and their fortuitous success is a defining characteristic of evolutionary models of policy change (John, 1999: 48–9). This 'garbage-can' process of politics recognises the changing nature of the selection mechanisms which couple ideas and interests. No single variable predominates, in that interests and ideas, as well as the actions of social actors and the design of institutions, all contribute to policy outcomes.

Herein lies the strength of synthetic accounts of policy change. They posit the constant interaction of ideas and interests, allowing for the contingent nature of policy change and recognising the role of strategically-placed actors. Through their emphasis on the articulating of interests and ideas, they avoid the reductionism of interest-based and ideational accounts. As such, they provide a powerful explanation of change which accepts the possibility of equilibrium and stable patterns of policy-making, but also recognises how sudden and radical shifts can occur. This acknowledgement of bandwagons towards change and the practice of serial processing offer an important insight in to how ideas 'take-off' and enhances our understanding of the process of dislocation and the logic of hegemony.

However, the absence of a coherent explanation of changing selection mechanisms betrays the inability of synthetic models to articulate the relationship between ideas and interests in a satisfactory fashion. Often, ideas are seen as quasi-independent variables that contribute alongside interests to policy outcomes (see Dudley and Richardson, 1999). In other accounts, short-term interests override beliefs and values to produce unexpected alliances between members of different value-based coalitions (see Hann, 1995). As such, ideas are almost secondary to interests, defined as a response to the functional needs of social actors who wish to achieve short-term benefits *and* satisfy their own need to be agents. Their success hinges upon the entrepreneurial skills and tactical awareness of social actors. They have no 'concrete existence unless they are taken up by interests and become part of the political agenda' (John, 1999: 43).

In fact, synthetic accounts appear to repeat the mistakes of both interest-based and ideational accounts, as they say little about the formation of preferences and how social actors identify with certain solutions over others. The linking of ideas and interests cannot be reduced to the vagaries of the 'garbage-can' of politics or be seen to follow from the likes of increased media attention or change in the environment. Unlike the socialised paths of policy frames, synthetic accounts offer few clues as to why certain ideas will link with particular interests. Yet, as we have said, only certain ideas will hege-monise a particular field of meaning. Thus, how social actors identify with such ideas and achieve hegemony through the construction of empty signifiers will be central to the articulation of ideas with interests. As with ideational accounts, this requires the recognition of the logic of hegemony, of how groups convert 'floating signifiers' into 'empty signifiers' that temporarily fix meaning. As we said earlier, policy change will actually only occur when groups construct empty signifiers that enable the group to cover over its internal differences and show the dependence of its own group identity upon the opposition of other groups. Here, once again, the experience of dislocation and the conditions surrounding the availability of empty signifiers, which are offered by discourse theory, can aid our understanding of policy change. In brief, only certain ideas will be 'persuasive'.

Conclusion

At the beginning of this chapter, we argued that discourse theory offers a valuable set of concepts and methods to investigate the issues surrounding policy change. We set out to complete two primary tasks. Firstly, we sought to demonstrate how discourse theory offers a middle path between the primacy of interests and the primacy of ideas by emphasising their discursive con-struction in conditions of contingency and undecidability. Secondly, we sought to show how such a conception of interests and ideas might inform mainstream accounts of policy change. Here we showed how discourse theory, with its focus on dislocation and the crises of structures, offers an important clarification of the role of agents in policy change. More importantly, it supplements existing accounts of policy change through its understanding of why and how certain ideas emerge at key junctures in time and space. The logic of hegemony provides a series of conditions which regulate the avail-ability of empty signifiers and determine policy change during periods of dislocation. These conditions can inform existing accounts of policy change and, thereby, provide a new research agenda for our understanding of the decision-making process.

This discursive agenda requires that future studies in the policy process refute the search for the objective causal explanations of social and political phenomena. Policy analysts need to discover the historically specific rules and conventions that structure the production of meaning in a particular social context. In other words, they should investigate how and why particular systems of discursive practice are constituted, function and change, as well as how and in what forms social agents come to identify with these particular systems of meaning (see Howarth, 2000). Central to such investigations will be the empirical study of the formation and dissolution of political identities, and the analysis of hegemonic practices in the policy process. It is only through careful empirical investigation that policy studies will be able to understand the importance of social antagonisms in constituting identity and social objectivity by the drawing of political frontiers between social agents. These are not marginal practices but are the key to explaining the formulation and implementation of public policy.

7

Globalisation and the Constitution of Political Economy

GLYN DALY

Introduction

What kind of an 'object' is the economy and what is its status? This question has taken on a particular centrality within 'modern' societies. As the figure of God progressively receded, the thinkers of the Enlightenment began to put their faith in the discovery of founding principles on which to base the construction of a rational social order, one that would, in turn, secure the conditions for human emancipation. Such principles became the essential focus for an emerging 'natural science' of political economy. If the medieval period was dominated by a theological project of interpreting God's laws, the success of the new age was largely seen in terms of working with the under-lying laws of economic reality. In this way, the economy was idealised as an object of first principles, an a priori foundation, around which a rational and moral social order could be constructed.

Through an analysis of what it saw as the logical and objective mechanisms of the economy, classical political economy aspired to intellectual mastery over the real. The economy was conceived as an autonomous realm in which universal developmental laws could be identified that would serve as a kind of anatomical basis for social progress and moral development.

However, the 'objectivity' of the economy was constructed in radically different ways. Liberal political economy, for example, stressed the fundamental importance of the so-called free market. In Adam Smith's famous conception, it is only through the unencumbered movements of an 'invisible hand' that the conditions for social equilibrium can be established. This naturalistic approach to the market was believed to reflect certain basic (metaphysical) 'laws of justice' that could be universally applied.

> Every man has perfect freedom, so long as he does not violate the laws of justice, to pursue his own interest in his own way and to set his enterprise as well as his capital in competition with the enterprises and capitals of other men. (Smith, 1776, *Wealth of Nations*, Book IV, Chapter IX)

Marxist political economy, by contrast, focused on the domain of production as the ultimate reality.

> It is always the direct relationship of the owners of production to the producers – a relation always naturally corresponding to a definite stage in the development of the methods of labour and thereby its social productivity – which reveals the innermost secret, the hidden basis of the entire social structure. (Marx, 1981: 927)

History was conceived as a law-bound structure shaped by the dynamic and contradictory playing out of the tensions between the forces and relations of production. Communism represented the inevitable outcome of the logic of history, capable of resolving the underlying productive tensions through collective ownership.

While the liberal and Marxist versions of political economy construct the 'objectivity' of the economy in characteristic ways, and are totally different in their prescriptions, they, nevertheless, share the same problematic. In both cases, the economy is an a priori unity whose internal logics, or laws, remain constant in every social formation. In other words, the economy exists as a conceptual model that can be specified in advance, an underlying structure of rationality around which a causal topography of the social may be logically constructed. Emancipation and moral progress were rendered dependent on a particular economic model: the free market (for liberalism); the socialisation of the means of production (for Marxism). In this respect, both types of political economy tend to be presented, by their respective advocates, as ultimate rational accomplishments embodying characteristic ends of history.

Using Husserlian terminology, we might say that a crucial task is to *reactivate* what has become *sedimented*, or forgotten, in the notion of political economy. Through routine use, the notion of political economy has tended to become sedimented within a tradition in which it has been made synonymous with generalised ideas about objective interests and positivistic truth – thereby concealing the traces of its own philosophico-discursive origins (see Laclau, 1990). Indeed, it is something of a paradox that the notion of political economy (in all its variants) has tended to eradicate the dimension of the political. That is to say, the ambition of political economy has been to master all ambiguity and contingency by establishing a final metaphysical ground – a set of immutable economic laws – on which to base an ultimate order of social rationality. In this sense, traditional political economy has aimed at an immaculate conception, a theology of reason, that cannot be politicised or put into question.

Against this perspective, we need to reactivate the historical problematic of political economy and probe the limitations of its construction. This problematic turns on a fundamental division between essences (in this case economic reality) and appearances (subjectivity, illusion, false consciousness and so on). In contemporary thought, however, this type of division has tended to become increasingly blurred. Heidegger, Wittgenstein, Foucault, Derrida and others have all contributed to a progressive deconstruction of the classical modernist problematic and an increasing emphasis on the discursive

nature of reality. At the same time, one could cite examples of various thinkers whose interventions have increasingly undermined objectivist-naturalist
approaches to the economy: Marx's own view of capital as essentially a social,
or power, relation (rather than simple reward for honest toil); Hilferding's
analysis of the organisation of social and economic life in ideological
(specifically nationalist) terms; Simmel's argument that money cannot be
referred to an absolute value the consistency of which depends upon a
broader structure of symbolic exchange; Gramsci's notion of historic bloc in
which the relationship of base to superstructure is reconceived in relational
(that is, non-causal) terms; Keynes's demonstration of how the economic
'ground' can be politically constructed and manipulated through state intervention. More recently, writers such as Aglietta, Lipietz and Boyer have shown
that the regulation of the economy is not an endogenous matter (as in classical
models). Rather, economic stability depends on the construction of an entire
mode of social regulation that transcends the economy as such. Each of these
thinkers, in varying degrees, alludes to the fact that the economy cannot be
regarded as a closed autonomous order but has to be considered in far more
contextual terms that reveal its discursive character (see Daly, 1991).

These types of interventions may be considered to contribute broadly to
the development of a post-structuralist perspective, constituted around two
principal assertions: firstly, that objectivity, or presence, depends on context;
and, secondly, that no context can constitute an absolute closure. Indeed, it is
this fundamental emphasis on the dimension of non-closure that prompts the
term *post*-structuralism. To this effect, the economy can never become an
'object' (a self-enclosed presence) but will always depend upon wider power
relations and those historical attempts to construct it in a certain way.
Evidently this does not mean that what we call the economy simply disappears
but, rather, that its dimensions and frontiers are always historically constituted.
At an abstract level, the term 'economy' can be understood as designating the
material reproduction of social life. However, the way in which that material
reproduction is understood and organised is finally a political matter. In
general terms, we might say that this entails moving away from the metaphysical realm to that of the metaphorical – that is to say, moving away from
the idea that economic truth is discovered and towards the idea that it is made.

This chapter analyses the evolution of post-structuralist themes in
relation to the development of anti-economistic thought, regulation theory,
systems theory and the discourse theory of hegemony associated with Laclau
and Mouffe. It then moves to a consideration of contemporary forms of global
capitalism. Finally, it explores the ways in which post-structuralism could
contribute to a reactivation of the dimension of the political in respect of the
economic imagination.

The Crisis of Economism

The classical Marxism of the Second International mobilised two main forms of economism that have been variously combined in contemporary thought: epiphenomenalism and class reductionism. With the former, 'superstructures' are regarded as a simple reflection of the economic base, playing no active role in the historical process. For this reason, the Second International saw little or no scope for political or ideological activity since everything depended on the objective movement of the economy. This led to a situation where, in interwar Germany, for example, socialists could abandon the ideological terrain, regarding the themes of liberal democracy as simply 'bourgeois'.

While this crude epiphenomenalism has been generally abandoned, stubborn residues can be discerned in even the most sophisticated forms of Marxist analysis. Laclau and Mouffe (1990), for example, point out that, while in Althusser and Poulantzas there is a conception of the 'relative autonomy of the state', this is immediately contradicted by an insistence on the deter-mination in the last instance by the economy. The shift in emphasis from the first to the last instance does not alter matters. There is a basic division in which the economic can be identified as independent and, ultimately, causal.

With class reductionism, on the other hand, social and political identity is conceived purely in terms of the position occupied in the relations of production. There were two main aspects to this. First, workers were seen to have an objective interest in socialism that would form the basis of their solidarity – the inexorable movement of the class in itself to the class for itself. Second, all political struggle under capitalism would eventually be resolved into a fundamental antagonism between workers and capitalists.

Both types of economism have been progressively eroded and the empha-sis of Marxist and socialist thought has increasingly shifted to contextual issues of actual political engagement. As it became increasingly apparent that the working classes were not only becoming less homogenous, but develop-ing a far greater predisposition towards social democracy and trade unionism (political perspectives that are quite compatible with, and even supportive of, the continuation of capitalism), socialist theorists began to affirm a crucial mediating role for intellectuals in order to actively stimulate a revolutionary class consciousness.

These tentative movements towards greater political intervention and prag-matism reflected a process whereby the logic of the contingent increasingly supplemented, or 'filled in' for, the failure of the logic of determinism and automaticity. For example, for Lenin, the vanguard party would be respon-sible for establishing broader class alliances (that is, between peasants and workers) and for developing a revolutionary strategy that effectively bypassed notions of teleological stage-ism. Socialism itself would bring about the modernisation and technological advances that were being denied by capitalist imperialism. But, as Laclau and Mouffe point out, the role of the intellectual tended to be restricted to explaining the objective (pre-constituted) character of class identity. For Lenin, the possibility of vanguard activity required the determinate conditions of economic crisis (Laclau and Mouffe, 1985: 36).

While versions of economic reductionism persisted in Marxism they were also to be found in liberal thought, often in the most doctrinaire of forms. The liberal idealisation of the free market has been at the root of some of the most authoritarian and inhumane political measures taken against the poor and excluded. One of the most notorious examples is that of the Irish potato 'famine' where, under Whig prime minister, Lord Russell, and in accordance with market orthodoxy, food continued to be exported from Ireland while a nation starved. While anti-Irish prejudice played a part in this disaster, it was underpinned by an economistic paradigm wherein a laissez-faire strategy was seen as the *only* 'rational' response. The overriding concern was to secure the long-term optimisation of prosperity and employment through a vigorous export-oriented economy. To depart from the 'invisible hand' approach would have been perceived as immoral and irrational. Far from a pathology of racist motivation, the tragedy of the Irish famine was, rather, the result of an economistic, conception of the good.

The response of contemporary liberals to such issues as underdevelopment, genocidal conflict and global poverty is that more capitalist modernisation is required. This is indicative of the liberal economistic myth in which the free market is portrayed as a universal panacea and as the very foundation of a holistic and emancipated society – indeed, the foundation for the final society as *the* outcome of history (as in Bell, 1965 and Fukuyama, 1992).

Deconstructing the Economy

The Austrian Marxist, Rudolf Hilferding, was among the first to embark on what can be called a deconstruction of the economy. That is to say, instead of looking at the economy as a self-enclosed order, Hilferding focused on the way in which the economy developed in relation to, and was affected by, such 'non-economic' factors as ideological and cultural practices – thereby destabilising the traditional economic/non-economic distinction.

With the notion of organised capitalism, Hilferding showed how twentieth-century capitalism was increasingly characterised by the concentration and integration of the various factions of capital (industrial, financial, commercial and so on) into what he called finance capital. The power of finance capital was further consolidated through a modern expansionist state and a virulent nationalist ideology. There existed, then, a fundamental interconnection between the economic and the politico-ideological. Far from the latter simply reflecting the former, Hilferding advanced a re-conceptualisation whereby the politico-ideological could be seen to provide the *conditional requirements* for the construction of the capitalist economy. It is in this sense that Hilferding began to effectively deconstruct the traditional economy/ideology division and to reformulate the connection between these elements in relational rather than causal terms.

The radical character of Hilferding's interventions also extends to his view of political subjectivity. In a remarkable passage that discusses the plight of Britain, he wrote:

> Class antagonisms have disappeared and been transcended in the service of the collectivity. The common action of the nation, united by a common goal of national greatness, has taken the place of class struggle, so dangerous and fruitless for the possessing classes. (Hilferding, 1985: 336)

Within the nationalist construction of organised capitalism, therefore, class antagonisms are subsumed under the construction of a generalised nationalist identity that unites both workers and the bourgeoisie. Political subjectivity is not simply given by the position occupied at the level of the relations of production, but depends on a politico-ideological context that transcends those relations. Hilferding alludes not only to the material character of ideology, but also to the ideological character of the material (economic) base.

However, Hilferding tended to view nationalist ideology as the naturalistic expression of finance capital. Thus Hilferding reaffirms a basic objectivism by presenting history in terms of a necessary outcome. Capitalism would inevitably collapse because of irreconcilable nationalist ideologies that reflected a determinate stage of development. Once again, the politico-ideological terrain is regarded as ultimately governed by an underlying economic reality.

With Gramsci there is a complete recasting of Marxist economic categories which radically undermines their aprioristic and objectivist status. Gramsci affirmed the material character of hegemony and ideology, no longer regarding the latter as a secondary effect expressing something that is already there (at the level of the economic base). Instead, it becomes the 'organic cement' for constituting an entire complex of political and cultural practices with economic and institutional arrangements in a 'historic bloc'. This is crucial because, if the economy cannot be identified independently of the superstructures that it is supposed to effect, then it loses its causal-objectivist status. Thus, in Gramsci's notion of historic bloc, the classical distinction between base and superstructure is dissolved. The economy is not separated from politics, ideology or culture but is articulated with these phenomena in a characteristic manner. The historic bloc – which may vary across time and space – may be said to constitute the very paradigm of social reality. It is a paradigm in which:

> precisely material forces are the content and ideologies are the form, though the distinction between form and content has purely didactic value, since the material

forces would be inconceivable historically without form and the ideologies would be individual fancies without the material forces. (Gramsci, 1976: 377)

Gramsci's perspective is crucial and clearly transcends Hilferding's view of the singularly nationalist orientation of capital. By developing a radically contextualist approach, Gramsci reveals that nothing automatically follows from the capitalist mode of production and we cannot predict whether it will be articulated with nationalist, apartheid, liberal, social democratic or some other term. In other words, a radical undecidability has been introduced whose resolution will depend upon the outcome of concrete forces in political struggle. This will have crucial consequences for the construction of the economic space and the types of practices carried out there.

Thus there exists no increasing conformity to a pre-given model of capitalism but, rather, unstable forms of politically contested historic blocs. It is in this sense that Laclau states: 'There is therefore no "capitalism", but rather different forms of capitalist relations which form part of highly diverse structural complexes' (1990: 26). If the economy does not stand outside history – if it is submitted to the contingent logics of contextual construction – then it must also be regarded as a fundamentally discursive construction.

Gramsci carries out a similar deconstructive operation in respect to the category of 'class' such that nothing automatically follows from the position occupied at the level of productive relations. Class identity is not given in advance (thereby negating any notion of 'false consciousness') and there is no guarantee that workers will eventually grow into revolutionary socialists. Indeed, in Italy, Gramsci was confronted with an extensive fascist mobilisation of the popular classes. For Gramsci, the particular orientation of a class wholly depends upon the forms of 'political, intellectual and moral leadership' – in short, hegemonic constitution. Again the concept of class is stripped of its transcendental aprioristic status and is placed back in history as a formation that can only take shape through contextual hegemonic practices. Indeed, Gramsci is concerned to drop the notion of class in favour of what he calls 'collective wills' in which a complexity of historical ideological elements (with no natural or pre-given class belonging) are involved in their hegemonic constitution.

Nevertheless, despite the ground-breaking advances of Gramsci in developing a context-based approach, there remains a residual economism in his thought (Laclau and Mouffe, 1985: 69). Even though Gramsci presents a thoroughly relational/articulatory view of class identity, he assumes that it is *only* fundamental classes which are capable of hegemonic practice. In other words, classes – because they are classes – are bestowed a privileged and predetermined role as the exclusive agents of hegemony. Once again, politics is seen to have a transcendental source – the relations of production – which fixes the identity of the players in advance and determines that hegemonic struggle is always going to be a 'zero-sum game' between the main classes (Laclau and Mouffe, 1985: 69).

Laclau and Mouffe are concerned to break definitively with this last residue of economism. They argue that it is simply impossible to predetermine the identity of a political actor independently of the processes of hegemonic constitution. There is not, therefore, an identity which can be identified in an objective manner and which subsequently engages in hegemonic activity. Rather, the distinction identity/hegemony is dissolved and, radicalising the Gramscian argument, hegemony itself becomes the very terrain for constituting identity as such: 'The logic of hegemony, as a logic of articulation and contingency, has come to determine the very identity of the hegemonic subjects' (Laclau and Mouffe, 1985: 85).

Two consequences flow from this. First, political/hegemonic activity does not possess an ultimate source of determination (human nature, gender, productive position and so on) but is, in principle, extended to all aspects of human engagement. Second, it is impossible to predict who the political actors are going to be independently of a historical context of hegemonic practices. Thus, in certain instances, it may very well be that ecological, feminist or gay/lesbian liberation movements constitute the most radical forms of hegemonic struggle against an existing set of power structures. The particular orientation of the workers, then, will wholly depend upon the articulatory forms of identification which are established with such movements and their struggles. In this respect, we could summarise the Laclau-Mouffe perspective by saying that there is no such thing as 'identity' only hegemonic (and, therefore, incomplete and vulnerable) forms of identification which never reach a point of ultimate closure or completion. In this respect, class loses its aprioristic status as providing an objective basis for unification or revolutionary transformation and we are fully in the discursive realm of historical and hegemonic possibility.

Regulation and Systems Theory: Autopoiesis and the Myth of Autonomy

The deconstructive approach clearly informs the type of regulation theory that has been developed by writers such as Aglietta, Lipietz and Boyer. Aglietta explains his intervention in the following way:

> The essential idea of *A Theory of Capitalist Regulation* is that the dynamism of capital represents an enormous productive potential but that it is also a blind force. It does not contain a self-limiting mechanism of its own, nor is it guided in a direction that would enable it to fulfil the capitalist dream of perpetual accumulation. (Aglietta, 1998: 49)

Aglietta's central point is that capitalism cannot regulate itself endogenously but requires certain conditions of possibility. Put simply, 'economic relations cannot exist outside a social framework' (Aglietta, 1998: 45). Moreover, in regulation theory there is an important stress on the interdependence between the political and the economic. As Boyer argues: 'There is not one but a multiplicity of types of accumulation in accordance with the consequences of political conflict and the processes of institutionalisation which develop in particular out of major structural crises' (Boyer, 1997: 75).

The term 'regulation', however, is perhaps unfortunate in that it raises all kinds of questions as to the nature of regulation and the status of that which is being regulated. In an attempt to resolve such questions, Jessop (1990, 1999a, 1999b) has sought to combine regulation theory with the systems theory developed by N. Luhmann (1995). A key concept in Luhmann is that of autopoiesis. Essentially, autopoiesis refers to the way in which a system is instituted through a process of self-referral in respect of a distinctive code (or principle) of organisation. The system of law, for example, is instituted through a legal/illegal division which itself depends upon the organising code of the former. Thus, for Luhmann, a system is autopoietic in so far as it manifests the 'recursive application of its own operations' (Luhmann, 1988: 336).

Jessop draws on the concept of autopoiesis to underscore his view that the economy – or, more specifically, the capitalist market economy – reveals a radical, and operational, autonomy (Jessop, 1990, 1999a). Despite this autonomy, however, Jessop maintains that a market economy can only be sustained through complex forms of regulation and what he refers to as 'social embeddedness' within the life world of a society (1999a).

There are problems with Jessop's conceptualisation of autopoiesis and his consequent view of regulation. In the first place, Jessop appears to link autopoiesis with the more traditional themes of independence and autonomy that we find in political economy. Moreover, although Jessop is at pains to avoid causal/deterministic arguments, it is questionable as to whether he succeeds in theorising a non-causal approach. For Jessop, the economy is connected to other social systems (the law, education, the media and so on) through a relation of 'structural coupling' (Jessop, 1990, 1999a). But what precisely is the status of this relation? If the relation is a non-causal one – if it is a fully discursive relation – then this would mean that the structure of the economy was essentially unstable, prone to dislocation and hegemonic recomposition. This, consequently, would undermine any analytic notion of independence or autonomy. But, in that case, it would seem more appropriate to speak of a logic of articulation, where the emphasis is on mutual deformation and modification, rather than structural coupling which retains too much of an impression of simple linkages between discrete elements.

This ambiguity is further compounded when Jessop characterises his theoretical project as one which focuses on 'the discursive as well as extra-discursive aspects of economic and political phenomena' (Jessop, 1999b). This runs the risk of reproducing a rather classical formulation whereby an extra-discursive x (which, in this case, surely connotes the economy – its 'structures', 'institutions' and so on) is presented as having a series of determinate effects throughout the social (super-)structures. To this effect, there appears to be a danger that regulation might be interpreted as a simple process of steering and/or legitimising an underlying, and autonomous, economic reality.

Perhaps Jessop's reading is too one-sided and an alternative approach to regulation may still be developed within the terms of systems theory. In particular, while Jessop focuses on the way in which systems can achieve autopoiesis, there is little analysis of what the idea of autopoiesis can tell us about the construction of systems in general or what might be called the systematicity of systems.

In this context, it would be useful briefly to refer to Kant who could be regarded as one of the first systems theorists. Kant's crucial contribution to moral philosophy was to show that an ethical system cannot be grounded in any a priori sense (Kant, 1993). The 'good' to which any ethical system refers is not an exterior but, on the contrary, is always constituted within the terms of the system itself – there is no sense of the ethical/unethical division prior to the system itself. In a similar fashion, Luhmann argues that systems can never be grounded in anything solid. Indeed, we could summarise Luhmann's position by saying that it is because of the radical absence of any ground that we have system. If there were an ultimate ground, then the logic of systematisation would cease to have any meaning; we would simply have infinite presence – a final domestication of the real.

Luhmann demonstrates this argument by reference to the legal system. In the first place, the legal/illegal distinction cannot be determined outside the system of law. Moreover, the question as to whether the legal system *itself* is legal or illegal is strictly unthinkable and undecidable (see Esposito, 1991; Staheli, 1995). Where a system's code encounters itself, the system is confronted with its fundamental lack of ground. To this effect, no system is capable of systematising its own principle of construction.

Every system, therefore, is marked by an originary 'violence' – an arbitrary 'line in the sand'. At the same time, through processes of routinisation, systems attempt to conceal this violence and the essential arbitrariness and undecidability of their constitution. Thus, for example, the system of law no longer appears arbitrary because of the numerous layers (sedimentations) of case study, precedence and so on, all of which can be seen as a way of repressing the fact that precedence law is without origin (precedence is precisely the illusion of foundation) and that the legal system cannot be based on any naturalistic conception of Law.

In this context, what autopoiesis shows is that the 'ground' of any system is merely the artifice of its recursivity; a phantom of its tautological construction. This is why, for Staheli, the 'self-referential system functions as a metaphor for the impossibility of the origin' (Staheli, 1995: 19). No system can find an edge and the more a system refers to itself, the more it serves to underline an essential lack of foundation. Recursivity is precisely that which acts as a stand-in for the absent foundation. At the same time, systems attempt to finesse their artifice by concealing the politico-hegemonic nature of their origins behind a particular idealism. In search of authenticity, the originary and arbitrary violence of a system is typically disavowed through some kind of naturalistic appeal to Reason and/or the presence of certain mysterious laws (of justice, nature, history, God and so on).

The effect of closure of a system (bearing in mind that such an effect is always partial and provisional) is entirely the result of the recursive processes of self-referral and exclusion; processes which Laclau and Mouffe designate by the term hegemony (Laclau and Mouffe, 1985). To this end, every system exists as an attempt to ground the ungroundable and to finally resolve the basic paradox of systematicity – that the lack of origins/foundations makes systems both necessary and impossible.

From this perspective, the concept of autopoiesis has to be strictly separated from traditional ideas of autonomy and independence. Indeed, we might usefully characterise autopoiesis as that which shows the impossibility of autonomy and independence. Or, to make the same point in different terms, it is because the latter cannot be formed that autopoiesis comes into being.

On these grounds, regulation can be seen as a process that reflects the autopoietic nature of systems, rather than any autonomy. Regulation is neither a steering mechanism nor a set of subsequent adjustments for something that is independently constituted. On the contrary, regulation should be seen as a process of autopoietically constructing the 'object' itself. In the same way that for Kant the 'good' is not prior to the ethical system, the 'object' of the economy is not exterior to regulatory practice. In this context, regulation can be understood in terms of Laclau and Mouffe's conception of hegemony – as a process of radical construction (Torfing, 1991). In contrast to the self-conception of orthodox political economy, therefore, those elements that are said to comprise the economy are not given in advance but depend upon how they are articulated in a regulatory framework.

The question of the market is a case in point. A number of Marxist-inspired writers (such as Pierson, 1993; McNally, 1993; Jessop, 1999a) conceive the market in naturalistic terms. For these writers, the market is usually equated with capitalism and is presented as having a generally negative impact on social relations. However, there is nothing that is essentially capitalist about the market (a point that is already well made by Marx). Market mechanisms pre-exist capitalism and are clearly in operation in all kinds of social formations, including those with a strong socialist dimension. Moreover, it is clear that a whole range of enterprises exist within the sphere of the market: credit unions, co-operatives of every type, housing associations, radical journals, green consumption, alternative technology, the new forms of cyberculture and so on. None of these can be regarded as having an unequivocal status as 'capitalist'. The ambiguity of such phenomena cannot be thought, within an essentialist identification of the market, as a fixed capitalist totality or homogenous *milieu*. Indeed, in many cases, market mechanisms can be seen as posing a direct threat to the monopoly forms of capital. By the same token, there is nothing necessarily positive about market practices. Against a background of widening demands for social and economic equality by various marginalised groups and vast disparities in wealth and resources, the liberal conception of a 'free market' that automatically establishes social equilibrium – or a Hayekian spontaneous order – can only appear as a metaphysical conceit.

The point here is that the market is not an autonomous construct. In Derridean terms, it is not a 'condition-less condition of possibility' (Derrida, 1987: 115) that can regulate itself according to endogenous laws. The relative degree of closure that is achieved for a market will depend upon the processes of autopoietic-discursive construction within a wider hegemonic framework of regulation. A market will always depend upon certain historical conditions of possibility that recursively affect its meanings, dimensions and its 'objectivity'. For example, market realities will be constructed very differently under conditions of feudalism, laissez-faire, the mixed economy, command statism or some other type of regulatory formation. It is on the basis of this undecidability, moreover, that the rigid divisions of traditional political economy – essence/appearance, base/superstructure, economy/society and so on – are increasingly destabilised.

As a historical example, take the case of 1920s Germany which is particularly informative in this respect. Against a background of widespread social dislocation and the disintegration of liberal capitalism, the Nazi movement began to assert itself as the only credible force that could impose order (see Laclau, 1990: 65–6). But Nazism was not merely a superstructural effect of an underlying movement towards organised/monopoly capitalism. On the contrary, Nazi discourse provided the very conditions of possibility for the latter to emerge *in that context*. And this had profound consequences for the organisation and dimensioning of everyday economic reality. The identification of a 'Jewish conspiracy', for example, became part of the official diagnosis of economic problems and this, in turn, led to the creation of enormous state bureaucracies to oversee the dispossession of Jewish people and to carry out a 'redistribution' of their property.

In much the same way as the later apartheid regimes, Nazism was able to establish a distinct form of autopoietic 'foundation' for the economy through nationalist/racist discourse. In this context, a new sense of closure was produced through the construction of exclusivist frontiers against the perceived threat of Semitic corruption and depravity. What enabled Nazism to redefine economic reality and to impose its characteristic mode of social regulation (a mode that could effectively articulate, and make sense of, the emergence of a new epoch of capital accumulation) was precisely the absence of any ground or objective mechanism of regulation.

This inherent instability is also apparent in the ongoing construction of meanings and identities of 'Europe'. Current developments tend to reveal that there is anything but a 'common market', much less one that would serve as a unifying structure for the different elements of this region. On the contrary, the very attempts to stabilise European markets have led to an increasing emphasis on the themes of conscious control that, in Derridean terms, function as a 'dangerous supplement' to the former. That is to say, European economic decisions increasingly have to take account of, and are modified by, a whole range of political concerns: environmental, social, cultural, regional and so on. At the same time, new European institutions and legislation reflect a multiplication of political struggles around such issues as social justice, poverty, workers' rights and the various forms of discrimination in employment and other social relations. These struggles, moreover, are progressively denaturalising the idea of a self-regulating market. Far from expressing an autonomous logic, the construction of the 'market' – and, more generally, the economic space – now has to begin from more far more sites of antagonism and political reconstitution than ever before. To this effect, the contemporary era is one that is marked by a constant displacement of any 'centre'.

Globalisation

Globalisation is widely regarded as a process that is affecting more and more areas of human life, from market interaction to popular culture, leisure, consumption and the numerous transformations associated with the internet and the World Wide Web. In terms of political economy, however, globalisation is a process that was already well known to Marx and Engels. In the *Communist Manifesto*, they showed how capitalism could only reproduce itself through a constant revolutionising of the means of production and a permanent search for new markets and resources to exploit: 'The need for a constantly expanding market for its products chases the bourgeoisie over the whole surface of the globe. It must nestle everywhere, settle everywhere, establish connections everywhere' (Tucker (ed.), 1978: 476).

According to writers like Lash and Urry (1987, 1994), however, globalisation may be contextualised in terms of the latest phase of capitalist development. As liberal capitalism was replaced by 'organised capitalism' and the rise of the regulatory nation state, the latter has now been superseded by the age of 'disorganised capitalism' that reflects the decline of the nation state and the increasing domination of transnational forms of corporate capital.

But, as Laclau points out, there is a danger in this perspective of simply replacing the absolutist myths of the previous phases – that of an autonomous market for liberal capitalism and a rationalist state for organised capitalism –

with an equally absolutist myth – monopoly capital as an all-powerful agency (Laclau, 1990: 58–9). If this were the case, then the dimension of the political would once again be eliminated within the terms of a new metaphysical closure – a new illusion of autonomy. Laclau's point is not that monopoly capital cannot emerge as a dominant force, but that this domination has to be understood in contingent and historical terms. Here we should recall Marx's basic insight that, far from expressing individual wealth/accumulation, capital fundamentally comprises a social relation of production. More specifically, it designates the reciprocal relation between a 'class that possesses nothing but its capacity to labour' and a class that monopolises the means of production. It is in the context of this relation that capital evolves as a force that is capable of 'maintaining and multiplying itself as an independent social power, that is, as a power of a portion of society, by means of exchange for direct, living labour' (see Tucker (ed.), 1978: 208). In other words, capital aims at establishing something like a universal system – a global (dis)ordering of social relations – in order to sustain a very specific relation of class domination/exploitation. This is why Marx insisted that capital was both radically cosmopolitan and intensely parochial.

    Moreover, in order to create a global system, capital seeks to conceal the politico-discursive violence of its construction through the autopoiesis, or gentrification, of that system. This is particularly apparent at the level of international financial speculation or, what Marx would call, 'fictitious capital'. As J. J. Goux points out, no other phenomenon illustrates the contemporary processes of globalisation more strongly than the international stock market:

> It is one of the most disconcerting features of world capitalism that sudden and devastating shifts in share quotation and price can make the difference between instant fortune and bankruptcy, the apparent soundness or frailty of companies and nations being determined by the fatal mobility of a few figures that encapsulate the activity of the financial market that day. (Goux, 1997: 22–3)

As Proudhon emphasised, the stock market takes on the status of a monumental source of capital exchange where the compass needles of 'value' spin. Like great secular cathedrals, the institutions of Nikkei, Hang Seng, FTSE and the Dow Jones Index constitute a kind of oracular network of global capital-information flows. And through this network, capital tends to be imposed as a global authority/ordering principle. In the very midst of the era of disorganisation, capital continues to evoke a certain trust through the movements of 'God's dollar'. Moreover, the symbolic authority of capital is further reinforced through a discursive process of imbuing the (arbitrary) cycles of capital events with a kind of human pathology. Thus the stock market is variously 'buoyant', 'confident', 'hesitant', 'anxious', 'stable' and so on. And this is perhaps capital's ultimate conjuring trick, that, as it destroys all traditional patterns of authority right up to the nation state itself, it is able to reinvent this authority through its own transnational symbolic order.

This process, moreover, is being accelerated by the next generation of stock markets that are principally associated with NASDAQ (the National Association of Securities Dealers Automated Quotation in association with the American Stock Exchange). According to its mission statement, NASDAQ is committed to creating 'the world's first truly global securities market ... A worldwide market of markets built on a worldwide network of networks ... linking pools of liquidity and connecting investors from all over the world' (*http://www.nasdaq.com/about/about_nasdaq_long.stm*). Based on internet technology and thereby transcending distance and differences between time zones, the new cyber stock market is one in which, according to F.G. Zarb, Chairman of the National Association of Securities Dealers Inc., 'trading securities will be digital, global and accessible 24 hours a day' (Zarb, 1999). The world according to NASDAQ is one in which 'the impossible is becoming routine and the routine is being rejected' (NASDAQ, 1999). At the same time, however, this very dissolution is reintegrated within a vision of a new world order of capitalist populism. As Zarb put it: 'The 21st century stock market will be multi-dealer, computer-screen based, technology-driven and open to all – because people will have access to information that they want to act on' (Zarb, 1999).

This illustrates Deleuze and Guattari's argument that capital is both a force of deterritorialisation and reterritorialisation (see Deleuze and Guattari, 1984). In this context, as the older type of citizen-based relations are deterritorialised, they are simultaneously reterritorialised as netizen-based relations in which individuals are reconfigured (re-interpellated) within the terms of a multi-dealer cyber network of financial decoding and transmission, locked into a world in which capital information, and the *belief* in that information, is paramount.

This new empire of the signs may be said to constitute an obscene simulation of Habermas's ideal of a universality of undistorted communication. Alternatively – and in the context of the progressive decline of the traditional sites of socio-political authority – we might say that such developments reflect the construction of an ultimate new age religion, complete with its orgiastic rituals of the trading pit at the centre of the stock market. Such rituals not only invest capital flows with what Lacan might call a sacred *jouissance*, they also act as a kind of barometer for monitoring the 'real' effects of such flows and in such a way that we take the endless calculations of (incalculable) value seriously.

What Marx demonstrates is that such flows – the *danse macabre* of capital – are made possible through the disavowed violence of exploitation and privation. In Luhmann's terms, he identifies the systematicity of capital's system. In contrast to Adam Smith, Marx shows that the real 'invisible hand' is not that of harmonious equilibrium but, on the contrary, that of power and social exclusion, naturalised through the myth of the liberal market. While the mistake of Marx was to assume that, apropos of metaphysical laws, such a condition would be resolved teleologically, the analysis of capital as a power construction (or, indeed, autopoietic system) remains compelling. What Marx alludes to is precisely that which, in the sense of Lyotard (1993), is *exorbitant* in capitalism – that which is beyond the system of valuations as such, but which nevertheless renders such a system possible. This is located at the level of human labour power and its creative energies. This is why Marx constantly referred to capital as a dead thing that, vampire-like, must feed off the forces of living labour.

At the heart of the seemingly neutral calculus and evaluations of capital lodges a fundamental incalculability – the exorbitant cost to human potential and its capacity for productive optimisation. While capital works ceaselessly to transform and commodify all existing social relations, what it refuses to bargain with (in fact, *cannot* bargain with) is precisely its exploitative conditions of possibility. In other words, what capital cannot conceive or calculate is *its own symptom* of global privation – the very principle of its calculus and its historical reality.

Perhaps the most striking feature of this incalculability is the so-called foreign debt. This debt is now so extreme, so permanent, that it cannot properly be evaluated within existing conventions and its quantification appears increasingly absurd and arbitrary. In the modern age, the foreign debt – a debt which, in practical terms, is beyond calculation and is exorbitant in relation to any possibility of actually being met – is, rather, the name (or one of the names) for the structural dislocation, the traumatic failure, of global capitalism as a universal system. As Derrida (1994) notes, an ideological symptom of this failure is the deafening contemporary disavowal of Marx and the ongoing attempts to exorcise his ghost(s). Far from confirming any historical triumph, such attempts reflect the fact that capitalism cannot finesse its systematicity and that it can never constitute itself as an objective order.

The attempt to gentrify capitalism as a world system is further reflected in the development of a Multilateral Agreement on Investment (MAI) under the auspices of the World Trade Organisation (WTO). The stated goal of the MAI is to grant all foreign investors the same legal protection as received by national investors (thereby overcoming the 'cultural exception' clause of the 1993 General Agreement on Tariffs and Trade (GATT) accords). The net effect would be that legal power shifts decisively away from nation states – thereby subordinating indigenous democratic demands and socio-economic needs – in favour of global capital interests. Under the terms of the MAI, sovereign states can be held legally accountable if, contrary to corporate profit maximisation, they refuse to be 'flexible' about standards concerning labour regulation, health and safety, environmental protection and so on. Measures such as food subsidies, agrarian reform, control of land speculation and the extraction of natural resources, forest protection and local bans on pesticides, pollutants and toxic dumping could all be legally challenged through the MAI.

This can be seen as an attempt to construct a kind of global super-structure that would gentrify/codify the dominance of corporate capital in legalistic terms. However, it is precisely because of the fundamental absence of an ultimate ground on which to base the legitimacy of the MAI that hegemonic resistance is made possible. Political mobilisation against the WTO and the MAI proposals has been extensive and it is through such mobil-isation that the practices of the former are degentrified and their politico-discursive violence exposed. Demonstrations against the summit talks of the WTO in Seattle are clearly an illustration of this and also reflect the fact that upwards of six hundred non-governmental organisations from around the world continue to join forces – chiefly through the internet – in order to oppose corporate domination of global agendas (*http://www.corpwatch.org/*). In the context of evolving supranational regulatory frameworks, such as the European Union, opposition to any single unifying capital-logic of globali-sation is even more evident.

Far from expressing a naturalistic movement, globalisation is a process of combined and uneven development with multiple points of rupture and challenge. It is essentially prone to dislocation, failure and all those forces of the political that persistently undermine capitalism's autopoietic pretensions to universalist autonomy. In short, globalisation is both a power construct and a power struggle.

Conclusion

In their classical modernist form, both liberalism and Marxism represent secular quests for the fundamental object that would serve as the basis for a rationalist reconstruction of the social. Although radically different in orien-tation, both perspectives identify this object at the level of the economy and treat it as the source of metaphysical laws for framing a transparent society.

The history of political economy, however, is one of progressive dislocation. That is to say, in order to function, the modern economy has come to depend upon more and more conditions of possibility (a vanguard, a state, the widening demands of disaffected groups and so on) that have mani-festly compromised any sense of autonomy or objectivity. Against this background, Hilferding and Gramsci sought to destabilise such distinctions as economy/ideology, base/superstructure and to place a much stronger emphasis on logics of articulation and recursivity. Similarly, the regulationists have convincingly demonstrated that the economy is incapable of regulating itself in its own terms. Moreover, by linking this insight to Luhmann's systems theory, we can see that the economic 'object' is not prior to the regu-latory system but, on the contrary, is constituted within the very terms of that

8

Complexity in the Wild:
action in local welfare

WILL MEDD

Complexity ... means being forced to select; being forced to select means contingency; and contingency means risk. (Luhmann 1995: 25)

Ontologies: note that. Now the word needs to go in plural. For, and this is a crucial move, if reality is *done*, if it is historically, culturally, and materially *located*, then it is also *multiple*. Realities have become multiple. (Mol, 1999: 75)

Introduction

This chapter is concerned with the problems raised by complexity for the understanding of politics. The problem of complexity refers to the impossibility of complete observation and the necessity of ignorance as a characteristic of claims made upon the world (Luhmann 1995; 1997). But this is not just a theoretical problem. It is a problem in the world, in the *wild*. The chapter uses ethnographic research to demonstrate the significance of post-structuralism for understanding the dynamics of social welfare. It will not address debates concerned with the ideological problems of post-structuralism for social welfare. These tend to confuse and conflate debates within post-modernism and its variations (for example, Taylor-Gooby, 1994) neglecting, as Penna and O'Brien, (1996) make clear, the complexities of different approaches and take a critical stance based on claims to objectivity and normativity (see also Fitzpatrick, 1996; Hillyard and Watson, 1996).

So, the chapter is not a theoretical exposition of post-structuralism and its relation to politics but, rather, an attempt to demonstrate, and to perform, the relationship between post-structuralism and politics through a story about collaboration in social welfare. This is a *story* is based on my observation and representations of collaboration in social welfare. It is not fictional. It is concerned with complex processes and my account of them could have been structured in other ways. My argument is that this problem of representation is not just a problem of needing more accurate, 'real', accounts. Rather, this is a problem *in the world* I am observing. Complexity is a problem in the world and this not only refers to a problem of representation (which is important) but also to the relations through which the world will become. Complexity

system. At the same time, Luhmann's identification of the auto]
of all systems, including that of the economy, is one that shows
character of traditionalist notions of autonomy and extra-discursi

Luhmann's perspective overlaps with that of Laclau and Mc
ever, the crucial contribution of the latter has been to affirm that ev
– right up to the system of objectivity itself – is constituted through
and antagonism – that is, through a conception of what a system 'is
from possessing a substantial basis, the 'ground' of any system depe\
the capacity of hegemonic practices to establish frontiers of exclus
given conjuncture. And this means that every 'ground' is essentially]
dislocation and political recomposition.

More widely, such interventions may be said to reflect an unravel
modernity in which positivism has increasingly given way to a new em]
on context and contextual instability – the fundamental themes of
structuralism. While post-structuralism, in and of itself, possesses no pol
or ethical consequences, what it does allow for is a crucial reactivation o\
dimension of the political in political economy (and in social relati
generally).

This acts as a good antidote to all those eschatological visions o\
universalist new world order – whether in terms of Rorty's Western liberalis
as that which embodies 'the last *conceptual* revolution' (1989: 63) or in term
of Fukuyama's highly provincial account of the end of history. By reactivatin]
the political, post-structuralism enables us to put into question all sedimented
notions of economic and social reality and thereby to sustain what Derrida
calls the promise of more radical forms of justice and democracy that are
always 'to come' (Derrida, 1994). Against every myth of a centre – be it liberal,
Marxist, nationalist, globalist or whatever – post-structuralism provides the
conditions of possibility (but no more than that) for developing a new type of
politics whose first and enduring fidelity is to non-closure.

makes perspectivism necessary but it also enables multiplicity, that is, multiple realities. The implication of multiplicity is *ontological politics*, 'in which 'the real' is implicated in the 'political' and *vice versa*' (Mol, 1999: 74).

This chapter is not just a performance. It is not just a story. It is the performance of a story which has implications for how we understand the politics of complexity in social welfare, which, in turn, has implications for proposals of solutions to resolving the politics of complexity in social welfare. This is important because collaboration ('partnership working' and 'network governance') play an important role in claims made for 're-inventing government' as enabling, providing, steering, rather than coercing, producing or rowing (Osborne and Gaebler, 1992; Dunshire, 1996; Jessop, 1998). Partnership working and network governance are the basis of attempts to create a new role for government by reconstituting social democracy as a 'Third Way' (see Giddens, 1998; 2000), able to deal with the complexities of our world. The implementation of partnership and network governance has been evident throughout social welfare policy, for example with policies for social care (DoH. 1998a), health care (DoH. 1999a), child care (DoH. 1998b) and housing (DoETR. 1999b). Indeed, few days now go by without reference to policy strategies based on 'joined-up government'. And yet, while debates about the possibilities of the 'Third Way' remain largely at the level of political philosophy, and analysis of network governance and collaboration tends to be limited to particular actors involved, less attention has been given to the processes of policy implementation which suggest limitations to the capacities of these new 'Third Way' approaches.

'Complexity in the Wild', as a study of policy processes and implementation, challenges both the extent to which collaboration (in its broadest terms, 'partnership working') can be taken as a 'good thing' (Hambleton et al., 1995: 7; Hudson et al., 1999: 236; Nocon, 1994: 1), and the extent to which policy networks (in broad terms, co-ordination characterised by reflexive negotiation) can achieve a 'common purpose' (Kickert et al., 1997: 9; see also, Amin and Hausner, 1997; Kooiman, 1993). Indeed, 'Complexity in the Wild' will demonstrate how collaboration and network governance, far from achieving 'partnership working' and a 'common purpose', involve dynamics that can be characterised by dominance, misinformation, mistrust, misunderstanding, and manipulation. The problem is not one of management, of needing better 'collaboration' (as recent government interventions suggest), but one of politics. Complexity necessitates the dimension of the political because it implies that ontologies are not given. It generates the possibility, the necessity, of ontological politics, problematising the development of a collective, rational and strategic solution to the politics of social welfare through network governance and collaboration. Complexity leads to multiplicity, necessitating selection, contingency and risk. The choice by which an option is selected is always political and always accompanied by ignorance. Such choices depend on not knowing as much as knowing.

As a performance, therefore, this chapter brings together the problem of complexity as a problem of observation *in practice*. In this sense, complexity is not just a problem for academic theorising – though this is important – but the observation of complexity happens in the world in which the selections made of complexity are contested.

Models of complexity, most notably 'complexity science', offer another account, another reduction, of the complexity of the world. Calls for understanding 'dynamic', rather than 'taxonomic', complexity (Chia 1999) are limited to metaphysical claims, and do not help us understand *what happens in practice*. Rather, as a problem in the world, to understand the dynamics of that world, that of politics in social welfare, we need to look at what observations are constituted in that world through which ontolog*ies* are performed. The problem is not simply that which entails perspectivism and pluralism. It is that complexity leads to multiplicity, for different representations imply the possibility (and necessity) of different relations, of different realities. These realities are negotiable and contested. They are political and have multiple effects. *Complexity necessitates ontological politics in the world.* Ontological politics is not about different claims to the truth but about multiple realities, characterised by the necessity of ignorance.

Complexity in the Wild

Imagine a project in a place which I will call *Webton*. It is characterised by its 'high and concentrated multiple social deprivation' and seen to be in a 'spiral of decline'. A project. This needs explanation. In part a plan, a focus on what will be done. But we live in a world of projects, a world in which the process of doing things is as important as what gets done. The project involves a plan but, just as much, it involves organisation and practice. In Webton, workers from different institutional agencies involved with social welfare had found their practices densely interconnected – so much so that they developed strategies of working together and collaborating. The different problems confronting Webton – housing, health, social care, employment and so on – could not be isolated from each other and neither could the work of each agency concerned with those problems. It was in the context of these problems that the project, which I will call *Interface*, emerged as a 'multi-agency resource centre'. Interface emerged through a combination of the strategies of 'street-level' workers (see Lipksy, 1980; 1993) and managers (see Clarke and Newman, 1997) at the planning level, and it was made possible largely by a pump-priming mechanism called joint-finance (funding administered through the health authority but managed jointly by it and social services).

Interface is faced with problems. The funding for joint-finance is due to end and the project must find continuation funding from elsewhere. This is where my story, *Complexity in the Wild*, begins. This story is about the processes through which Interface secures funding and about what happens to Interface as part of these processes. It is, as you will see, about the politics of the complexity, its *ontological politics*. It is about the politics of observing Interface, the politics of making decisions about Interface and the politics of what Interface will become.

Before I continue, I want to make a small, but important, note about Interface. Interface is a voluntary project. As a plan, an organisation and a practice, Interface is performed in, by and through the voluntary sector. The project is overseen by the District Council for Voluntary Service (DCVS), and it is managed by a subcommittee of the DCVS. This subcommittee consists of members who we might expect to manage a voluntary project: a chair and treasurer of the DCVS executive, voluntary sector representatives and Webton residents. Interface is also run by volunteers and it provides services for other voluntary sector organisations. And yet, Interface is also performed in the statutory sector, in different statutory agencies. Interface was set up by statutory funding. The subcommittee which manages the project includes district council officers, health authority officers, social services officers, housing association officers, county council officers. The day-to-day management of the project is carried out by two full-time paid employees and the project hosts the provision of statutory services. Interface is, therefore, complex and this complexity is the very condition of its possibility. As a project to deal with the complexity of Webton, Interface must be complex. This enables, and leads to, the multiplicity of relations through which Interface is performed. Here begins ontological politics. Interface is multiple, multiply related and negotiated.

Observing

My temptation (desire?) is to tell you what Interface is. But is this possible? Would this help you understand the politics of the complexity of Interface? The politics of the complexity of Interface is not about what the project actually is but, rather, how different claims about the project are made; different claims which have different implications for who should fund the project; different implications for what the project might become. How would my claims capture the complexity of Interface any more than those of someone else? What medium would I use? What observations, descriptions, representations could I make? Should Interface be represented by a diagram, some statistics, photographs, pictures, poetry or by songs? All of these media could be, and have been, used to capture the complexity of the work of Interface. Yet none of them offers the possibility of a complete representation of Interface. None of them can '*repeat* the system' (Cilliers, 1998: 10). All of the representations require selections of Interface, selections which could have been otherwise, could have offered different stories.

The politics of complexity in the story of Interface begins with a problem of representation. This is a problem because the representation will be a re-duction of the complexity of Interface which is a problem for self-description and self-representation in order to communicate (Luhmann, 1990 and 1995). This is not just my problem for telling the story. It is a problem for the managers of Interface who want to secure funding. How should they represent Interface in order to do so? What accounts of Interface will secure funding? How might these representations affect what Interface will become?

This politics of the complexity of Interface begins with a review of the project by two managers from social services on behalf of the joint-finance committee (the joint-finance contract involved a review of Interface being undertaken prior to the end of funding). The joint-finance review has the objective to 'review the operation of the Interface project against its original objectives'. But, the review notes, this is in a context where 'decisions regard-ing the future of the project are required'. The stories, the representations, of the review have implications for future funding.

While the review cannot capture the complexity of Interface, what is captured is encouraging for the managers of Interface. The review states that 'demand exceeds expectations' and that the project has 'met or exceeded the objectives set at its inception'. Interface is 'acknowledged as significant in reducing stress in the area and seen as a preventative influence in alleviating poverty' and 'to discontinue a successful project is bound to both increase demand on other services ... and attract negative publicity'. So the project has done more than meet its objectives – it is seen to be needed, but it needs funding to continue. Who might want to fund the project? How can this be decided? And upon what will this depend?

One possibility for the project is non-funding, in which case it would close. But the review suggests this will attract negative publicity and lead to an increased demand on other services. The managers of Interface agree with this – indeed, they might well generate this publicity, if necessary. Further-more, Webton had been successful in gaining regeneration funding from the Single Regeneration Budget (SRB) and this could provide some funding for Interface, which would mean the potential of 'good value for money' for other funders. Another possibility, then, is that the district council should fund the rest because one story of the review is that the majority of clients have hous-ing problems which is the district council's responsibility. The council contest this. They argue that the housing problems also reflect problems of health and social care. The managers of Interface also contest this for they argue that housing is often just the presenting problem when, in fact, individuals' housing problems are often densely interconnected with other health and social care issues (and they know sole funding from the council is unlikely). Alternatively, the additional money for the SRB could be funded by the district council, the health authority and by social services, together. This would reflect the stories of the managers of Interface who argue that the different issues cannot be separated and that their work is of significance to housing, health, social care and community development. So, closure is a problem and the district council cannot afford sole responsibility. Therefore, the only option appears to be a collaborative funding agreement between the SRB, the health authority, the district council and social services (as part of the county council).

At this point, the politics of complexity takes another turn. The problem of funding is no longer just a problem of representing Interface – though this is still important – but also a problem about how the decisions to fund the project can be made.

Decisions

Imagine the complexity of the funding decision processes. To secure funding, there needs to be a channel for formal funding processes. The funders will need to have adequate resources to fund the project. They will need to be able to demonstrate to audit that these resources were being used 'effectively', 'economically' and 'efficiently'. They will need to consider the project in relation to other forms of provision, or possible provision, for which the resources could be used. Imagine the problem of such decisions. For the SRB there is not such a problem because funding for such a project was part of the overall regeneration strategy, although the official decision is still to be made and will depend on collaborative funding from the main agencies.

For the other possible funders the situation is more problematic. For funding to be secured, the formal decision-making processes will have to have taken place. But each funder will want to know that, once they have com- mitted their funds, the money will be spent – they cannot afford to under- spend in a climate of under-funding. And, to be sure of this, they will need to know the other possible funders were willing to be committed. Without this knowledge, there will be the risk of under-spending in their budgets, com- mitting more money to the project than they can afford or being left with a project which does less work than they had wanted for the money. So, to make the formal decision, each of the agencies wants to know if the other agencies are committed. But each agency wants to know this before making a formal decision. This is a Catch-22, a Prisoner's Dilemma. The 'solution' to this problem does not depend on predefined rationalities, as Game Theory might suppose. Even simultaneous decision making cannot resolve this problem. The agencies are negotiating their rationalities.

For the formal processes to occur, the funders will need to make informal agreements with each other. Each needs to be confident of the other's position. So the politics of the complexity of Interface now extend into a politics of decision making through informal relationships. The processes to secure funding, 'the funding game', consists of a complex web of dynamics to resolve, or avoid, these issues. Imagine how, for the managers of Interface, the decision-making processes of the potential funders could threaten their project. They are not going to sit back and wait. They want to persuade. They want to do what they can to ensure that the project will continue. They want to show that the project is needed and wanted by the 'community' of Webton and that it is important for all mainstream agencies to support it. And they want to do this before the current funding ends. In fact, they need a decision earlier because of the potential need to give staff notices, close contracts and run down the project. They want commitment as soon as possible. Commitment which is not possible through the formal process alone. What they need is to secure commitment through informal processes.

The politics of the complexity of Interface and the politics of decisions surrounding the funding of Interface are densely interconnected. Interface, a project set up to deal with the complexity of deprivation and service provision in Webton, has now become a part of the complexity about which the agencies must make further decisions.

Informal processes? Do these simply involve persuading the various funders about what Interface is? To some extent this is so. For example, imagine how the managers of Interface spend time demonstrating that the high number of housing inquiries is just a reflection of the presenting issue, behind which lie a complex array of problems for individuals and the 'community' of Webton. To communicate these issues to potential decision-makers, the managers write their own paper as a background to the joint-finance review. They also spend time with local councillors and members of the local community. They explain why the work of Interface does not encourage people with problems to the area but, rather, helps these people to find ways of helping themselves – for example, through support groups and by directing them to appropriate services. So the managers of Interface do try to tell their story of Interface to inform the decision-making. But there is more than this. To understand the politics of decisions in 'Complexity in the Wild' we cannot look at Interface in isolation. We need to take account of the wider *network* of dynamics through which these decisions are made and through which Interface is performed.

Through networks, the managers of Interface know people. Imagine the position of Claire who is the day-to-day manager of Interface. She is involved in various collaborative meetings about community development and other particular projects (for example, HIV awareness work). Through these meetings she has contact with representatives from health services, social services, the district and county councils, local traders and other voluntary sector organisations. Through these networks, Claire keeps 'plugging' the importance of Interface for different areas of work in Webton. She raises the support of these various people. With the exception of local councillors, however, most of those Claire engages with are not the decision-makers at the level of strategic funding in their agencies. So, while there might be support locally, although about this we cannot be sure, there is still the problem of persuading key decision-makers.

Imagine the situation of Ann, who is the coordinator for the District Council for Voluntary Service (DCVS) which oversees the management of Interface under the joint-finance agreement. As the coordinator of DCVS, she is a key representative of the voluntary sector, as it is known. Ann has regular contact with all the agencies concerned with Webton. Sometimes this is one-to-one, perhaps just to share information and discuss, informally, possible directions for service provision. Through these meetings, Ann learns about the situation in the different agencies. Ann also has regular contact with the agencies through the vast array of inter-agency/sector meetings at the strategic level. For example, she is a member of the SRB executive, of the Joint Commissioning Team and of many council steering groups which want input from the voluntary sector. Through these various committees, Ann knows who is who and, often, she knows them personally. Imagine the opportunities she has to inform these people of the importance of Interface and of the need for funding. Imagine the opportunity for her to find out what is happening in the agencies and to find if they have made decisions or who she needs to speak to. Through these networks Ann can negotiate. She can have information. She can know who to trust. She can know what is going on. As a representative of the voluntary sector, Ann can contribute to the processes of the 'Third Way'. Or can she? Imagine what happens when Ann disagrees with some of these people in meetings. How does this affect the negotiations about Interface?

Take, for example, a local councillor in Webton who has 'some reservations about Interface'. This councillor, as chair of the district council Development Committee and chair of the SRB executive, issued a press release about a new project being funded before the SRB executive had made the decision. Should Ann, as a member of the executive, confront the councillor about this? Note this is in a context where Ann was trying to persuade this councillor to support Interface.

Or take, as another example, a meeting where social services demand that new contracts with the voluntary sector for rural services should involve monitoring criteria for the processes and not just the services outcomes. Should Ann, who wants to refuse to agree to this, have voiced her opinion strongly in a context where the representatives of social services had mentioned (threatened?) that a link between the general DCVS funding contract and the specific Interface contract could be made (thus reducing DCVS funding)? Should Ann risk 'rocking the boat' over rural services when she wants to persuade social services to find separate funding for Interface?

Imagine what happens when Ann is given information about the different agencies. In a context of complex interconnected processes, how should

Ann deal with the information? This requires wisdom. The problem for Ann is not how to clarify her knowledge. It is dealing with rumour, reputation, as well as habits – 'know-how', rather than 'knowing'.

Ann is in regular contact with the Director of Community Services in the Priority Services Trust, a provider of services for the health authority, potentially in competition with DCVS for funding from the health authority. He tells her he offers full support for Interface and that the Trust could not provide such a service, 'it is beyond health alone'. He does say, however, that the GPs in Webton are lobbying for funds from the health authority and that Ann should be careful of the 'power of non-decision making' in the health authority. How should Ann respond when the director of primary and community care tells her funding is unlikely? She explains to Ann that the health board were beginning to consider funding Interface but, in doing so, had found out that funding from the district and county councils was unlikely. She tells Ann there is, therefore, no need for a decision from the health authority. She explains how the district council said funding was unlikely because of the restrictions for growth funding and Interface did not fit in with Social Services funding criteria. Anyway, the director tells Ann, projects like Interface are the responsibility of the Community Trust. Who should Ann trust? Whose information is reliable?

As part of these networks, imagine how Ann checks the claims. A district council officer tells her the health authority had not been told this and that no decisions have been made. Indeed, Ann is told that funding has been looking positive and that an officer from housing is offering a commitment and bringing Interface into private housing's funding to ensure its success. Ann then speaks with representatives at the Priority Trust who confirm there is nothing detrimental coming from them and that the health authority is under pressure from the GP lobby in Webton. This representative also says there is a tendency in the health authority to avoid decisions until it is too late. Ann does not speak with social services. She does not need to. There is no reason to suppose that the director from the health authority was representing their position accurately, since the other information had been inaccurate. Imagine how Ann then goes back to the health authority and tells them they can consider funding because the information upon which a decision was not being made was false. Imagine how Ann and Claire judge how far to push the processes. How far should they 'bite the hand that feeds them' or 'rock the boat'.

The SRB are in support of Interface and the coordinator of the SRB helps Claire write their bid for funding. He encourages her to bid for additional 'growth' funding to extend the work of Interface in the community. Imagine how surprised Claire and Ann are, however, to find that the coordinator has then recommended to the SRB executive that 'the project should consolidate its role as a one stop shop … and curtail some of its community development work'. He also steps down from the DCVS sub-executive committee, which manages Interface, explaining he cannot advocate the community development role of the project. Ann and Claire also think the council is likely to fund Interface, having been told they have the support of the housing department. But then they discover that the director of community services in the district council has put forward the proposal that continuation funding from joint-finance should be given to 'prevent premature abandonment' of the project. The director explains that funding is unlikely from the district and county councils due to budget cuts and that two-year extension funding from joint-finance will buy the project time and enable the main possible funding agencies to consider how to keep the project funded in the future.

Imagine Ann and Claire in this situation. They cannot be sure where they stand and, as they explained, they take 'three steps forward and four steps back'. The response from health authority representatives on the joint-finance committee was that funding Interface through joint-finance was not an option because it had already been decided Interface was not suitable for priority funding, and the health authority thought the project was not good value for money. Now what should Ann and Claire do? If funding from health, as well as from the district council and social services (county council), is unlikely should they persuade decision-makers that joint-finance is an option? Should Ann, as a voluntary sector representative, push for joint-finance to fund Interface, which would mean other voluntary projects might loose their funding? Where should her priorities lie? Now the problem is not just 'rocking the boat' or 'biting the hand that feeds them' – it is about causing a storm which could mean other smaller boats might sink or never get afloat.

Imagine that the decision for joint-finance is postponed and an 'emergency' meeting is planned . That meeting lasts five minutes. In that five minutes, as well as noting apologies, the health authority representatives explain that they are committed to funding Interface; the county council representatives also say they are committed to funding Interface; and the district council say they are also, reluctantly, committed to funding Interface. Interface has funding(s).

The story has jumped. Decisions have been made. But how? I do not know. The managers of Interface do not know. They are surprised to hear this news. They are relieved to know that they did not cause a storm and sink the smaller boats, for the time being at least. And the point is, not knowing does not matter. They, as well as those on the committee for joint-finance, do not need to know. Joint-finance do not need to make decisions. It is no longer important. They can live with the ignorance of how the decisions were made. They have to. No one can be sure of how the decisions were made, nor the rationale behind them. Note that these have not been formal decisions. We cannot identify a clear process, a clear authority, through which these decisions happened. Indeed, we cannot even identify if there were moments at which the decisions were made. We do not know how they came about. Yet these public statements of commitment, recorded in minutes, are a pretty good security that the process is over. The project will get funding. But we, the managers of Interface and those of joint-finance, can live with this ignorance.

Along with the politics of the complexity of Interface and the decisions to fund Interface comes ignorance. And it is not just our ignorance of the decisions which is important here. The decision makers in the different institutional agencies must also live with ignorance. In part, I refer to the ignorance of each other and their different, unknown, rationales. But, in part, and in particular, I refer to their ignorance of Interface. They could not know Interface. They could not have a complete representation of Interface. Indeed, most had never been to the project, to the building within which, and through which, Interface happens. Upon what selective basis they made their decision we remain ignorant, just as they cannot be sure what ignorance was involved. The politics of the complexity of Interface leads to a politics of ignorance. Ignorance of Interface cannot be overcome and there cannot be a complete representation. The decision makers must make selections and cannot observe the process of making those selections without further selections. And they cannot observe the others making their selection. They must live with ignorance. But ignorance involves contingency. What ignorance, what contingency, what risk is accepted? What ignorance of Interface will they allow? What will they allow Interface to become?

Ontologising

The jump in my story is a jump back to the politics of complexity of Interface with which I began. Interface has secured funding but this is not the end. I have already lost some of the story about the ontological politics of Interface. I have not given an account of the problems that Interface suffered through the funding game, of how staff had been given their notice or how contracts for services had been closed and developmental projects stopped. I have not explained how agencies using the project had begun to look for other projects. These are important but they are not what I want to focus on. I want to tell the story of how the politics of the complexity of Interface, which posed the problem of how to represent Interface, re-enters the problem of the ontological politics of Interface, the problem of what Interface will become. The key here is the problem of establishing upon what conditions funding was secured. Had funding been given for Interface to develop as it wished? Did Interface have a general contract through which to continue and develop its work?

Imagine a meeting between the managers of Interface and the representatives from the different funding agencies to discuss the contract with Interface. This is the first time (except for the coordinator of the SRB) that these representatives had actually been to the project. What is clear is that what Interface would become is different for each of these funders. The SRB director gave seven outputs – from employment to women's self-defence – according to which the project would be assessed. The representative from the health authority wanted to make sure the project generated outputs for their inter-agency strategies for community care. The representative of social services also wanted the project to meet to their community care outputs and the objectives of the anti-poverty strategy for the county council. The representative from the district council wanted clear monitoring of clients in relation to housing and other council services. They all told the managers of Interface that it was no longer to do 'case-work' with individuals but to refer them to appropriate agencies. They told the managers of Interface that they should no longer involve the project in community development and they told the managers of Interface that they would have to increase the monitoring and representation of their work to show that they met the criteria of the funding contract. This was all for one year of funding, following which the future would need to be negotiated.

My story is close to the end now, although Interface continues with a yearly contract. It is a yearly contract which directs Interface to meet the criteria of different funding agencies. The project works to those criteria. The project works to those separate criteria. Imagine how the project changes over time and how the project is related to the different funding agencies. Imagine the complexity of Interface and the ontological politics that continue.

Conclusion

Enough of the *Wild*. Well not quite, but enough about the story. Now it is time to explore how we can begin to approach the problem of complexity in theory. *Complexity in the Wild* is a story which, as I noted in the introduction to this chapter, demonstrates that any account we claim about the 'reality' of these dynamics, be they those of Interface or of the decisions about Interface, will be one of ignorance. We will have to ignore what we cannot represent, what we do not know and this includes ignoring ourselves (reflexivity refers this to another level, to another blind-spot). This is the reality of complexity. But this is not just about a problem of representation, it is also about ontologies. It is about how we deal with the problem that there is multiplicity.

Let me remind you about Interface. What is Interface? We cannot understand Interface away from its relations and the relations through which Interface is performed, through which Interface is, are, multiple. The reality of Interface is generated through these relations. And these relations, as we saw, are multiple, contested and political.

Perhaps the problem of complexity is a problem of our understanding. Perhaps what we need is to find the mechanisms of complexity, to find the underlying rules which generate complex dynamics. This would be the way of the 'third culture' (Brockman, 1995). The 'Third Way' meets the 'third culture'?

Maybe Brockman is right, the insights of complexity science might after all 'affect the lives of everybody on the planet' (1995: 19). Then the task of social science, of political science, can be to use – with a critical stance, of course – the models from complexity science to understand the complex social world (see, for example, Byrne, 1998; Cilliers, 1999). But how would we deal with the essence of complexity? The multiplicity that complexity generates? What observations would the modelling require? What selections of the modelled would be assumed to represent reality? What relations would need to be mapped and modelled? What would happen when we know about this? How would the models accommodate our 'capacity to reflect upon, and to contradict, any mathematical description made of [us]' (Castoriadis, cited in Tsoukas, 1998: 305)? Could the models incorporate within themselves their own consequences on the dynamics of what they model? Could they accommodate what would happen when the 'Third Culture' meets the 'Third Way'? Just how would the modellers imagine this complexity (Shackley et al., 1996)? How would the models capture 'Complexity in the Wild', and what would happen if they did?

Complexity, it seems, would still be a problem, if for no other reason than that we could not know the consequences of our modelling. We could not anticipate the multiplicity of relations through which our models would be produced and performed. Instead, then, what if we keep complexity as a problem? What if we complexify our thinking (Chia, 1998)? Perhaps we could move beyond the temptation of capturing complexity, of 'taxonomic complexity', and recognise 'that the current established system of symbolic expression cannot adequately capture the sense of fluent indeterminacy and temporality intrinsic to life' (Chia, 1998: 350). Instead, we could recognise this 'dynamic complexity'. In this sense, we would not juxtapose the simple and the complex but, instead, recognise that we cannot know the totality of anything, now we know the atom is not the ultimate unit. We must always make distinctions. This is how we deal with dynamic complexity, and this is also why dynamic complexity alone does not help us understand the dynamics of 'Complexity in the Wild'. The dynamics in the wild involved selections which exposed and hid, produced and undid, enabled and constrained; selections which were necessary and yet contingent, which enabled Interface and yet constrained what it could become.

This is how we can think about and imagine, complexity. Dynamic or unstructured, complexity refers to the possibility of infinite interconnectivity. Everything is interconnected yet, we structure to cope with this forming selective relations. Paradoxically, these selective relations form 'immanent constraints' to relations and further selections. That is to say, immanent constraints to connectivity (Luhmann, 1995: 24), a structured complexity which limits further connectivity, complexifies and further limits interconnection. In this sense complexity is self-conditioning and temporal (Luhmann, 1995: 43–5).

With infinite time, infinite connections could be made. But a system cannot afford to synchronise fully to its environment because this would require the possibility of all possible connections simultaneously. Instead, systems 'gain time' from their environment, generating their own temporality (Luhmann, 1995: 46). So, dealing with the problem of complexity generates complexity. We saw the complexity that Interface became to deal with the complexity of Webton and we saw that Interface became part of the complexity of Webton. Complexity is not just dynamic, therefore, it is also structured and structuring. It is self-conditioning and it is a problem.

The problem that complexity presents is the problem of ignorance. Complexity forces selections, and selections force ignorance. Our models of complexity, our third culture, unless they could claim to *repeat the system* (Cilliers, 1998: 10), have to ignore what they see as unimportant, as trivial, what they cannot see. An important part of what they could not see is that they could not see themselves seeing in time. One cannot observe oneself in one's environment without observing within that environment. We live in an 'ecology of ignorance' (Luhmann, 1998). Interface could not represent itself without selections which would exclude and ignore the processes of Interface representing itself. The funders could not represent themselves without selections which would exclude the processes of representing themselves. They had to live with the ignorance of each other.

It is not just living with ignorance that is important. It is living with ignorance which makes things possible. How could one proceed if we needed to know everything, if we needed to, and could, understand everything? This raises problems for the normative basis of literature on policy networks and collaboration. For what could 'shared understanding', one of the clichés of networks, collaboration and the 'Third Way', mean in an ecology of ignorance? How could this occur? Instead, we need to think about how things happen, how Interface exists, in the ecology of ignorance.

Complexity is the key, for complexity enables relations and, therefore, multiplicity. It is the *possibilities* of relations enabled by complexity through which multiplicity can occur. This does not mean that complexity simply leads to multiple perspectives but, rather, that complexity leads to multiple relations, with multiple effects, and, therefore, to multiple realities. As we saw, these are contested, they are not given, and the ontologies are political. The complexity of Interface enabled its relations to different funders. It enabled Interface's multiplicity, its multiple realities in the relations through which it was performed. It was because of this complexity and the necessity of ignorance that this could occur. The funders would have to accept their ignorance of the multiplicities. But they accepted this with a condition, a submission. If *their* targets (their future observations) were not met, not secured, or, if another funder pulled-out for any reason, they too could pull out. So the necessity of ignorance, of contingency and risk, was accepted, but it was limited, constrained. This meant the funding could happen and that the funders could have their relations with Interface because they could be ignorant of the others. The risks were limited by selecting relations, generating further complexity. For now, the multiplicity includes Interface's relations to the *different* funding agencies and the funding agencies relations with each other about Interface. Complexity is then self-conditioning, it leads to multiplicity, to further ignorance, to further ontological politics.

9

Political Science and Complexity

PAUL HAYNES

Biological, social, cultural, mental, etc. systems work upon the same basic principles
– ones embodied in creative processes of component-systems. (Kampis 1991: 460)

We require just a little order to protect us from chaos. (Deleuze and Guattari 1994: 201)

Introduction

There is little controversy in suggesting that social and political organisations
are complex. The question that I will be concerned with, however, is the degree
to which accounts of such complex behaviour can be described in terms of the
models and methods developed in relation to complexity science. I will consider what is at stake for politics, particularly in its relationship with science,
in applying aspects of the complexity science paradigm to the study of politics.

Until recently, perhaps as recently as the 1960s, methods developed
within the discourse of Enlightenment thought had remained, in a modified
form, the dominant forces in the development of political theory. In political
science, modernity was ushered in with a series of methods related to those of
the natural sciences. Since these early beginnings, when the methods of social
science had subordinated themselves to those of the natural sciences, there
has been a slow but continual separation of methodological principals to the
point that an antagonism developed between political and natural science.
This friction created a tension between the methods inherited from science
and the ideology that surrounds such methods within the realm of social
science. My intention is to show that modernity can, finally, be ushered out
with a re-evaluation of the relationship between natural science and social
science (natural philosophy and political philosophy) that ends this antagonism. This re-evaluation can be seen to be active in, and with the development
of, both post-structuralism and complexity. Both complexity and post-structuralism represent a series of responses to an attempt to totalise knowledge –
responses that centre on the problem of reflexivity and the way in which
information feeds back into these systems of knowledge.

Post-structuralism begins its break with structuralism with the conclusion that systems are dependent upon conditions that cannot be reduced to

those structures or systems themselves. These systems were designed to explain the totality of an object of study and, though there is an attempt in structuralism to deal with reflexivity, such structures were unable to account for their own part in the process. Post-structuralism sets itself the task of exploring these reflexive conditions in order to create strategies with which to relate such conditions to the systems they describe.

Similarly, complexity science breaks with the assumptions of classical science by showing that interaction always involves feedback and, thus, cannot be mechanistic, linear or deterministic. My method in this chapter will be to use the assumptions of post-structuralism and complexity science to examine the complexity of systems and the forces and dynamics that are said to shape them. I will, thus, use theory from social science to evaluate methods developed within natural science and theory developed within natural science to evaluate features of social science. I will show that natural science, as much as social science, has developed beyond the assumptions of modernity and that social science, as much as natural science, has outgrown Newtonian assumptions of cause, change and organisation. These changes in the scientific paradigm, I will argue, have important implications for political science. Symmetrically, recent developments in political science have fundamental implications for the status and methods of science. It is clear, for example, that observation and self-reference pose problems as much for social science as for science. Problems arise as scientific, political and social theories are recognised as parts of the system they attempt to theorise. Niklas Luhmann states this problem in the context of social theory with great clarity: 'Sociology can no longer use the distinction between Subject and Object, as if sociology was the Subject and society, or the social system of science, the Object' (Luhmann 1994: 133).

In science, Claude Shannon's definition of information as divorced from meaning has similar implications for observation and interpretation (for a full discussion, see Hayles 1999: 50–84). The rise in popularity of the paradigm of post-structuralism and complexity is a response to the perceived limitation of science and social science in addressing the difficulty posed by the reflexivity, interactivity and the connectivity of systems.

Complexity and post-structuralism reflect the limitation of the more traditional approaches to method in natural and social science. The genealogy of these methods and the politics involved in their rise to a position of dominance for more than two hundred years is instructive. This chapter will briefly examine the relationship between Robert Boyle and Thomas Hobbes, as discussed by Shapin and Schaffer (1985), in order to demonstrate the political, or at least non-neural, aspects of models and methods for natural and political science. The relationship between Boyle and Hobbes offers us a case study on the relationship between science and politics and its examination will help us understand the emergence of complexity science and its application beyond the boundaries of natural science.

From Boyle and Hobbes to Luhmann

In their book *Leviathan and the Air-Pump*, Steven Shapin and Simon Schaffer examine the boundaries and methods of science in relation to questions of political philosophy. The story they develop is that of the relationship between scientist Robert Boyle and political philosopher Thomas Hobbes or, rather, the science and political thought of Boyle and the political thought and science of Hobbes. Shapin and Schaffer emphasise the remarkable agreement between the ideas of these two figures. Both approach questions of method through mechanistic philosophy and expressed a similar epistemology developed within the rationalist tradition. Politically, they agree on the ideal of both a king and a parliament and a subservient and unified church. Such a degree of harmony between Boyle and Hobbes is not interesting in itself but it creates a space for engaging with their areas of disagreement. These areas include the status of experimentation, a difference found in the approach of Boyle and Hobbes to the air-pump.

The air-pump, developed by Boyle and Robert Hooke, came to exemplify the former's observational and empirical method. Indeed, the air-pump is referred to by Shapin, though not necessarily in his own voice, as 'the Scientific Revolution's greatest fact making machine' (Shapin, 1996: 96). Boyle's empirical method relied upon the credibility of reliable witnesses whose senses were corrected and disciplined by scientific instruments and 'the discipline enforced by devices such as the microscope and the air-pump was analogous to the discipline imposed upon the senses by reason' (Shapin and Schaffer, 1985: 37).

Boyle, like Galileo and Newton, was interested in that which was perceptible. The air-pump was an effective tool in that it controlled conditions for drawing out the relationship between various percepts. Hobbes opposed this method of observation claiming that the only method able to gain universal consent was that of mathematical demonstration: 'In Hobbes's view, Boyle's experimental solution to the problem of order was not possible; it was not effective; and it was dangerous' (Shapin and Schaffer, 1985: 80–1) because it separated knowledge from power. Hobbes argued that his own method, rather than that of Boyle, was truly scientific. The opinion of witnesses could not be made universal and mathematical but was formed on the basis of inconclusive experiments and the (demonstrably) deceptive senses. According to Hobbes, the very basis of order had been undone with such experimentation. In the name of nature, or of the facts produced by such things as the air-pump, academics and scholars challenged not just the king's authority but the traditional notion of authority itself. For Hobbes, then, the method of science must defer to the needs of the political, with scientific authority, in a very real sense, subordinated to political authority. But for Boyle, the methods of science were a model for discovery and the gaining of knowledge in all disciplines. For him, the needs of politics must be subordinated to the type of knowledge generated by science.

Shapin and Schaffer draw out an immanent critique of Boyle's methodological assumptions. They indicate that Boyle develops conditions for the establishment of facts and that these depend upon various conditions of credible witnessing. Such witnessing was to be public and collective, but the conditions for being part of the reliable witness community or being an appropriate public site were developed by Boyle in a way that is neither intuitive nor unproblematic. Hobbes took Boyle's conditions to almost exemplify the practices of a secret society, a strange form of public space that Haraway compares with a top-secret defence lab (Haraway 1997: 25).

Boyle's model of reliable testimony was that which displayed a certain sort of morality and modesty, only asserting statements that could be proven in experimental trials. Testimony was to be obtained from men who hoped to advance natural philosophy rather than their own reputation or interests. Theories, hypotheses and speculations were to be spoken about with caution. A witness could speak confidently only of matters of fact because they were considered empirical truths. In disputes over matters of fact, experiments, and not rhetoric, would decide the case. Such evidence would enable those in error to renounce their former position: 'Till a man is sure he is infallible, it is not fit for him to be unalterable' (Boyle, 1772: 311, quoted in Shapin and Schaffer, 1985: 74).

The dispute between Boyle and Hobbes, then, becomes a dispute about the extent to which scientific discovery can be understood as shaped by social institutions and structures of authority and, indeed, the extent to which it contributes to, and itself shapes, those structures. Shapin and Schaffer conclude that: 'Knowledge, as much as the state, is the product of human actions. Hobbes was right' (Shapin and Schaffer 1985: 344). In her response to Shapin and Schaffer, Haraway (1997) takes Boyle's personality and gender to be at stake, centring on his advocacy of modesty as a condition for reliable testimony in experimental narrative and pointing out that contingent factors have been important in structuring the assumptions of people that have steered science and social science in particular directions. In this regard, Haraway does not disagree with Shapin and Schaffer. It is clear that there is no method of science that has a logic and set of principles that can crank out truths like a machine. It is also true, however, that deducing truth about the world from firm foundations, Hobbes's preferred method, is as unhelpful for a practising scientist. Very little could be done with a strict adherence to either methodological principle.

If Haraway, Shapin and Schaffer take the side of Hobbes, as Christopher Norris (1997) concludes, then it is the side of a rather peculiar Thomas Hobbes, who becomes almost a proto-critical sociologist who recognises something about the constructed nature of knowledge. Norris rejects such constructivist assumptions and advocates a critical realist epistemology that enables a clear distinction between the historical context of discovery and the social context of justification. Thus, Norris, like Haraway, Shapin and Schaffer, presents an ethical argument as to the validity of observation and experimentation as methodological principles for science. These principles are as contested for social science as for natural science and rely upon a firm distinction between discovery and construction. But it is just such a distinction that is rendered problematic by Niklas Luhmann, who suggests a more fundamental and radical approach to the relationship between subjects and objects.

Luhmann argues that, historically, social science, like natural science, has approached its subject matter in one of two ways: either it emphasises positivism or it advocates a critical approach. In its empirical guise, social science analyses latent structures through manifest features, while in critical form it maintains that social reality is not as transparent as it appears. Luhmann argues:

> All attempts at building a unified theory of society on the basis of a critical/positivist distinction had lead into the paradox of treating appearance and reality, or latent and manifest structures, as one and the same thing. The situation is now changing in radical ways which sociology has yet to appreciate. (Luhmann, 1994: 126)

This, of course, presupposes that there is a purpose in creating a unified theory of society, otherwise it is merely a choice of which side to take. The 'situation' that Luhmann refers to here is that of the emergence of interdisciplinary discussions of self-organisation, modification, generation and reference represented by the work of the Santa Fe Institute, and other gatherings, on the wider use of complexity science. Luhmann concludes that: 'We can draw upon these recent discussions in order to understand society as a self-observing system that defines its own identity while, at the same time, leaving an "unmarked space" for the possibility to describe society in quite different ways' (Luhmann 1994: 126).

Examining social systems as though they were complex autopoietic systems suggests, for Luhmann, a method with which to trace the process of observation through its many layers of reflexivity. In the following section we will turn to the arguments that have influenced Luhmann.

Chaos, Complexity and Autopoiesis

Dynamics is the study of change and has been a focus for scientific analysis since the time of Newton, Leibniz and the method of calculus. Such early accounts of dynamics, associated principally with classical science and Enlightenment thought, emphasised the mechanistic and deterministic way in which component features interacted with each other. Change was about the attainment of equilibrium, the regaining or retaining of stability. The theory of change that these methods and models suggested had been extremely powerful in the early development of science. They also remained relatively powerful and unchallenged once they crossed over into the realm of social science. Though long since superseded by other models in physics, for example, thermodynamics and quantum physics, these assumptions have not been rigorously expunged from the assumptions of social scientists. Since recent developments in complexity science have further emphasised the limitation of the Newtonian paradigm in science, it might be appropriate to examine the degree to which assumptions about change within the social sciences can benefit from a re-evaluation, in accordance with the assumptions of complexity science.

Complex dynamical systems, the type of systems that are appropriate to the features under examination here, tend to elude formal analysis and depend instead on computer simulation and conceptual modelling. Notions such as chaos, attractors, genetic algorithms, autopoiesis and self-organisation can be set to the themes of bifurcation, feedback, non-linearity, conservation and dissipation which form the basis of the vocabulary of complexity. But there is often confusion over the terminology at stake or the demarcation of different aspects of complexity science. Many accounts of complexity adapted to social science mention chaos or chaos theory (see, for example, Eve, Horsfall and Lee, 1997; Kiel and Elliot, 1995) and chaos is often used as a generic term for processes developed within complexity science. Chaotic systems are important in that they have the property of being both simple and maximally complex at the same time. Complexity is important because it seems to spontaneously emerge and increase in systems. The two concepts are useful in understanding each other but they cannot be subsumed under a single category. To conflate the two terms is unhelpful.

Chaos theory is often represented as a revolutionary way to explore complex phenomena and to explain the disorganised order of the world. It is clear that understanding the world in terms of non-linearity problematises the type of thinking associated with Newton. Non-linearity is a necessary condition of chaos. It is, therefore, supposed that chaos theory questions the whole foundation of Newtonian physics. As one populariser puts it: 'Where chaos begins, classical science stops' (Gleick, 1987: 3).

This is correct only in so far as many aspects of complexity theory contradict the assumptions of classical science. Chaos theory, in its technical sense, has relatively few real world applications. The most familiar idea associated with chaos, the butterfly effect (sensitive dependence upon initial conditions), merely signifies that tiny differences, such as the flapping of a butterfly's wings, may, relatively quickly, become amplified by feedback into immense differences. But chaos theory does not explain such feedback mechanisms or the emergence of order. As Ben Goertzel, a mathematician trained in chaotic dynamics, argues, 'Where chaos is concerned, there is a rather large gap between the philosophical, prospective hype and the actual, present-day science' (Goertzel, 1994: 1). An additional reason why an emphasis on chaos, rather than complex systems, is unhelpful is that theories of complex and self-organising systems also share a heritage with General Systems Theory.

It is no coincidence that such systems thinking should make a return to dynamic modelling at a time when the computing power sufficient to run complex simulations is freely available. There were many reasons for the failure of cybernetics and systems theory in the 1940 and 1950s, not least the exaggerated claims made in its name (not a failing that all advocates of a complexity theory approach to social science have made a full note of). However, there were also considerable successes for such thinking in their application to the social sciences (such as in the work of Greg Bateson and Niklas Luhmann). While a return to systems theory is not, of itself, likely to be a profitable enterprise, complexity can act as a corrective to some of the limitations of general systems theory. Though complexity science is not an academic discipline as such, there are a number of centres, research institutes and research groups that specialise in research in a wide range of complex systems dynamics. Chief amongst these are the Santa Fe Institute and the Brussels School, centred on the research of Ilya Prigogine.

Complexity itself can be described in terms of mathematics. The complexity of a system is related to the length of a schema used to describe the regularity of aspects of that system. Though it is useful for the sake of clarity to have a formal sense of complexity, these measures and methods only indicate the signs of complexity-increasing mechanisms, rather than explain the dynamics of these mechanisms (for a clear introduction to measures of complexity see Gell-Mann, 1994). There is no unity to the various themes of complexity, but there is a family resemblance between related concepts. The key assumption is that there are particular patterns that are shared by, and reflected in the behaviour of, self-organising systems. The most obvious of these is the existence of elaborate feedback mechanisms and the emergence of order and organisation. Complexity is said, then, to spontaneously emerge in systems and complexity and self-organisation are described as emergent properties of the chemical/biological/social system in question (for different contexts of complex systems, see Prigogine and Stengers, 1984; Kampis, 1991; Byrne, 1998; and Cilliers, 1998).

Complexity science has crossed over into social science in a number of ways (see Thrift, 1999). However, the most influential model to make the transition from complexity science to social science is autopoiesis (see, for example, Zeleny, 1980; Luhmann, 1990; Jessop, 1990; Mingers, 1995). There are a number of reasons for this. Primary amongst these is the negative reason that there are limitations to the alternative systems derived from complexity science when applied to social organisation. Systems such as chaos, catastrophe theory, dissipative structures and complex adaptive systems, for example, produce their complex output by making use of the store of input and, in this way, are merely complexity-preserving mechanisms and, as such, are fixed. An entirely different class of complexity occurs when a system is able to give itself a new input with the production of each new adjustment to the system. Autopoietic, self-modifying and self-generating systems are models that describe exactly such increases in complexity, as opposed to being merely descriptions of complex features that fixed systems possess. As social, political and cultural change seem not merely to preserve complexity but to be examples of increasing complexity, models such as autopoiesis would appear, therefore, to accommodate themselves better to an understanding of the mechanisms involved in such change. Autopoiesis presents a mechanism with which to describe the process of creative complexification. It is also the most highly developed model from complexity science to be applied to social phenomena. For these reasons, I will examine this class of systems in detail, rather than giving an overview of the general paradigm of complexity (see Gell-Mann, 1984 and Cilliers, 1998 for an overview in relation to science and social science respectively). However, in this analysis, autopoiesis will represent an exemplar of complexity approaches to social science in general. I will then make some recommendations about the use of particular elements of complexity as tools for modelling socio-political phenomena and the limitation of such measures.

Autopoiesis has been the most influential of this class of models for social science (see Luhmann, 1982 and 1990; 1994; Jessop, 1990; Teubner, 1993; Mingers, 1995). Autopoiesis was developed principally by Maturana and Varela in the 1970s, in an attempt to model some general aspects of life. They wanted to model living systems through a distinct mode of existence and a new type of logic based on a consistent approach to self-reference.

An autopoietic system can best be thought of as a closed network of component-generating processes. This involves complete and identical temporal replication within self-maintaining processes. That is to say, the components of the system, through their interaction, generate recursively the same code which produced them. Autopoiesis, then, can be best understood as the ability of any particular pattern, for example a life form, to maintain its integrity when set against the adaptational pressure of the external features of its environment. This can, typically, be described as a process in which a system produces its own organisation, that is to say the set of its defining relationships, and maintains itself within that particular structure and space. Autopoietic systems are typically dissipative, in other words, they are not conservative in relation to energy, merely in relation to structure, and are generally homeostatic. Varela, in *Principles of Biological Autonomy* defines an autopoietic system as that which is:

> Organised (defined as a unity) as a network of processes of production (trans-
> formation and destruction) of components that produce the components that:
>
> 1. through their interactions and transformations continuously regenerate and
> realise the network of processes (relations) that produced them; and
>
> 2. constitute it (the machine) as a concrete unity in the space in which they [the
> components] exist by specifying the topological domain of its realisation as such a
> network. (Varela, 1979: 79).

Such self-production can be contrasted with allopoeisis, that is to say, other
forms of production which assemble elements that are materially distinct and
occupy an external space to that which produces them. Varela also introduced
a broader class of systems, that he termed autonomous systems, which maintain their organisation but need not be thought of as producing and regener-
ating their components. Thus, autopoiesis is considered a special class of
such autonomous systems. Furthermore, autopoietic systems do not manifest
the linearity associated with causal systems because they are within a self-
producing cycle and there is no original or initial element. Varela's sense of
autopoiesis makes a virtuous circle from the vicious circle contained in the
notion of the self-causation and the more general notion of self-reference.

Autopoiesis, particularly in its account of cognitive systems, starts from a
phenomenological basis. According to Maturana, the notions of object and
other are the most important notions for a system because it is through the
making of this distinction that the system can become an observer. For
Maturana, this is important in that:

> Observing is both the ultimate starting point and the most fundamental question in
> any attempt to understand reality and reason as phenomena of the human domain.
> Indeed, everything that is said is said by an observer to another observer that could
> be him or herself. (Maturana, 1988: 27).

Though autopoiesis might develop into a useful tool for social science, there
must be a degree of caution when dealing with the concept. Despite the fact
that autopoiesis has received a fair amount of attention recently, it does not
seem to have offered more than a series of generalisations about what must
be included if a system is to describe self-generation. For example, Maturana
and Varela give no specification of the set of conditions under which the type
of organisation associated with autopoiesis occurs and offer no explanation
for the component-producing processes.

Luhmann, the key social theorist associated with autopoiesis, uses the
idea merely as a point of departure with which to consider the problems of
designing a system to account for self-reference and self-generation. While
influenced by Maturana and Varela's approach, Luhmann has not invested in
the systematic use of their ideas. His work is a thorough and sophisticated
view of social systems on the grand scale and his ambition stretches further
than drawing a simple parallel between social systems and different types of

complex system. He attempts to reformulate questions and enable particular problems to be taken into account that cannot be accommodated by other theoretical approaches. He also, importantly, discusses what a social system actually is. Like Maturana and Varela, Luhmann uses a constructivist framework. However, the latter also plays with the abstract, metaphorical and heuristic features of systems thinking that constitute its meaning. As an abstraction, Luhmann's theory is concerned with society as a whole and the most significant systems that reflect this structure. However, as heuristics, such systems enable understanding of the world by describing patterns, relations and behaviours. Luhmann's theory also indicates the problem of complexity for the social, which includes the complexity *of* the social as an embedded dynamic. Luhmann both indicates *and* addresses the problems of complexity which have implications for a social theory developed in relation to themes from complexity science.

The reason for the need to develop a separate social theory of complexity, with all the difficulties this entails, should be clear. Societies or socio-political institutions are not exactly like anything else – machines, an ant colony, a body or an eco-system. These are all different nodes in a taxonomy of dynamic systems. A general account of features such systems have in common will be too vague to be of any use to the political scientist. Models that are used to explain one system are unlikely to explain the features of another without being adapted to the specificity of the second system. It is in the use of such a system as a heuristic or as a way of thinking beyond the limitations of existing social and political theory that complexity and post-structuralist assumptions are most useful. We will now consider the uses and meaning of such models for natural and social science and suggest some approaches to social investigation that can be developed as an alternative to Luhmann's social systems.

Politics, Complexity and Post-structuralism

Arguments developed in post-structuralist theory and the assumptions that they express are diverse. In many ways post-structuralism is as complex as complexity science. But post-structuralism as a paradigm suggests a series of interesting problems that are directly related to problems exposed by complexity. According to the paradigm of post-structuralism, the limits of knowledge are models, metaphors and strategic representations. These limits are necessarily reflexive and are difficult to represent as a totalising model or a unified narrative. Indeed, such difficulty seems to anticipate the end of attempts to construct grand narratives (see Lyotard, 1984). As with complexity science, post-structuralism is a term that describes a wide variety of theoretical practices but we will here exemplify the post-structuralist approach through the work of Gilles Deleuze.

Deleuze argues that understanding the world depends upon generating concepts and models. Shifting between discourses and overstepping traditional demarcation boundaries are important for this process to occur. The purpose of this engagement is not to reduce one discipline to the deeper truth of another, nor is it to set up a superficial unity between different areas of study. Instead, it is important because of the way in which:

> Someone's own work can lead to unexpected convergence, with new implications, directions, in other people's work. And no special status should be assigned to any particular field, whether philosophy, science, art or literature. (Deleuze, 1995: 30)

Deleuze's work urges the reader to conceive of the world in as many different ways as a concept can be thought about. He acknowledges that there has been a fragmentation of knowledge but this does not lead to the impossibility of constructing systems, he argues, but is only a reason to be more careful in the claims that are made about them.

> Systems have in fact lost absolutely none of their power. All the groundwork for a theory of so-called open systems is in place in current science and logic, systems based on interactions, rejecting only linear forms of causality and transforming notions of time. (Deleuze 1995: 31–2)

Those describing such systems must, therefore, also be aware of the problem relating to the status of concepts and models in constructing, and being constructs of, reality. It is here and in this way that the creation and use of specific models has a political import. Let us return to complexity science.

In science, themes associated with complexity emerged in an ad hoc way from various attempts to model the interaction of gravitational bodies, in explanations of variable sensitivity in simulations and from more abstract theorising on adaptation and change. The problem of unifying such concepts, for the social scientist, relates to the question of which aspects of the theory are to be adapted to social science and which phenomena they are to be used to explain. This, itself, is a matter of cultural and epistemological bias. Dave Byrne, for example, claims that communities *are* dissipative structures, that Prigogine's model to explain how chemical clocks work describes how the world functions:

> Every PhD student in everything should get to grips with the 'chaos/complexity' programme, not for reasons of fashion or even legitimate career building but because this is the way the world works and we need to understand that. (Byrne, 1998: 161)

To simulate social phenomena with models developed within science is to work within the constraints of the assumptions developed within science to explain something that facilitates itself to such an explanation. In this way, to apply such a model uncritically to political science, as though the world functioned according to the laws of the model, would merely be subordinating political theory once more to the dictates of the natural sciences. The implication is that individuals can be quantified into homogenous units, though these units tend to form complex organisations. But how are the model and the actual world related? Here complexity can be used to exemplify the politics of model construction.

Consider, for example, the way in which ideas developed within complexity science have captured the public imagination. These ideas are represented in popular films (from *Naked* to *Jurassic Park*) and television adverts (from *CITCO* to *Nike*), and have entered the vocabulary of corporate managers, business and marketing consultants and policy advisors (for a clear example of chaos theory in management narratives, see Cefkin, 1998). Decision-makers, all the way up to the level of the United States government, seem fascinated by considerations generated within complexity science. The Santa Fe Institute, one of the key centres for research into complexity science, is almost entirely financed by big business. The Defence Evaluation Research Agency (DERA), the research agency for the ministry of defence, has recently commissioned a series of reports into the application of complexity science to specific organisational considerations. Additionally the Economic and Social Research Council (ESRC), often in partnership with business, has funded a number of large research projects and seminar series to examine the utility and efficacy of complexity science to social science. The interest illustrated in these examples is often stimulated by researchers who are themselves interested in maintaining a circulation of new ideas. As Nigel Thrift argues: 'in an increasingly mediatized world, complexity theory is, to an extent, just another business opportunity. It is up for sale and it is being sold' (Thrift 1999: 33). The same might be said of post-structuralism, as used to sell art or, in a more sinister way, as a means with which to bully those not initiated into its vocabulary. Post-structuralism does, at least, anticipate such a possibility and, again, this ability to deal with reflexivity will be useful in examining the system of practices that the political scientist works within.

Autopoiesis and complexity, in general, cannot be applied directly to social science in any meaningful way. Autopoiesis is a mechanism that explains how an organisation can change while retaining its structure. This might prove to be an insightful analogy. Indeed, there are many social and cultural processes that seem to display feedback mechanisms and emergent properties and, thus, seem to resonate with other complex systems. However, to say that these processes, let alone society or its socio-political structures, are auto-poietic or a series of self-organising systems is senseless and to miss the point of what such a model is meant to do. Relocating a model from the scientific realm to that of politics does not necessarily imply that there is an assumption of a uni-directional influence from the sciences to the social sciences. Katherine Hayles, for example, argues that similarities between natural science and social science are not the result of a direct influence, but a parallel that has its basis in a common cultural matrix (Hayles, 1990: 174). This implies that there is no need for a unification of methodological principals. Instead, the question of method is not merely a problem for science and the sociology of science, which then extends into the method of the social sciences and humanities, but, additionally, becomes the most significant question at the root of the status and epistemology of social science.

How and why specific models gain currency are important and complicated issues (see DeLanda, 1991; Deleuze and Guattari, 1994; Haraway, 1997; Hayles, 1999). What seems to be clear, however, is that models that can be generated, and can remain self-sustaining, gain a degree of durability over time. It is as though models, as forms of discourse, become written into the fabric of the world. New models alter the way in which the world is perceived and new perceptions alter the way in which the world is modelled. These processes, and the descriptions derived from them, are always in the making and never complete. They cannot be easily governed or systematised. It is this type of process to which post-structuralism and forms of complexity science are both sensitive.

Conclusion

Models are, in a broad sense, always political. By this, I do not suggest that judgements of truth should be suspended in order to apply a sociological approach to knowledge, as Shapin and Schaffer seem to imply. Clearly, their approach is as ideological as any governance of method. Instead, the degree of quasi-transcendence concepts acquire through duration (see Latour, 1993: 127–9; Deleuze and Guattari, 1994: 255–6) implies a methodology that reflects the ungovernability of the elements that it helps to decode. Models, metaphors and concepts, in a very real way, take on a life of their own.

This approach, instead of leading to a denaturing of the social, as with Luhmann, leads to a strategic type of denaturing of social experience. It is strategic in the sense of being a type of narrative that is critical of the narrative form being used as a type of representation. As a cultural narrative, it is caught in a recursive loop between social theory and social and cultural change that resists any final analysis. As Katherine Hayles concludes in her book on chaos and complexity: 'Other times have had glimpses of what it would mean to live in a denatured world. But never before have such strong feedback loops among culture, theory, and technology brought it so close to being a reality' (Hayles, 1990: 295).

In this way, it is only through the multiplicity of complexity themes that the specificity of the political can be drawn out of what would otherwise be a false analogy with the motion of fluids or organisms. The exact form such models take is the complicated question. What makes a good model is difficult to recognise. Einstein is reported to have claimed that a good model is one that makes the ugly difficult and the beautiful easy. I would add to this that a good model also makes the mundane impossible. Knowledge is not merely the product of human action, either as a discovery or a construction, any more than the state is. In this regard at least, Boyle and Hobbes were both wrong.

PART THREE

Critique and Political Thought

10

The Horizon of Community

ALAN FINLAYSON

Introduction

There are few concepts that can surpass 'community' for their ubiquity in political theory and ideology. Whether it be in the abstract (general conceptualisations of the idea of community or the basis to solidarity) or concrete (specifications regarding particular communities such as a nation or a people of some sort), theory and ideology have a primary concern with discourses, problematics and practices of community or communities. Think, for example, of the general deployment within political rhetoric of community as a 'signifier', its use in describing certain policies ('community care' 'business in the community', 'community policing') or the way in which politicians, activists and various spokespeople may claim to articulate the feelings of 'the community'. The community can even be some kind of subject. It has emotions, needs and desires – 'the community is very unhappy about this' or 'we in the community are demanding an immediate response' and so forth.

In politics the idea of community necessarily has a special place. Political thought is concerned with relationships – between individuals, between individuals and society or between societies. As such 'communality' and 'solidarity' inescapably form a central concern of political thinking. Political philosophy is concerned with the meaning of 'we'. It does not ask 'What am "I"?' but 'Who are "we"?', 'What is "we"?' or 'How should "I" relate to others?'. In short, it organises or specifies a way of conceiving 'we'. Indeed, we can go so far as to state that politics is this practice.

Thus, political theory or political ideology always proposes or implies a social theory of some kind. It is not concerned simply with the physical presence of community or the features necessary for its taking particular forms (though these certainly form a part of many political discourses, from Plato's ideal city to Rousseau's sovereign republic). Politics is also concerned with how community is to be understood and valued, how its relationship to the overall understanding of social life is to be thought and, ultimately, with a more general conceptualisation of the experience of collectivity – of ways of being together and the political consequences derived from this. Discourses of 'community' define ways of comprehending our social relationships and of imagining how we are connected to each other, shaping our understanding of the social world and participating in the process of making it meaningful in particular ways. Political theories and acts function through their 'staging' of particular versions of communality. That is to say, they constitute a form of community upon which they then act.

As such, the thinking of community has determinate effects. Constructions of community may simultaneously define their subjects – who they are, who is and is not to be counted as a member – and what they are to be like. In short, community 'interpellates' (see also Chapter 1). But also, as a necessary part of such an operation, concepts of community provide an origin and point of legitimisation for various political theories or ideologies. Prescribing subjectivity and offering a grounding for theoretical-ideological claims, concepts of community place politics within a determinate and limited location. Conceiving of 'we' through the terms of community entails a presupposition of organisation – an already-existing set of bonds that are prior to the thinking of politics. This forms an origin, a baseline for thought. It is an origin that may be conceived of literally as a moment of historical foundation (in the 'ancient past', with 'The Revolution' or 'national liberation', for example) or, figuratively, as the starting point for thinking, the first thing needed to make thinking of the political possible.

For example, an ideology, such as Conservatism, may function by positing the national community (or a Burkean community of prejudice) in order to demonstrate the inflexibility of the status quo, its fundamental aversion to the dictates of liberal reason (see Eccleshall, 1990; Hall, 1988; Howarth, 1995b). Conversely, some forms of socialism may proceed by positing the natural solidarity and community of 'the class' or of 'all mankind'. In both cases, the community is imagined as indicative of a spontaneous, 'given' order that forms the foundation to our political thinking – its natural basis without which we cannot even begin to think politics, justice or peace.

But, precisely because it is a fundamental point within the geography of political thought and practice, community is not always afforded an explicit theorisation by political philosophers. There is often a focus on the ways in which it should be dealt with by, for example, a moral theory of justice, but, as such, community becomes an object to be taken account of by political theories rather than a concept or practice on which those theories should dwell. The concept of community circulates within political thinking implicitly and unthought, rather than explicitly and always rigorously conceived. In brushing up against the limits of the community, political discourse strikes against its own objectivity. It must operate within a horizon of community to be meaningful and so cannot make that horizon itself a matter of explicit political-theoretical engagement. It is a 'myth' in the sense given to that term by Ernesto Laclau (1992 and 1996), a point of closure beyond which there can be no contest.

This logic of 'closure' needs to be understood and can be analysed through employing some of the tools and concepts of post-structuralist thinking. We will explore this by considering further (though in general terms) the way in which community has often been conceived in political thought. We will illustrate some of the ways in which political thought in the Western tradition has been shaped by the need to stage communality as a prelude to engaging in political theory. We will then consider some ways in which this critical approach to community suggests the need for some kind of reformulation of our understanding of community – a reformulation that places community at the contested centre (rather than incontestable limit) of political thought and action.

Community in Political Thought

The inhabitants of the democratic Athenian polis clearly manifested a concern with the origins of, and basis to, their political community. Claims about that community helped to justify the right of the polis to take precedence over tribal or familial patterns of social organisation and obligation. With the establishment of a social order beyond that of kinship, it became necessary to limit the extent to which ties of aristocratic friendship could disrupt the unity of the democratic polis and the rule of its law. In this process the polis itself became an object of veneration and the source of its own authority. In the words of Nicole Loraux (1986), the Athenians 'institutionalised an ideology of the city' and developed a political thought that aimed to preserve social order and to contain potential discord within a commitment to it. Indeed, the polis engaged in numerous practices (competitions, festivals, public funerals) that affirmed the existence of the polis and the place of citizens within it through the provision of a moment of internal self-reflection (see, for example, Goldhill, 1986: 57–78 and 1987).

In the *Politics*, Aristotle overcame the clash between the laws of the family and the laws of society by making the state into a natural entity, emerging from the development of social relations of necessity into those that take on the task of securing the good life. We are the political animal who, by nature, lives in a state, exercising that speech which enables differentiation of right from wrong. Accordingly, we come to share a common view on these things and thus constitute a city. The state is a natural form of association for us, emerging from these bonds of household and friendship. A natural communality forms the conceptual and practical horizon within which individuals, families and ultimately forms of the state are understood – and the processes of legislation and education that will make the virtuous individuals of the virtuous community.

This leads, amongst other things, to a concern with size and number (see also Derrida, 1997). The polis must not be too large because, for example, foreigners may become difficult to detect and they may become citizens. Furthermore, 'it is necessary that the citizens should know each other and know what kind of people they are' (1326b: 11). The polis is too large if a herald cannot make himself heard (1326b: 6) or if the citizens cannot know each other (1326b: 14–15). The correct size of polis is that which makes it straightforward for it to talk to itself about itself, where it can be, as it were, identical to itself. There must be unity between the political structures, the shared culture of the citizens and the individual life. But there is a danger that over-investment into the community will cause it to become detached from its basis in the organic and natural interaction of the people. Aristotle fears that the political community might become separated from this basis and its representation detached from its sources – hence his concern with limitations of number and the avoidance of the sort of division and differentiation (be it political, ethical or derived from the social structure) that might necessitate a projection or an imaginary of community. Unity is established through limitation and exclusion – by a discounting, as well as a counting.

Aristotle's conceptualisation thus, necessarily, entails a limited, bounded and strictly balanced communal order that forms the basis to political inter-action and can foster virtue without that unity becoming a representation with a life of its own. His concern with establishing the ideal number of citizens is a concern with the scale of community such that it can be self-sufficient, not only economically but conceptually, able to conceive of itself without having to draw on anything outside of itself – except negatively, in the sense that it has excluded or expelled that which might disrupt it. Community must be the real and functioning horizon of political life with nothing beyond it. It cannot even be beyond itself.

Modern liberal political theory appears to break with notions of bounded self-present communality through its embrace of individual reason and rejection of romanticism. Indeed, this would appear to be a large part of the point of liberal modernity – freedom from the shackles of traditional bonds and forms of invested authority, an avoidance of a necessary communal unity into which individuals are subsumed. Rather than members of enclosed communities of fate, the archetypal liberal individual is able to enter freely into social relationships that have been chosen or consented to, in contrast to having been imposed through tradition. But one only has to think of the connection between liberalism and nationalism to sense that the break with earlier forms of communal 'imaginary' is not so complete. In any case, a political philosophy predicated on individualism is, itself, a way of conceiving of community and not necessarily a break from it. The idea of a community of rational and willing liberals is such an embedded presupposition for liberal political theory that it can barely even be noticed by proponents, let alone mentioned. It cannot be acknowledged as a community for this is usually taken to suggest some kind of comprehensive communal doctrine that, for liberals, is reducible to a mere particularity, as opposed to the universality upon which the liberal polity is supposed to stand.

Consider Kant's enlightened public exercising its reason as part of a community of literate citizens. Here the community that can communicate with itself turns into a community of communicators. Communication, and the community it engenders, becomes the criteria for the judgement of right reason – the tribunal that evaluates it. Kant links duty, theory and morality with the very existence of humans as that species destined to fulfil the promise, and realise the capacity, of the reason given to them by nature. The Kantian subject is oriented towards cosmopolitan hospitality because of his capacity to reason, to be edified by rational publicity. And this level of publicity necessitates both communication and others to communicate with. The human subject can only realise the essence of his humanity as part of a universalised citizenship. And to be a citizen – to be a free and reasoning subject – every institution, every nation, must embody that cosmopolitan rationality. Humanity itself is the community with both essence and telos that makes this necessary. Community, the world and history become one with thinking itself because only the species not the individual can progress in this way (see Balibar, 1994).

This is the amazing promise of such liberalism – that the community may be the community of all humanity. But, as we know, this may turn out to be a bounded community, defined by a specific conception of rationality and the reasoning subject and limited to those 'independent' subjects freed from relations of subordination. It may, indeed, be a community that is 'difference-blind' (see Taylor, 1992: 25–73). Those who sell their labour, the 'primitive' peoples and women, do not form part of the body of active citizens. Kantian liberal individualism calls on a concept of community that turns out to have a gender and a class – and it is only those within the community who can fulfil the destiny of the species (see Campbell and Shapiro, 1999; Mendus, 1992).

Liberal society is that within which the community is defined by its capacity and need for free, open and transparent speech and discussion. But this transparency is made possible by the positing of a pre-existing universal and natural community. Speech which does not conform to the rules and limits of that community is, therefore, not speech at all or, at least, not 'rational discourse', being little more, perhaps, than the old braying of the barbarians. Faced with the gulf this opens up (between principle and the social division that contradicts it), liberal theory has increasingly turned to the theorisation of communication and dialogue in an attempt to refound a community forged out of a perfectly symmetrical, and hence just, mode of communicative exchange. Thus the Habermasian approach, as with the straightforwardly Kantian, displaces power relations and concomitant modes of identification/subjectivation (the relations that constitute public spheres and communal blocs in heterogeneous ways), along communicative networks of inter-subjectivity held in place by procedural frameworks for deliberation made manifest via the law. Habermas regards this as a 'subjectless form' of communication. That is to say, the community that does the communicating is not conceived of as a community. It is interesting, then, that Habermas should advocate a 'constitutional patriotism' that, while he claims it is distinct from a communitarian-republican conception of a shared political culture, manifests the same features of a limiting horizon within which a discourse ethics can be made possible. Through the constitution, it becomes an empirical fact that holds down and allows to function around it a speech community that can constitute a tribunal of public reason. In other words, while contemporary theories such as that of Habermas are quite aware of the dangers of an immanentist conception of community (in Habermas's case especially aware and keen to avoid it), they find it hard to imagine any way of establishing what might be just or right or fair without its having a basis in a community that is first unified (by its capacity to talk coherently with itself). The problem is thus conceived of as that of how to constitute such a community – one defined only by a doctrinal attachment to the coincidence of its own potential transparency with the promise of universal reason.

Recently, John Rawls has claimed that the 'well-ordered democratic society' is not a community (1993: 40). But he does this by narrowly defining a community as an association united by a 'comprehensive doctrine' of a sort that the modest Rawlsian democracy, refusing such unity of purpose, could never have. Yet, for Rawls, a democratic society is 'a complete and closed social system. It is complete in that it is self-sufficient and has a place for all the main purposes of human life' (1993: 40). It provides a framework within which political deliberation can occur and which is sufficient unto itself. The point of the principle of justice is to form the horizons within which character and outlook are formed as it is only in this context that moral powers can be realised (Rawls, 1993: 41). This only avoids being a community because the Rawlsian principle of justice is not counted as a comprehensive doctrine since it says it is not and defines itself against such things. Rawls advocates a 'social union', self-sufficient to itself, contained within itself, in as much as its core principles of organisation are to be found within the organisational form that defines it – what, in *A Theory of Justice*, he called the 'community of humankind', where the members 'enjoy one another's excellences and individuality elicited by free institutions, and they recognise the good of each as an element in the complete activity the whole scheme of which is consented to and gives pleasure to all' (Rawls, 1971: 523). It is a community that is historical in the sense that its capacities are formed within the context of an ancestral tradition and cooperation 'is guided at any moment by an understanding of what has been done in the past as it is interpreted by social tradition' (Rawls, 1971: 525). What is specific to the liberal mode of conceiving community is that it focuses more on the conditions that make the liberal community possible than on a substantive notion of a particular community. This may mean that, in sub-stantive contexts, liberal theorists may tend to have in mind the sort of communities in which they already live and seek only to clarify the conditions for the improvement of that mode of community. But it is this 'minimal' mode of conceiving community that gives rise to conflict with the so-called communitarians who prefer to concentrate on substantive notions of com-munity, although, even here, the specification of community is vague. It is 'a mode of self-understanding partly constitutive of the agent's identity ...' and 'describes not just what they *have* as fellow citizens but also what they *are*, not a relationship they choose but an attachment they discover' (Sandel, 1982: 150, emphasis original). Here, again, community is conceived of as a con-tainer and it is only within it that political values may be legitimated.

So, we see a certain kind of repeated problematic that we can designate as a political metaphysics of community. It is the presence (both actual and metaphysical) of community that makes good politics possible. Any perceived failing in political practice can be understood as a failure of the community to be fully present or of politics to be faithful to the community which it serves. The remedy is a return to community (as sought by organic conservatives or those labelled by Marx as 'reactionary socialists'), the substitution of a 'bad' or 'false' community by the true one (a form taken by various ethno-nationalisms but also by a certain kind of revolutionary class-warrior) or a revision of our understanding of community so as to give to it a solid and rational foundation by focusing on the necessary conditions for justice which is taken to be equivalent to community (the essence of the liberal tradition as interpreted in this context).

The Communal Horizon of Modernity

A discourse of community forms the horizon of that which is considered politically intelligible. Politics is identified as the process by which certain sorts of collective are maintained but it is also a process that can only proceed if there is such a collective already in place. For there to be politics there must be a foundation on which it rests – the self-identical community that cannot be subject to any internal contest or collapse or be dependent for existence on anything outside of it. Consequently, disruptions to community are most often figured as external contingencies imposed from outside – capitalists, foreigners, foolish human reason (see Žižek, 1989 and 1993).

But this has also meant that political contestation has been possible pre-cisely on these grounds. Challenges to dominant conceptions of political community have been able to emerge from within the horizon of that which they attack in the form of a questioning of the location of the boundaries of community, accompanied by the insistence that they be expanded to include subjects not previously regarded as members of the community. For some civil-rights-based movements (around issues of gender or race, for example), this has proved an effective ideology.

But, as the means of communication has expanded, along with the possibilities for travel and movement within and between actually-existing communities, the capacity for groups to communicate within themselves has expanded and fractured. The self-discursive community need not be geographically contiguous. Communities of fate can be imagined, instead, as communities of affect, of those who believe they share a sensibility or some set of cultural attitudes. At the same time, the existence of functioning cultural 'communities of fate' within the heart of the supposedly chosen community of willing liberals becomes a problem because they may conflict with the horizon of the liberal community and, in so doing, render that horizon visible, exposing its contingency. Hence there is anxiety within liberalism about what to do with those distinct cultural communities that exist within liberal society yet do not submit to its rules and norms and, in some instances, actively oppose them.

This shapes the contours of some of the political disputes that define the present conjuncture. There is a tension in democratic practice between a radical moment that seeks to challenge the community, and its self-definition through boundaries, and that which wishes to work within the current boundaries for fear that the community will fall apart and, with it, the meaningful horizon. On the one hand, is an attachment to the purity or authenticity of community which may be radically exclusionary in some forms (such as racisms and fascisms) but can also be open to the admittance of others, so long as they assimilate to communal norms. On the other hand, is that form of politics which seeks to contest the boundaries by asserting the rights of communities to be different from each other.

However, there may not be such a gulf between these positions as it first appears. For the dispute here may only be between different communities rather than different conceptions of community or between theoretical traditions that focus on community at levels that are at variance with each other (as in the split between liberal and communitarian approaches). To caricature things slightly, we may say that one position, while denying that it is a community at all, seeks to defend itself from anything that might disrupt or destabilise the communal horizon that secures it. The other claims to perceive a multiplicity of communal horizons on to which it will not impose anything. But this, of course, requires seeing these varied communities themselves as unified organisms, as if they are super-subjects deserving of rights analogous to those afforded to individuals because the disruption to a communal horizon is an attack on the authentic being of that community and its members.

These positions share a logic of 'objectivity', where the essence of the community must be found to coincide with its existence such that the political becomes derivable from it. Except that this is not exactly what takes place.

Rather, the community becomes a desired object, something to be founded so that politics of the right sort can begin to take place or, at the very least, its deficiencies remedied.

That there should appear to be a form of continuity from the ancient to the contemporary ought to be worrying. Surely modernity represents some kind of break with traditional forms of thinking? It entails the rejection of groundings built on absolute criteria or claims such as divine right, natural inheritance or the traditions of the community. Political modernity is precisely the capacity to 'think for oneself', to free oneself from these habits of thought. But this is not a repetition in any simple sense. Repetitions are always also alterations. Contexts change and conceptual structures operate in new conditions. The change wrought by 'modernity', in this context at least, is a change in the causal location of the political – the introduction of an ambiguity. Where classical or Christian political theory could regard community as mythically or divinely founded (such that the task of philosophy and activism was to ensure that politics conformed to its requirements), in modernity, the political or, at least, politics – practices of governance, strategies of organisation and negotiation – seems to come 'before' community, having, as it does, the function of ensuring that the community is enabled to be present to itself and is defended from disruptive elements. In the form of nationalism, this has consisted of political leaders and activists working towards the establishment of the natural national community in whose name they then claim to be acting – as if they were only bringing about what is already present. Here, politics becomes a matter of engendering a self-consciousness of community and regularly gives way to a demand for the authenticity of nostalgia, a return to what is 'really' there, an original, naturally sanctioned solidarity. Politics thus assumes priority over community but only in as much as it acts to bring about that which has been lost – indeed, this can become the benchmark against which politics is judged.

In liberalism, this movement is more complicated. As we have seen, it is not that liberalism refuses to think communally. But community cannot here be thought in terms of this nostalgia, for liberalism seeks to free individuals from the strictures of the communal, while submitting them to the dictates of a higher, universal-communal reason. Thus, it founds communality and solidarity through the establishment of a commitment to a shared law and focuses on the necessary conditions by which a polity may bring communality and justice into harmony with each other (which is what will happen when everyone endorses the tenets of liberal political theory).

Durkheim is instructive here. Where some theorists of urban modernity had despaired at the decline in communality wrought by industrialisation, Durkheim found the very force of dislocation to be the basis of social solidarity. For him, the function of the division of labour is 'to create in two or more persons a feeling of solidarity ... to cause coherence among friends and to stamp them with its seal' (1933: 56). Hence, 'it must have a moral character, for the need of order, harmony, and social solidarity is generally considered moral' (1933: 63). The 'collective consciousness' of 'traditional' community is not destroyed but made abstract, becoming transcendental and universal. Community is not restricted to societies based on the mechanical solidarity of likeness. It is something that will develop in liberal societies organised by civil law and united by the 'cult of individualism'. The division of labour represents the binding of complementary differences in 'a true exchange of services'. Community shifts from the position of threatened ontology to promised eschatology. But it too must be manifested and represented. Durkheim recognised that the *conscience collective* of traditional communities was a force for social regulation, manifesting itself in a community's collective representations. While he considered the form of social solidarity found in industrial societies to be rational rather than mythic, he also recognised that 'there can be no society which does not feel the need of upholding and reaffirming at regular intervals the collective sentiments and the collective ideas which make its unity and personality' (Durkheim, 1987: 233). And we can see in political modernity the increasing concern to manifest, at the level of collective culture, just this kind of unity. Increasingly, culture, rather than social structure and ascribed positions in a hierarchy, becomes the locus of identity formation and expression.

To be sure, liberal theory begins with the 'fact' of plurality. But it does so in order to then rein in that plurality and manage it, so as to restore to the political community its self-identity – an identity formed from 'interests' that meet, compromise and combine in order to find a desired 'consensus' on which the management of society and economy can then be based. Increasingly, this is figured on a global scale. The project of liberalism has become that of establishing communal unity at a global level and it is believed to be made possible by the globalisation of 'culture'. Such an expansion is justified as it is merely bringing about what is already there – finally expressing and bringing to self-consciousness the truth of Kantian cosmopolitanism. Here, politics can be declared to be at an end because all that is left for it is to accept its 'John the Baptist' role and bow out, having delivered the new age.

But it would be wrong to employ a standard post-modern critique and simply argue that liberalism manifests a particular in the form of a universal. It certainly does recognise particularity. But its response is to try to refound universality and objectivity somewhere else beyond, rather than on top of, particularity. For Habermas, it is founded inter-subjectively via the validity claims implicit in language. In a more sociological vein, Gellner has argued that industrialisation and the expansion of social scale introduce contingency into the regimented order of feudal society. Consequently, culture comes to replace structure as the integrating force of social solidarity. Thus, modernity reverses the relationship between the communal culture and the political.

Where, for Aristotle (and also for Roman and early Christian political thought), the purpose of politics was to bring about the virtuous community, working in harmony with it and maintaining its boundaries, under the conditions of modernity, culture begins to be conceived of as the prerequisite to virtuous and rational politics. Such a conceptualisation complements the potential expansion of 'imagined communities' made possible by the revolution in printing and the spread of literacy, as well as by the unification of territories and the development of new networks of commercial trade and governance represented in the rhetoric of techno-globalisation. Here, universal rationality will be manifested in a shared world culture formed out of the circulation of commodities and the interdependence this is believed to necessarily foster.

Community without Commune

Is it possible to form another thinking of community, one where it is conceived not as a limit but an opening, as something other than the point where a form of sociality closes in on itself ? Jean-Luc Nancy (1991) has proposed understanding the political as 'the place of community ... the place of a specific existence, the existence of being-in-common, which gives rise to the existence of self'. His concern is to explicate the Heideggerian notion of '*mitsein*', 'being-with', and to place it in relation to the political which then becomes understood as the place where 'community as such is brought into play' (Nancy, 1991). Nancy opposes community in the sense of a 'common being' to that of a 'being-in-common'. The former conceives community as a transcendent essence based on the sharing of a prior and full identity. By contrast, 'being-in-common' emerges from the commonality of finitude. It is not concerned with a notional togetherness into which all else is subsumed but, rather, with relations. Instead of community being the necessary a priori of the political, it is conceived in terms of a dynamic sharing of finitude. In a sense, what we share in common is the absence of a common being, of a super-subject into which all are absorbed.

For Nancy, community is always exposed to something outside it, its own division and differentiation:

> What such a community has 'lost' – the immanence and intimacy of a communion – is lost only in the sense that such a 'loss' is constitutive of 'community' itself. It is not a loss: on the contrary immanence, if it were to come about, would instantly suppress community or communication, as such. (Nancy, 1991: 12)

To identify community with a specific object or place or form of social association unifies the horizon of what is politically possible or acceptable with the horizon of community that gives it shape. As such, politics comes to an end since it is merely the working out of what was already there, contained within the telos of the community. This is a conception at odds with the idea of democracy which consistently undermines such attempts at communal unity.

There is a particular and special relationship between the concept of democracy and that of community. The two are linked most tightly by an overlapping concern with the notion of 'the people'. Clearly, a conception of community is concerned with a people of some sort and their commonality. But democracy also gives the people a special place since they are the origin of sovereignty. But that space of sovereignty is itself ambiguous. It is not something that the abstraction 'the people' can ever fully possess or occupy. Indeed, it must never be fully occupied if democracy is not to lapse into anti-democratic forms of populism. No force, including the people, should ever absolutely occupy the place of power. The Ancient Greek criticism of democracy was concerned with precisely this possibility – for Plato and Aristotle, a likelihood that the people could become despotic over themselves and that the Demos could put itself above the law and the constitution. This is why democracy rests on the preservation of what Lefort has called 'the empty space of political power' (Lefort, 1986: 304). But the concept of community, which makes that conception of democracy possible, also seeks to close over that emptiness by uniting the people as one across time and space, making them the solipsistic source of their own power to find themselves to be a community. In this sense the democratic concept of the political places it in between the community and its own horizon of unification. Politics is the ongoing process of constituting the 'we' of community, rather than something contained within a prior communal shell. In Nancy's terms, the community is 'inoperative' or 'unworking' (Lefort, 1986: 304), it continually undoes itself. To put this in classical terms, we might say that democracy is comic not tragic.

Conclusion – The Democratic Comedy?

If the Platonic vision of the truth-seeking philosopher involves a descent into darkness after which there is a journey upwards to the light and the realisation of a higher truth, the democratic represents the comedy of continual (and potentially joyous) failure. Comedy draws attention to its own staging of itself as a fiction. It undermines the possibility of enchantment by the theatrical. Where the tragic seeks to take particulars and present them as general or universal exemplars, the comic generates laughter at the failure of particularity to sound the sonorous notes of the universal harmony (see Taplin, 1996) As Simon Critchley (1999: 217–38) argues, modern philosophy (particularly in the Kantian mode) substitutes the aesthetic for the religious as the privileged sphere for the exploration of meaning in human existence. In so doing, it also privileges the form of the tragic, advocating a heroic response to the fact of finitude. One might also point here to the post-Kantian tendency to extol the virtues of straight talking, the search for meaningful dialogue that abhors the disruptive gestures of the partisan, parodic or polemical. The tragic favours the suffering of the elite icon but comedy exalts the ordinary member of the demos that laughs at those who would rule over us, the fool who refuses to pursue polite and rule bound discourse and (often enough) finds comedy in taking things literally.

The comic is solidaristic, it is infectious and dangerously hysterical. But it has a different relation to finitude. Finitude consists of the fact that whatever the community demands of its members (who are themselves that community) is more than they can ever give. The solidarity demanded by community is something I cannot fully give. If I give myself entirely to the community, becoming subsumed within it, then I am no longer myself and no longer one who can take the decision, and take the responsibility, on behalf of my community. If commitment to community is something that is to be maintained, then it depends on the presence of a permanent surplus between 'I' and 'we', a certain 'paradox of magnitude' to steal a phrase from Jacques Rancière (1999). I can never know everyone in my community and, even if I did, I cannot know everything there is to know about them, there is always something more, to which I can never have access. If there were not, then they would not be other and there would be no need for community since we would already be a unified and ever-present unity. But I cannot be certain about the other, certain that they are as communal to me as I am to them.

Political discourses of community are concerned with affirming or creating just this kind of impossible certainty. It is this that the tragic celebrates but the comic, as Critchley puts it, 'recalls us to the modesty and limitedness of the human condition, a limitedness that calls not for tragic affirmation but comic *acknowledgement*, not heroic authenticity but a laughable inauthenticity' (Critchley, 1999: 224).

This is not to suggest that democracy should be conceived of as nothing but the constant blowing of a raspberry in the face of attempts to manage or organise the community. It is not to suggest a purely anarchic or schizophrenic attitude. Rather, it is to suggest that there is something comic to be found in our attempts to impose order and then face their continual repetition and failure. The comic maintains the gap between the community and its own coming to self-presence – always points to the thread left untied and loose – and, in this, we find the democratic spirit of community. The democratic citizen identifies with the demands and desires of citizenship, yet knows that these will not be forthcoming without continual struggle and effort – knows that the relationship entered into is one that is endless. It is a community that, rather than basing itself on a presumed immanence, finds nothing beyond the ceaseless process of negotiating our own communality, of failing to constitute a universal 'we'.

Politics, then, is not the attempt to reflect a community or to constitute a space within which it can represent itself (to itself or to others). Rather,

politics entails the staging of forms of communality. It is forever concerned
with the establishing and disestablishing of the forms taken by sociality and
interrelationships. The thinking (or doing) of 'we' and the thinking (or doing)
of the political are intimately related but the relationship is not one of simple
identity or complementarity. The moment of the political demands a thinking
of the nature of relationality in such a way that it uproots the 'natural' order of
communality by positing (perhaps) another communality or (more often) a
communality that is not accounted for by accepted forms of communal
identification. Many aspects of our tradition of political theory (as we have
seen) seek to do away with this questioning, to assert or establish a given form
of communality (however distorted or evaded they may claim it to be). They
seek to turn democracy into a procedure for the management or the maintenance of the 'health' of a community that is itself not up for question. But
the question of community is the question of democracy – indeed, we might
go so far as to say that enlightenment (and the promise of modernity)
demands this process of questioning community which is itself the nature of
the modern political community. It is not to be thought of as the principle of
unity (hidden from direct view but underlying and guiding our interactions),
nor as the spontaneous outcome of our individuated transactions and
contractual relationships (be they financial or inter-subjective and linguistic).
The community, in Rancière's terms, does not add up to itself – it is always
greater and lesser than its parts.

Politics is concerned with the attempt of the community to grasp itself, to
establish what it is exactly, in order to have a ruling principle by which to
judge all applications of the body of the community itself – a standard against
which a principle of distribution may be measured. An ordering principle, in
other words, that is, itself, not subject to the contestation of politics. But this is
a concern for order above a concern for community. The community that
refuses to universalise such a 'we' but, rather, opts to make the finding or
creating of that 'we' its endless purpose is the politicised community of democracy – the community that finds itself and founds itself out of the
commonality of finitude. In this way, perhaps, without enthroning ourselves
and our speech as the determining centre of political organisation, acknowledging instead the permanence and the promise of the spaces between us,
we can pull ourselves away from our self-incurred immaturity. This means
accepting that the state cannot, and should not, embody the will, the communal universality, of the people of whom it is made up. But neither can the
state withdraw and leave behind a natural community formed of the spontan-
eity of anarchistic 'brotherhood' or neo-liberal self-interest. For the community is, in the last instance, ungrounded. It stands on nothing other than the
facticity of people who live and die and necessarily come across each other in
the process. In so doing, we meditate (and argue, fight, win and lose) over the
notion of 'we'. The logic of the political is the logic that insists that this

question never be closed, never be objectified by a claim to the 'reason' of unification. To be sure, this runs risks. Such a politics exposes us to instability, confusion even, but, without the possibility of error and of evil, there can be no true responsibility or freedom. This is the real 'politics of risk' and it is a risk we have no choice but to take. To refuse it is to refuse the political itself and to dream instead of preordained order. And that is never comic. It is the realm of tragedy.

11

Critical Theory and Democracy

MARK DEVENNEY

Introduction

All disciplines, including political science, are conservative. Disciplines police institutional boundaries in defining appropriate objects of study, in authorising methodological principles and in legitimising accredited subjects as their agents. It is unsurprising, then, that post-structuralist theory is viewed with scepticism by many political scientists, since it entails a critical interrogation of the objects, subjects and tools naturalised by disciplines. This hostility is frequently justified by invoking the spectre of the relativist, who decries the fundamental tenets of democratic theory and practice. Critics variously contend that post-structuralist theory: (i) undermines all moral justification for the critique of inequality (normative Political Theory); (ii) disputes the competence of social scientists to generate objective statements about society (behaviourist Political Science); (iii) undermines the autonomy of the subject responsible for its own actions (a fundamental tenet of liberal democratic states); (iv) relativises the legitimacy of the representative institutions of liberal democratic societies; and (v) casts doubt on processes of democratic will formation.

Such reproaches pivot on a collective fear of relativism. The inference that knowledge is never independent of power elicits opprobrium from defendants of scientific neutrality and purveyors of moral universality. However, it is the contention of this chapter that an adequate defence of radical democracy, far from being undermined by post-structuralism, in fact, relies on it. This argument obliges, first, a working definition of post-structuralism – no elementary task, given that the term is a banalisation of, and commits conceptual injustice to, a broad spectrum of theoretical work. Thus, I begin by developing a definition of post-structuralism through a discussion of the problem of limits and sovereignty in political science. The second section demonstrates the pertinence of post-structuralist theory through an immanent critique of the key terms in democratic theory and debate. In the final section, I propose a 'promissory' note for radical democracy, the skeletal fragments of which haunt triumphalist apologias for liberal democracy.

Post-structuralism and Politics

At face value post-structuralism is concerned with two themes:

1. structures
2. that which exceeds or undermines structures.

In the case of political science, this entails reflection on the structuring of modern societies and on the conceptual presumption of the social scientist claiming knowledge of these structures. A post-structuralist approach begins with a critique of the idea of structure, undermining the presumption that modern democracies are constituted as self-defining systems. Indeed, many political scientists use, without necessarily dwelling on it, the concept of structure (or system) in order to describe modern states and structures of power. This entails four related, though often implicit, claims:

1. that the political system comprises certain elements which act reciprocally on each other
2. that these elements may be arranged in a variety of different ways
3. that social scientists can predict how the system will react, should one or more of the elements be transformed
4. that the facts of politics are rendered explicit through the model(s) used to analyse society (adapted from Lévi-Strauss, 1963: 279–80).

Contemporary political science supposes the 'democratic' nation state as its key unit of analysis; the nation-state is deemed to comprise a number of key institutional features (parliament, bureaucracy, parties, citizens, a legal order, regional and local authorities, international relations and so on) which may be organised along a number of different structural matrices; the consequences of transformations within the political system are deemed predictable; and different models are built depending upon the relation between these variables. As a consequence, predictions can also be made about those societies 'not yet' democratic. Depending on the relationship between variables – for example, the strength of the landed aristocracy in relation to the military – the transition theorist, for example, seeks to predict the conditions which will ensue in democratisation.

We will now turn to some different approaches to such political study and, through a critical analysis, advance some post-structuralist claims regarding politics. In looking at Bernard Crick's noted definition of a political system, Michael Saward's analysis of, what he terms, the problem of political boundaries and the problem of induction in relation to behaviourist political science, we find that, in each case, a similar, though distinct, problem arises – the exception, which proves the rule, but which is unavoidable.

In an addendum to his classic study *In Defence Of Politics*, Bernard Crick characterises political systems as clearly defined societies, with territorial boundaries, in which there is a certain amount of complexity, no overarching conception of the good, a large middle class and a degree of political equality (Crick, 1993: 171–4). For Crick, a political system establishes limits on the remit of its actions, with reference to their legitimacy within the predefined limits of the system. Thus, 'The political system exists within a prior frame-work of order' and the study of politics (as opposed to international relations, or sociology) is properly limited to this order (ibid.: 181). As a consequence, 'International Society is not a political system. It is a proper subject for the study of government; but because it has no common government at all, sadly it cannot exhibit normal political behaviour' (ibid.: 181).

Strangely, Crick does not treat the establishment of such systemic limits as, itself, a political act. Instead, he naturalises 'normal political behaviour' and excludes from the remit of political studies that which is not a 'political system.' There is a treble exclusion and establishment of 'appropriate bound-aries' at work here – Crick (i) defines normal political systems through the exclusion of international society on the grounds (ii) that it has 'no common government' and thereby authorises (iii) the marking off of that which is appropriate to the study of politics. Crick insists that political systems are not defined by consensus:

> Those who say we desperately lack a consensus of values, and have such a thing to offer, (usually a fighting faith for democracy, or else monotheism), are in fact simply trying to sell us a particular brand of politics, while pretending that they are not, as it were, in trade themselves ... Where such an articulate and systematic consensus does seem necessary is in an autocracy. (Crick, 1993: 177)

Yet he simultaneously presumes consensus about the appropriate limits of the political system without thematising this prior system of order – that which defines the properly political system. What, though, of conflicts regard-ing the limits and remit of this system? What is excluded from the study of politics and what is neutralised as non-political, if these restrictions are accepted? In the case of democracy, Crick presumes that the question of the limits of sovereignty is resolved. The political scientist thus studies conflict within this system but these seem not to effect the system itself. A key issue for the post-structuralist is precisely this prior system of order and its relation to the conflicts.

Let us turn to a second example where the problem of sovereign legiti-macy is glimpsed, only to be instantly side-stepped. In a recent work, *The Terms of Democracy*, Michael Saward contends that conflict concerning the proper remit of sovereign authority can be resolved through democratisation.

> The problem of political units – supposedly intractable within democratic theory – is not as intractable as it is often presented as being. In principle, what really counts in democratic terms is whether or not a given existing unit is democratically governed. Many empirical disputes over political boundaries would be avoided if the unit in question were fully, or even partially, democratic. (Saward, 1998: 142)

Saward presumes that democratisation within a given existing unit is, in most instances, the solution to intractable disputes concerning the remit of sovereign authority over disputed territorial claims. Unlike Crick, he maintains that the nation state is not *the* unit of political analysis, concedes that the problem of political boundaries is generally taken for granted in 'political theory' and acknowledges the difficulty of finding a principle to guide the legitimate limitation of territorial sovereignty. Yet he recoils from exploring the theoretical implications of this problem, settling for the weak empirical claim that democratisation solves most disputes regarding territory.

> Why does an embryonic sub-unit demand some degree of autonomy? Because it lacks the security that democracy, and democratic rights in particular, can provide? Because it lacks the cultural or religious freedom that a properly democratic constitution would guarantee, and which democratic courts could protect? Because basic democratic freedoms, like speech and association, are denied in part or in whole? Because of the fact of past, or the fear of future, persecution and oppression? One suspects that the reasons behind demands for a degree of autonomy from an existing political unit can normally be characterised in one or more of these ways. (Saward, 1998: 128)

But, this conclusion begs the question Saward poses. While democratisation may 'solve' certain of these disputes, this symptomatic solution occludes the violence which the maintenance of 'democratic boundaries' necessitates. Saward avoids a problem which does not have a solution, comfortable within the terms of democracy he proposes. The political system (as Machiavelli and Weber among others knew) relies on force and any analysis of democracy must acknowledge the underlying violence which maintains the unity of any 'given unit'. No principle of justification, regardless of its remit, escapes this necessary imbrication in the politics of statecraft and hegemony. Indeed, more often than not, such tools of justification lend credence to the exercise of force. Saward's commitment to liberal democratisation results in a misrecognition of the key problem at the very moment he identifies it.

> If the boundary problem is largely, though as we shall see not solely a symptom of a lack of democracy in existing units, then we can say that often it will be most effectively addressed by exploring how democracy might be instituted or deepened in these territories. (Saward, 1998: 128)

The boundary problem may, indeed, be a symptom of failed democratisation but it is also symptomatic of a dilemma at the heart of democratic theory. Similarly, Crick's unquestioned commitment to democratic dissensus relies on a prior commitment to maintaining the order of the political system which is, itself, unthematised. Georgio Agamben, following Carl Schmitt, highlights the centrality of this dilemma in terms of the exception which proves, and gives force to, the rule (law).

> The paradox of sovereignty consists in the fact that the sovereign is, at the same time, outside and inside the juridical order ... the sovereign is the one to whom the juridical order grants the power of proclaiming a state of exception and, therefore, of suspending the order's own validity. (Agamben, 1998: 15)

This paradox has the form of an aporia – all law should be valid and the sovereign only acquires authority from this validity. However, the sovereign reserves the right to suspend all constitutional means of acquiring validity or, put simply, the sovereign has the legal power to suspend the law. This is the structure highlighted by Hobbes's *Leviathan*. The *Leviathan*, as source of the law, is not subject to that law. Yet the sovereign only exists as a consequence of the establishment of a legal order which requires a principle of sovereignty in order to function. The state of exception (or state of emergency, as many states term it) alludes toward a founding violence which secures the remit of sovereign authority and, thus, the terms of reference for its own validity. This conclusion brings into the question the assumptions shared by both Saward and Crick. It suggests that the legitimacy of a democratic system is maintained by a violence which is intrinsic to the legitimate 'political system'.

We will now go on to see that a paradox with a similar structure underlies political behaviourism and its assumption that a science of politics should ultimately have reference to objective facts.

The question of the relation between word and world was a key moment in the dominance of positivism within the social sciences, and notably political science, in the English speaking world. Mid-century political science in America and Europe generally rejected the investigation of normative questions as being beyond the scope of the social scientist. Stanley Cavell writes of a

> climate in which positivism was pervasive and dominant in the Anglo-American academic world from the mid-1940s to the 1950s and beyond, almost throughout the humanities and the Social Sciences, a hegemonic presence more complete I believe than any of today's politically developed or intellectually advanced positions: positivism during this period was virtually unopposed on any intellectually organised scale. (Cavell, 1995: 51)

Logical positivism, stated most simply in A. J. Ayer's *Language, Truth and Logic* (1971), provided the conceptual justification for the behaviourist domination of political science. In essence, Ayer contended that language admits of two forms of truth verification – logic and representation of objective facts. The upshot of this view is that most of the language we use is non-sense, as it is unverifiable either by traditional logic or with reference to a realm of objective facts. This move robbed political studies of the ability to make normative statements which were deemed to express the bias of the speaker, as opposed to the objectivity of the scientist. The scientist speaks from a position of neutrality in describing the world – his statements are true, the theorist speaks (interesting) nonsense.

However, the political scientist relying on these premises has a problem characterised in philosophy of science as the 'problem of induction'. Let me give an example. A conventional methodological conceit is to isolate a number of different factors – say class, political identification, gender and race – and, through a complex analysis of the relative importance of each, to explain the occurrence of an event. Crucial to this explanation is repetition. A statement is said to have generality if it holds in a number of different conditions and has not been falsified by any empirical event. However, the principle of induction, which secures the validity of the claim to empirical truth, is, itself, neither an empirical nor a logical statement. The principle that truth follows from the generalisation of the particular is, itself, not a statement which is either empirically or logically verifiable. It can be termed a principle of demarcation or a stipulative statement but, in terms of Ayer's initial criteria, it is simply nonsense. This conclusion is somewhat ironically evinced by Ayer's lifelong, but unsuccessful, quest to establish an adequate principle of verification for meaningful statements. Indeed, he acknowledged, 'the continual failure of attempts to formulate the criterion in such a way as to find a middle ground between the over-strict requirement ... and the over-indulgent licensing of gibberish'. (cited in Hahn, 1992: 302)

Various attempts have been made to resolve this aporetic consequence but of interest here is how it parallels the conclusion, noted above, with respect to sovereignty. The principle of induction is the exception which proves the rule. It demonstrates that the attempt to demarcate meaningful from non-meaningful statements cannot, itself, be justified. This suggests that there is no proper or necessary fit between language and world. This is not for the conventional, idealist reason that we can only access the world through language, a claim which runs the risk of reducing the world to language. Rather, as post-Marxist discourse theory insists, it is because any access we have to a world of meaningful objects presupposes the discursive organisation of those objects within a meaningful discourse.

The concept of over-determination specifies the implications of such an analysis for political science methodology. Over-determination implies that simple determination (that is, uni-directional causality) and multiple determin-ation, as methods for explaining the occurrence of events or analysing socio-political institutions, are inadequate. Over-determination implies a mutual implication of factors and the isolation of independent factors as mere method-ological artifice. The isolation of pertinent factors orders the theoretical expression of an event. The abstraction entailed in restricting research to these relevant factors does violence to the event thus discursively constructed. The attempt to understand an event in its totality commits an injustice, insofar as it implies a blind point which slights the object under investigation (see also Brunkhorst, 1999). This failure is a structural necessity, which cannot be controlled by its dismissal on the grounds of either an insufficient knowledge (which will be achieved with time) or a failure of methodology which experience will correct.

This is not to suggest that dominant structures should be ignored or that our relations in the world are wholly arbitrary. This is a crucial point, insufficiently emphasised in what often passes as post-structuralist work. The critique of structurality points to the final contingency of the life-world; however, this contingency only makes sense in relation to the ways in which we make sense of and control the world. If, relying on the thesis of an essential contingency, we assert that there are no structural limits to political identity, we advocate an abstraction which presumes a subject undetermined by any social structure. This abstraction misses the essential relation between contingency and those structured totalities which are the unconscious backdrop, often un-thematised, to our everyday life. A post-structuralist (discourse theoretical) account begins from a place immanent to these structures and theories. In thematising their often unthought assumptions, it questions social relations disguised in the alluring garb of 'nature'.

Thus far, we have seen how a number of theoretical approaches to the definitions of politics and democracy and of the forming of methodological paradigms rely on the exclusion of an element or moment that they are themselves incapable of accounting for without risking the collapse of their intellectual edifices. The unruly effects of these aporetic structures is not simply a matter of theoretical nit-picking. On the contrary, it has capital consequences for the understanding and analysis of democratic politics.

This conclusion allows us to develop an immanent critique of deliberative accounts of democracy. This requires a perturbation of the conceptual ideal and justification of liberal democracy – that is to say, the presupposition of autonomous subjects who communicate their collective will via representative institutions, which then act on their behalf. I discuss, in turn, these themes of autonomy and representation by relating them to the defence of democracy on the premise of communicative rationality advanced by Jürgen Habermas (see Habermas, 1997).

Autonomy

The concept of autonomy entails self rule – the right of the subject to make sovereign decisions regarding his/her beliefs and conduct. The term is often extended to describe groups of people capable of effecting a sovereign collective will. Since the Treaty of Westphalia, which ended the Thirty Years War in 1648, this conception of autonomy has been articulated to the nation state. The treaty institutionalised what are generally considered to be the normative foundations of the international order: territoriality, sovereignty within that territory, autonomous control over internal and external affairs and the consent before international bodies before intervention in the affairs of other states.

A defining debate within democratic theory concerns the relationship between public and private conceptions of autonomy. A sovereign individual exercises autonomous control over the decisions affecting him/her, yet most states, democratic or otherwise, intervene to limit the exercise of private autonomy. Constitutional states limit public sovereignty by guaranteeing fundamental rights and liberties; by the same token, the protection of essential social goods in most liberal democracies entails the limitation of private sovereignty. This suggests a tension within liberal rights discourse, judiciously summarised by Claude Lefort.

> The rights of man appear as those of individuals, individuals appear as so many little independent sovereigns, each reigning over his private world, like so many micro-entities, separated off from the social whole. But this representation destroys another: that of a totality which transcends its parts. It discloses a transversal dimension of social relations, relations of which individuals are only the terms, but which confer on those individuals their identity, just as much as they are produced by them. (Lefort, 1986: 257)

Considered in this light, rights do not receive their justification from a natural order but through the enabling and limiting role they play in the constitution of democratic society. Because of this, private and public autonomy are mutually constitutive and mutually delimiting. This is the founding premise of Habermas's recent defence (1997) of deliberative democracy. He contends that the enshrining of autonomy in a rights based constitutional order is not a means of limiting the sovereign people but is constitutive of sovereignty. From this perspective, the violation of fundamental (individual) rights by the sovereign is an attack on the principle of sovereignty itself. Thus, individual rights are deemed conditions of possibility for the exercise of sovereign authority. For example, no form of democratic sovereignty is plausible without the protection of the right to freedom of expression. Limitations of this freedom may endanger the 'rational' expression of sovereignty.

The concept of sovereign autonomy is intrinsic to a second key delimitation of modern political thought – territoriality. The proper, autonomous exercise of sovereignty by citizens requires legally defined borders and the clear specification of spheres of authority. This depends upon four clear delineations: who the sovereign is, what the territorial limits of sovereign authority are, why this authority is justified and the specification and division of the right to exercise this authority. In brief, the 'proper' remit of sovereignty requires specification. It is no mistake that most nation states struggle, internally and externally, to define and redefine these limits. Political science, for a long time, relied on an exposition of democratic autonomy which tied the citizen to the nation state and justified the existence of that state through the rights the citizen exercises as a sovereign subject with a free will. It is now clear that no nation state has the capacity to exercise sovereign authority over either its own territory, economy or people. Global institutions, environmental crises, technological changes and the restless progression of multinational capital, all threaten the ability of representative institutions to exercise sovereign authority on behalf of their constituents. The attempt to draw clearly defined boundaries for the exercise of democracy may have the opposite effect – that is to limit possible responses to unpredictable and previously unthought challenges to democratic rule.

Let me relate this to the discussion of the sovereign exception in the previous section. There, drawing on Giorgio Agamben's work, I noted that the sovereign is entitled to suspend the law yet is also subject to the law. The status of this exception is intrinsic to the maintenance of democratic order. In logical terms, the power of the sovereign relies on the maintenance of a structural presupposition which has no grounding. Once this presupposition, without foundation, is seen to hold the empty place of the universal, which theories of sovereign right attempt in vain to ground, we are compelled to reassess the various strategies of (universal) justification which characterise debates in contemporary political theory. It is significant that Habermas acknowledges that communicative rationality is an impossible ideal and that Rawls has to presuppose a veil of ignorance in order to adduce the difference principle. It is this final lack of justification which persuades Ernesto Laclau to conclude that 'the universal is an empty place, a void which can be filled only by the particular, but which, through its very emptiness, produces a series of crucial effects in the structuration/destrcturation of social relations' (Laclau, 2000).

This recognition implies a different rendering of autonomy. We can agree that autonomy is a peculiar and particular achievement of modernity. We can recognise the repressions and exclusions constitutive of modern forms of autonomy – the constitution of unreason in the definition of the reasonable. We can also recognise the potentially repressive affects and effects which the attainment of the ideal of autonomy might entail. Finally, we can recognise the exclusions constitutive of both public and private autonomy. All of this leads to an avowedly political conception of autonomy, rather than one derived from an ethical ideal which transcends the particularity of social and political struggles. This suggests two problems. Firstly, the linking of private autonomy to public, state autonomy is rendered contingent – it is the act of sovereign fiat which belies justification. Secondly, the limitation of autonomy to nation states is revealed as a contingent political act which is today under threat.

Critics of post-structuralism more often than not present a caricature of this rendering of autonomy in order to dismiss its pertinence. Maeve Cooke, for example, writes thus of the post-structuralist challenge to liberal autonomy:

> For writers such as Butler and Flax the notion of autonomy is problematic from two points of view: first because it postulates an ideal of self, thereby effecting a closure; second, because it affirms the value of attributes such as coherence, resolution and

unity at the expense of values such as fragmentation, fluidity and multiplicity. (Cooke, 1999: 181)

Cooke chastises this post-structuralist exposé for two reasons. First, she claims that post-structuralism treats subjectivity as a purely linguistic effect and identity as the effect of systems of meaning; second, she contends that post-structuralism, as political theory, makes normative claims which it cannot justify. The norms invoked seem arbitrary. However, she misconstrues the implications of post-structuralism on both counts.

The post-structuralist critique of autonomous subjectivity analyses the limits of subjective expression in language. It does not assume that subjectivity is an effect of language. This is implied in the relation between constituting and constituted subjectivity. The failure of any discourse to fully delimit the 'real' entails the possibility of resistance to established convention. This should not be confused with the defence of fragmentation, fluidity and multiplicity. I have noted already the necessity of addressing seriously those structures that delimit everyday life and not simply valorising fluidity. Moreover, in recognising the implicit normativity underlying any claim to represent the universal, post-structuralism addresses the question of normativity head on. This is in stark contrast to Habermas's argument that a universal claim to morality is implied in all communication. This move neutralises morality by presenting it as necessary to any interaction and, thus, independent of politics. In this case, the wager of taking seriously our moral commitments relies on a universality which warrants the wager, before it is even taken. The discussion which follows suggests that the ideal of sovereign representation is beset by similar problems.

Representation

If the proper conceptual limits of autonomy and sovereignty are inherently undecidable, then the concept of representation is plagued by similar difficulties. In political science, the term representation binds at least three discursive practices:

1. It is a term used in debates regarding the relation between words and things and, thus, concerns the verifiability of statements social scientists make in representing the world.
2. It is the most common form of democratic legitimation within the nation state.
3. It refers to the objectification of 'nature' associated with the expansion of productive activity over the past two hundred years.

The relation between language and the 'real' has already been discussed with regard to logical positivism. The present discussion examines the uncertainty pervading the conceptual economy of the term 'representation' as used in the other two discursive practices.

Democratic theory contends that government has a duty to represent the interests of its constituents. Systems of representation vary, from Rousseau's republican defence of the idea that the executive is merely the administrative body of the general will, to the liberal conception that government acts on behalf of the people having being elected as their representative (thus exercising its will without constant recourse to referenda). But, the principle remains the same – government represents the best will of its constituents. Democratic theory is, however, beset by the threatened distortion of the relationship between the representative and the represented by sectional interests. Thus, Rousseau resists the term representation, viewing it as a distortion of the purity of the general will. *On the Social Contract*, for example, variously details a struggle to maintain the purity of the general will against the private, corporate and common wills. The manifest intent of Rousseau's text betrays itself, demonstrating that representation is necessarily hegemonic, impure, and that sectional interests will always compete to represent universal interests. Ernesto Laclau expresses this point well:

> The task of a representative in parliament does not simply consist in transmitting the wishes of those he represents; he will have to elaborate a new discourse which convinces other members – by, for instance, arguing that the interests of the people in his constituency are compatible with the national interest, and so on. In this way he inscribes those interests within a more universal discourse and, in so far as his discourse also becomes that of the people of his constituency, they also are able to universalise their experience. The relation of representation thus becomes a vehicle of universalisation. (Laclau, 2000: 212)

Today the representative powers of national governments are challenged by global powers, such as multinational corporations and international bodies, which impinge upon their capacity to represent a clearly demarcated people (see Held, 1991: 225). Representation is an impossible ideal, always beset by uneven distributions of, and differential access to, power and resources. This is especially important in respect of political doctrines which hold to the ideal of fully transparent representation. Not only would such an ideal, if achieved, mark the end of representation tout court – its achievement would sanction the repression of the pluralism which is essential to any democracy.

We should note, however, Laclau's insistence that representation becomes a vehicle for universalisation. At first blush, this statement seems contrary to the popular conception of a post-structuralist politics. The insistence on the importance of universalisation belies the uninformed misconception that post-structuralism is simply about the particular, the contingent, about exclusion and not inclusion. Laclau insists on the necessary link between universal and particular – representation suggests that particular interests are hegemonically represented in discourses which extend beyond their particularism. He makes the point that the two ideals, that of particular interests that are completely self enclosed and that of a universalism with no reference to particularity, would, in fact, mirror each other. They are impossible ideals which, if achieved, would signal the end of all representation. Representation presupposes the necessary failure of universalisation, as well as the continued struggle to achieve the ideal. If there were no such failure then the need for representation would evaporate.

The problematic of representation may also be traced in the critique of instrumental reason that has been a keynote of Marxism since Adorno and Horkheimer's *Dialectic of Enlightenment* (1985). This brings us to the third of the discursive practices of representation listed above.

On this account, the autonomous subject, represented in liberal democratic polities, is constituted by a system of oppression of which she is a symptom. The autonomy, so highly prized by democratic society, has a flip-side – the internalisation of authority and participation in a system dominated by the particular interests of state and capital. The autonomy of the enlightened subject is wrought at the expense of an objectification of the material world, the subject and her body. This analysis braids together the modulations of representation delineated above – the autonomous subject of democratic society, who represents himself, and is represented by public institutions, is deemed a constituent element of, and participant in, an inequitable social structure. Nevertheless, the liberal claim to autonomous representation is not simply false – in its ideal formulation it functions as an implicit critique of the failure of the autonomous subjectivity to meet its own promise.

These different conceptions of representation all fall foul of defining the limits of what is proper to the self which represents itself. This is precisely the subject presupposed in both Habermas's and Rawls's accounts of democracy. The invocation, by the former, of an 'ideal speech' situation and, by the latter, of an original position, both presuppose perfectly symmetrical subjects, whose speech is not distorted. I suggest that an essential asymmetry distorts any such idealised account of symmetry. This asymmetry, inflected towards a critique of contemporary democratisation, challenges the legal and political status of the proper self, the relation of this proper subject to property and legality, and the relation between instrumental rationality and the autonomous self. The post-structuralist critique of representation urges wariness of the illusion that property (both individual and objective) is natural and it links the two in suggesting that the liberal conception of autonomy underpins a system of inequitable property relations. It parts from the Marxist critique of capitalism in refusing the suggestion that political transformation is effected as a consequence of further instrumentalisation of the external world and insists on the necessity of a hegemonic struggle for radical democracy, a struggle with no warranty.

This critique of representation holds implications too for Habermas's reliance on communication as the premise of democratic deliberation. Classical political theory rarely theorised communication but it is intrinsic to any consideration of democratic accountability. Democracy presumes that the people are capable of communicating a clear and stable will that can act as the basis of decision-making. This is the case whether decisions are made by a representative legislature or by the sovereign acts of a general will. The contingency of the principles of autonomy and representation suggest that this ideal of communication requires revisiting. The apparently legitimate communication of a sovereign will always represents a particular expression thereof. This does not mean that the communication of a democratic will is anathema to politics but recognises the politics underlying the claim to represent the general will. Expressed in other terms, the communication of an apparently sovereign will inevitably reflects the hegemony of a particular conception of the good; communication is not controlled by any sovereign utterance but is a site of undecidability inherently open to contestation. Habermas's projection of a community of ideal communication performs the dual task of providing a non-ideological standpoint, which is neutral as regards particular life practices, and of securing a semantic space undisturbed by the sonorous argument of constituted identities. Both of these moves enact the classic task of founding a pre-political realm to justify political action. However, the attempt to found such premises already entails the operation of a political will attempting to justify its politics. This strategy of occluding the violence of the moment of founding is of the essence of politics.

Post-structuralism, Deliberation and Democracy

It is often claimed that post-structuralism cannot provide a defence of democracy to supplement the deconstruction of key tenets of democratic theory, such as subjectivity, autonomy and representation. There is widespread suspicion, moreover, of an alleged ethical void at the heart of post-structuralist theory. These challenges rely on the two strategies touched on in the preceding discussion: empiricism or rationalism. The empirical political scientist claims to discover certain facts beyond a hermeneutics of suspicion; the theorist of rationality (in this case communicative rationality) relies on a claim to reason implicit in any communication. Let me briefly summarise that discussion in order to weigh the limits of such interventions.

Representation of (social) facts, I suggested, depends on forms of signification which are essentially contested. Brute data is always interpreted data. Furthermore, the isolation of social facts cannot do justice to the meaningful activities of which the facts are selective abstractions. Charles Taylor makes a similar point in arguing that the political scientist ignores the inter-subjective meaning of social acts, that social facts are practices, not individual actions, and that, as a consequence, their interpretation can only proceed along hermeneutic lines. This behaviourist reduction of social practices presupposes an oft criticised form of autonomous subjectivity. Subjects are viewed as atomistic individuals, in full control of their actions and responsible for them. This ignores the social discourses which interpellate and structure possibilities for individual choices and action. Lastly, the political scientist cannot justify the move from universal to particular without relying on premises which s/he would reject. The problem of induction indicates that the decision to derive general claims from particular facts cannot itself be grounded in facts or in logic. The empiricist response to the post-structuralist – either to return to the facts or face relativism – rings hollow if the empiricist cannot herself justify the theoretical decisions made without the invocation of a principle which appears arbitrary.

If empirical political science escapes contested signification by presupposing a realm of social facts, the rationalist opens the latch with different keys. Habermas's notion of communicative rationality, for example, seeks to escape the double hermeneutic of the social sciences – the problem that the language of the social sciences uses the same language as that of the domain it seeks to understand, potentially placing understanding in a context bound vortex of interpretation – by reconstructing universal presuppositions of validity underlying all communication. This reconstruction provides a critical orientation for the exercise of judgement by autonomous subjects, in control of the significance of their utterances. Habermas presumes that what orients communicative action is the claim to universal semantic and pragmatic agreement. This presupposition orients a leftist political project, coordinated by the ideal of autonomous interaction between rational subjects. But what if the speech act is a site of enunciative struggle which does not admit of such idealisation? What if consensus cannot escape the implication of a power which is never finally justified and such a consensus always represents the hegemony of particular not universal claims?

It is this conclusion which post-structuralist theory endorses. While Habermas can acknowledge that any actual consensus is not equivalent to the ideal of communicative rationality, he cannot admit that this failure is necessary and not simply empirical – that failure is intrinsic to any claimed universality (see Devenney, 2001). My discussion of autonomy and representation connotes an irreducible negativity which cannot be domesticated within any discourse, democratic or otherwise. Diana Coole is acutely aware of the resistance of the negative to description in her *Negativity and Politics*:

> [The negative] to borrow Derrida's phrase, has many non-synonymous substitutes: dialectics, non-identity, difference, différance, the invisible, the semiotic, the virtual, the unconscious, will to power, the feminine. These cannot be reduced to the various signifiers of a common referent. (Coole, 1999: 2)

This resistance of the reduction of the negative to the precarious signifiers of a common referent signals the febrile terrain which post-structuralism mobilises. A key question in the context of this article is the bearing of the negative on a conception of democracy. Any such answer must reveal, even as it dissimulates, the blind spots of democratic theory. What is more, post-structuralism does not presume a direct link between these conclusions and a particular political project. If theoretical premises implied the privileging of particular forms of action, then the responsibility for those actions is seconded to the theory. It is understandable that political theorists concerned with the extension of equality and liberty in democratic societies should chafe at such scruples, but I would contend that such scruples are crucial contributions of post-structuralism to the ongoing discussion of democracy. The conclusion that a post-structuralist perspective does not prescribe either an ethical or a political project would seem to leave the critic concerned with radical transformation of existing institutions at an impasse. This is not the case.

Conclusion

In concluding then, I suggest the pertinence of a post structuralist intervention to a deliberative conception of democracy. This entails considering the ethics of decision and responsibility, the contingency of democratic community and the logic of autonomy in relation to a deliberative conception of radical politics.

Most accounts of morality and democracy seek principles which either guide the taking of decisions or shift responsibility for decision-taking on to the principles. Post-structuralism refuses this link between universal principles of justice and legitimate decision-making. The radical absence of such principles does, however, have implications for political action and choice. An example demonstrates this. Think of the fascist confronted with the spectre of radical contingency. For the fascist, contingency should not be identified with but overcome through the introduction of a principle of order. The fascist identifies with the principle of order as the basis for the organisation of political life – the state, the body politic, the fraternity of Aryan man and the like. By contrast, the radical democrat sanctions contingency as necessary and, ironically, not contingent. This recognition entails (social) identification with radical contingency and the insistence that all political decisions require justification. A properly ethical decision does *not* rely on any principles or laws which precede it. This has the slightly bizarre consequence that a properly ethical decision would be taken by a wholly indeterminate subject, independent of all social practice. Given that such an ideal of subjectivity is precisely what post-structuralist thought rejects, this ideal of sovereign decision-making requires revising. It returns as the condition of possibility for autonomous action *and* the condition of its impossibility. Sovereign decisions cannot be taken but they must be taken. It is this structure of indeterminacy that opens a realm of freedom in which subjects can begin to question the laws given to them and recognise that the following of a law presupposes the taking of a decision every time the law is followed. This does not mean that the validity of the legal order is simply suspended. Rather, it is to recognise the violence which goes hand in hand with the forms of legitimation intrinsic to liberal democracies.

Identification with an ultimate contingency implies that the ethical, as an impossible ideal, should be contrasted with any particular normative order which attempts to achieve that ideal. The starting point of a democratic order is the recognition that no principle precedes those principles that we give to ourselves, thus constituting ourselves as a community of selves. This forces the acknowledgement of the contingency of the community of selves thus constituted and the possibility of disruption of the community thus constituted. Connolly terms this a democratic politics of disturbance which requires a constant contestation of all those rules which demarcate the demos, a constant reinvention of the laws which also means their constant amelioration. The identification with contingency, and thus with an essential value pluralism, distinguishes the radical democrat from the liberal. The liberal endorses value pluralism without acknowledging that this pluralism is constituted by a radical moment of indecision, which undermines the claimed legitimacy of the decision. Thus, the liberal struggles to justify the exercise of force in order to maintain the norms previously endorsed. The radical democrat, in recognising the contingent foundation of any order, also recognises the (illegitimate) violence required for the maintenance of that order. This is why the radical democrat can take responsibility for the decision which underpins the exclusions constitutive of the community and take on the burdensome task of their constant revision.

I suggested above that no principle of justification can finally justify the forms of order constitutive of political community. If this principle underlies the constitution of democratic community, it requires not just exclusion of those who would endanger such contingency but ongoing deliberation between those who do. Where Habermas defends deliberative democracy on the grounds of a universal ideal of communication implicit in the structure of the speech act, the radical democrat endorses deliberation precisely because the speech act does not admit of such an ideal. In recognising the failure of any principle of justification to ground a particular politics, the radical democrat insists on the proliferation of the spaces and places in which politics takes place and refuses the limitation of the political to the state or to the ideal of perfect community. But this endorsement of deliberation runs hand in hand with the acknowledgement and defence of the creation of antagonistic political frontiers between interlocutors. Often, even in a democratic state, these interlocutors will not acknowledge the validity of the arguments put forward by the opponent. No appeal to higher principles, to the facts, to a common humanity will resolve such disputes. These debates are won through persuasion and manipulation of the public political agenda, not through cautious rational persuasion.

The radical democrat then, drawing on post-structuralism, insists on the precarious institutionalisation of fora of debate and decision-making which allow both for rational deliberation and for the agonistic, sometimes antagonistic, struggles to dominate public space and the policy agenda. She critically appropriates democratic theory, specifically deliberative accounts of democracy, without falling foul of the positivist mistake of hypostasising what is as what should be. This leech-like appropriation of classical conceptions of democracy relies on the acknowledgement that certain structures are hegemonic in contemporary societies and that alternative hegemonic visions must be articulated. In so doing, post-structuralism makes a radical and innovative contribution to the promise of a democracy which never comes, but faithfully insists on being taken seriously.

12

The Singularity of the Political

ROBERT PORTER

Introduction

Contemporary politics, throughout Western Europe and North America, often invokes the necessity of pragmatism. In the UK, the spin doctors of 'New Labour' would have us believe that their party is not overburdened with any idealised assumptions or doctrinaire impulses. Such things, they might aver, cloud judgements and deflect government from the 'hard choices' of 'real politics'. The implication of such a claim is that there is some sort of gulf between ideas or ideologies – the (soft) concepts of politics – and its (hard) reality.

But this is, of course, a doctrinaire impulse derived from a set of idealised assumptions. The thought that there is such a gulf presupposes that 'the reality' and the concept of that reality are obviously distinct and that the mere concepts of the traditional ideologue can be easily contrasted to the clarity of vision possessed by the pragmatist. On the contrary, this chapter will argue, concept and reality are inextricably linked. The concept is involved in creating the political reality that it supposedly implies and reflects upon as a set of necessary conditions. The 'pragmatism' of current politics produces the situation about which it claims to be necessarily pragmatic. To put this in the form of a slogan we might say: *there is no reality behind the concept, only the concept through which the real is invented.*

This slogan condenses an intuition taken from the work of Gilles Deleuze and Felix Guattari who affirm the importance of the concept in as much as they show the way in which it invents and gives consistency to the reality of a political order or what they call a 'possible world' (Deleuze and Guattari, 1994: 17). It is the intention of this chapter to elucidate this thinking and to indicate its importance for the way in which we think about politics.

We will begin by considering a hypothetical example, that of an international human rights case, in order to establish something about how Deleuze and Guattari would conceive of the processes involved in the bringing of such a case. This will introduce us to the idea of 'singularity' in relation to a concept of the political. Then, using the thinking of Plato, Kant and Habermas for illustration, we will explore the way in which a logic of singularity functions in the formulation of the concept of the political. It will be seen that, in formulating a concept of the political, these three thinkers construct a 'problem position' or perspective that subsequently can be shown to singularly impact on the social field as an implicit (political) limit or order.

Then, drawing on Deleuze and Guattari, we will define the challenge facing the critical thinker as that of being sensitive to the implicit orders and limiting demands that remain hidden in such conceptual formulations of the political. If the challenge of thinking critically amounts to being aware of that which limits or orders our understanding of the political, then the potential of such a critique is simultaneously one of transgression, of moving beyond the limits set for us by the thought of others. But such transgression is constitutively dependent on certain limits of its own. Consequently, the third part of the chapter will explore the relationship between transgression and limit from the point of view of a logic of singularity.

By way of conclusion we will consider more directly how this notion of singularity can be pressed into the service of thinking critically about the concept of the political. How, we will ask, can it guide and help us in thinking critically about the political and what might be the ethics of such a critique?

The Singularity of Human Rights

Let us begin with an example. Consider the 'possible world' of an individual in the situation of having to assert or fight for 'human rights'. Say, for instance, that the individual's life is under threat. Her property has been taken from her or destroyed and she has been given the choice to leave the territory she occupies or be killed. She duly leaves but only to return with a view to hauling her aggressors before the law for their violation of her human rights. What is the 'possible world' referred to by this idea of human rights, in particular the notion of such rights that are 'universal'? Consider the following rights:

Everyone has to right to life, liberty, and security of person.

No one shall be subjected to torture or to cruel, inhuman or degrading treatment or punishment.

No one shall be subjected to arbitrary arrest, detention or exile.

No one shall be subjected to arbitrary interference with his privacy, family, home or correspondence; nor to attacks upon his honour and reputation.

Everyone has the right to the protection of the law against such interference or attacks. (United Nations, 1948)

These form part of the 'Universal Declaration of Human Rights'. The action taken against the individual in our example appears to be a straightforward contravention of 'human rights' as laid down in the UN declaration. Certainly her rights to life, liberty and security could be said to be under threat. She could also be said to be 'degraded' in so far as her 'home' was destroyed, her 'privacy' invaded, her person forced into 'exile'. All of this could be said. But by whom?

As the articles are legal principles devised with the approval of the members of the United Nations, then presumably those with the power to level these charges would be legal practitioners, with some kind of international political back-up. The fight against those violating 'human rights' would, in this sense, have to be subject to a specific legal intervention. Lawyers would say all the things we want to say about our exemplary individual.

Such an intervention, according to the logic of Deleuze and Guattari, is always inventive or conceptually innovative. Imagine that the 'human rights' case being built by such a legal practitioner turns decisively on the accusation that certain individuals or parties have engaged in acts of 'genocide'. The legal practitioner, in the first instance, must work within the confines of the conceptual-legal definition of such a crime. If genocide is defined in international law as the destruction or obliteration, 'in whole or in part', of an 'ethnical' 'group', then the connection between an individual case of maltreatment and this legal definition would have to be explicitly made. Suppose that there is clear evidence suggesting that an individual has indeed been issued with death threats and forced to leave the territory on which she grew up. The legal practitioner could, by making the conceptual connection between territory occupied by individuals and their 'ethnical' group identity, suggest that the 'forced exile' of the individual was undertaken for purposes which can legally be determined as 'genocidal'. That is to say, by making a case for suggesting that the territory on which an individual grows up has a bearing on the formation of 'ethnical' group identity, the legal practitioner could innovatively use concepts in the service of a demand (in this case the legal-political demand to treat individual acts of 'forced exile' as instances of 'genocide').

In the light of this example, we need to clarify certain issues. Firstly, we need to make clear that the 'possible world' brought to life by the legal practitioner cannot exist independently of the concepts through which it takes on concrete sense. The legal practitioner does not simply *show* that a violation of human rights has taken place. She is always already involved in *creating* the event of 'violation'. To put it back into a slogan we might say: *there is no reality of a 'human rights' violation behind the concept, only the conceptual innovation (namely, the accusation of 'forced exile' as 'genocide') through which it is realised.*

Secondly, and importantly, we need to emphasise that this activity of conceptual innovation is not simply a matter of individual will. On the contrary, such conceptual innovation always already implies a social matrix (what Deleuze and Guattari would call a social or 'collective assemblage of enunciation') at work in the conceptual formulation of any 'possible world' (Deleuze and Guattari, 1988: 78). The 'collective assemblage' that would immediately inform the possibility of formulating the case against 'human rights abuses' would consist of, at least, an international court of law, legal practitioners versed in this law, evidence compiled on behalf of the victims of 'human rights abuses' and a determinable notion of what constitutes a 'human rights abuse'. Furthermore, each conditional element in this collective assemblage itself expresses a social reality. An international court with real powers to prosecute presupposes international political convergence on its establishment. A determinable notion of a 'human rights abuse' presupposes formulation and consent to a qualitative distinction between what is human and inhuman. The existence of evidence of 'human rights abuses' is conditional on subjects or agencies, such as 'Human Rights Watch' or 'Amnesty International' bearing witness to the atrocities committed.

The third point that needs to be firmly kept in mind is that the social matrix or collectivity at play in bringing the 'human rights' case is not simply presupposed by it but actualised in a new way. Deleuze and Guattari do not refer to the collective presuppositions but to the collective *assemblage* at play in the formation of 'possible worlds'. We need to take seriously the terminology that is being used here. *Assemblage* literally means (and Deleuze and Guattari insist that we should always take them literally) the putting together of something that is different and uniquely irreducible to what it produces (see, for example, Deleuze and Parnet, 1987: 98). In this regard, the social matrix or collectivity at play in the 'human rights' case is not simply presupposed or given. The legal practitioner's demand to hold 'human rights violations' to account literally makes no sense unless the social or collective aspects of the demand (the legal convention, evidence and so on) are produced in accordance with the terms (the call for a conviction on the grounds of 'forced exile') of the specific and unique case that is being assembled or put together.

The fourth and, for our purposes, most important point is that, in urging us to focus on the irreducible and unique way conceptual innovation produces or assembles new or different 'possible worlds', Deleuze and Guattari are providing us with a *singular* logic that can help us think critically about the concept of the political. The Deleuze-Guattarian notion of singularity implies no previous determination and only makes sense in the irreducible and unique way in which it is assembled or produced (see Deleuze, 1993: 64).

However, the question remains as to the connection between Deleuze and Guattari's notion of singularity and its use in the service of thinking critically about the concept of the political.

The Concept of the Political: inventing the problem

There is no point in defining the concept of the political unless we show how the defining moment of the political itself involves a political act of limitation or ordering. From a Deleuze-Guattarian perspective, we can begin to work through this idea by focusing on how the limits of the political are set through the conceptual formation or invention of a 'problem position' (Deleuze, 1987: 1). To help illustrate this, we can make brief reference to three (one ancient, one modern and one contemporary) influential thinkers of the political: Plato, Kant and Habermas. But, before doing so, we need to be clear on two things. Firstly, when we use the language of 'invention', of assembling a 'problem position' in describing the thought of Plato, Kant and Habermas, we are imposing upon them a conceptual vocabulary which, clearly, they would not recognise as their own. Plato, Kant and Habermas do not explicitly formulate a 'concept of the political'. It is something which we find implicit in their arguments. But this does not lessen the impact of the critical remarks we will make with respect to their thought. On the contrary, it actually brings certain terms of the criticism into focus. We shall see that Platonic, Kantian and Habermasian thought is, from a Deleuze-Guattarian perspective, criticisable precisely because it remains unconscious of the 'problem position' it innovatively adopts in order to conceptually account for the reality of the political.

In *The Republic*, Plato formulates a 'problem position' which turns decisively on the possibility of nourishing or cultivating a *just* social order in light of the 'knowledge' and 'truth' that is to be found radiating from, what he calls, the 'Form' of the 'good' (Plato, 1976: 203). Thus, Plato's concept of the political is defined in conjunction with the innovative problem of how the social order can be governed (under the guidance, Plato insists, of a specific class of 'philosopher Kings') in light of this 'Form' of the 'good'. Plato's idea of a 'Form' of the 'good' implies a form of reality that is distinct from the assembled or invented concept through which it is brought to life (Deleuze and Guattari, 1994: 6). To put it another way, Plato assumes that the problem of the political (that is, the problem of accessing or gravitating toward the 'Form' of the 'good') reflects a reality independent of the concept or conceptual innovation in which it is realised and given sense. Plato, in this regard, is not conscious that the political reality he takes for granted (a reality governed by 'Forms') is one that he has constructed; he is unconscious of, what Deleuze and Guattari technically call, the 'constructivism' of the problem as concept (Deleuze and Guattari, 1994: 35–6).

Kant circumscribes the concept of the political by thinking of it in conjunction with the problem of morality. 'True politics', as Kant says, in *Perpetual Peace*, 'can never take a step without rendering homage to morality' (Kant, 1949: 340). The form of the moral in Kant (what he calls the 'moral law') is constructed in such a way as to take into consideration the political *rights* of those who must assume responsibility for its formulation. 'All politics ... must bend its knee before ... right' (Kant, 1949: 340). The moral affirmation of 'right' operates, in Kantian terms, as a conditional limit (or what Kant would call a 'condition of possibility') of politics. Although obviously different to Plato's 'Form' of the 'good', Kant's moral affirmation of 'right' logically functions in a similar manner; that is as an implied reality, supposedly independent of the concept ('moral law') through which its is realised. Kant, in this sense, is not conscious that the concept of political reality he takes for granted (a reality governed by the morality of affirming 'rights') amounts to a problem or 'problem position' he has constructively adopted.

Habermas follows Kant in conceptualising the political in accordance with a problem of moral legitimation. In order to legitimise any form of politics, we must, in the Habermasian view, constitute it in terms of an inter-subjective communicative exchange. Such a discursive exchange is moral, from this perspective, if it is constructed on the basis of inclusion and reasoned agreement; that is, the institutionalisation of moral laws or norms are conditional on the requirement that they express the consent of all those affected by the consequences that flow from their inter-subjective formulation (Habermas, 1990: 197). Again we witness the positing of an implied concept of political reality (namely, that the problem of morally legitimising any form of politics is necessarily conditional on securing inter-subjective consent to the laws constituted in discursive exchanges) that is, in truth, given only through its assemblage as such.

Looking at Plato, Kant and Habermas in this way allows us to critically raise the notion that an invention of a 'problem position', vis-à-vis the political, always already involves the construction of concepts whose function is to limit or order political reality. It is not that Plato, Kant and Habermas do not think hard enough about the conceptual presuppositions that underpin the theoretical edifices they construct. Rather, from a Deleuze-Guattarian perspective, the process of conceptually positing an image of the political is instantly caught up in an ordering complex. This surrounds us with certain dangers (see Deleuze and Guattari, 1988: 227–31). Deleuze and Guattari want to argue – and in this they are thoroughly Nietzschean – that the activity of constructing concepts ('philosophy', as they technically define it) can be a very *dangerous* business (see Deleuze and Guattari, 1994: 42).

For example, Kant's moral law is not only rights based, as implied above, but is also based in a *duty* and in a *responsibility* that supposedly transcends mere egocentric interest. A fundamental difficulty facing any positive affirm-ation and acceptance of such a concept of moral law is that of confronting the potentially dangerous or even monstrous consequences that may flow from consistently following it through in any given situation. The terroristic ethic of a 'suicide bomber', for example, would seem to be an exemplary case of an ethically and politically motivated agent following a course of action dictated in accordance with a moral law that is irreducible to mere egocentric interest (that is, the expression of a *duty* and a *responsibility* to an ethno-religious 'law' or 'cause', no matter what the cost to the self and so on). This is not to accuse Kant of justifying 'terrorism' (for a passionate defence of Kant against this charge, see Žižek, 1997: 231). Rather, it is to sober us up to the reality that, in as much as philosophical concepts (such as the moral law, the 'Form' of the 'good' and so on) become sedimented in thought, their authority can be called upon to order, limit and impact on political reality in the most dramatic and potentially devastating terms. Also, the adoption of a 'problem position' vis-à-vis the political is not exclusively the preserve of the public philosopher (such as Plato, Kant and Habermas) – it is also bread and butter for the political activist in the social field. Perpetrators of 'politically motivated violence' ('holy war', 'armed struggle' and the like) are well schooled in the conceptual art of persuading us that their actions are the product of an unavoidable problem that governs the present political predicament.

The challenge posed by the Deleuze-Guattarian critique is one of remaining sensitive to the implied orders or demands that often remain hidden in conceptual formulations of the political. To justify or bolster a political 'position' or perspective, by suggesting that it is merely reflective of an unavoidable political problem or predicament, is to make an implicit demand or order. Such a demand would be difficult to institutionalise, were it an explicit imperative that must simply be obeyed. Yet, by passing off certain demands as conceptual rather than authoritarian, the political agent can limit or order the social field accordingly. Those who seek political authority, who desire to have political opinion on their side, come to us with common sense, as pragmatic realists responsive to the needs of the populace (see Deleuze and Guattari, 1988: 75–6).

To order or limit (for our purposes, the terms are interchangeable) the social field in conjunction with a posited political perspective is to engage in a *singular* activity. The *singularity* of the act of conceptualising the political is given consistency or is defined by the *irreducible* terms of its assemblage or production. These terms, understood in accordance with the specific 'problem position' adopted vis-à-vis the political, are *irreducible* to the extent that *nothing in them is predetermined before the specific and unique conceptual invention or creation through which they are realised*. The critic, in this Deleuze-Guattarian sense, must believe in the singular (unique, specific and irreducible) power of the concept in summoning forth or assembling that which limits or orders (the problem of) the political.

Limit, Transgression, Singularity

If the challenge of Deleuze-Guattarian critique is that of remaining sensitive to the implied orders or demands that often remain hidden in conceptual formulations of the political, then its potential is simultaneously one of *transgression*, of moving beyond such limits. But, at the same time, this transgressive activity is constitutively dependent on certain limits of its own. There can be no transgression without a limiting infringement; conversely, there can be no institutionalisation of a limit that does not give rise to the potential for transgressive violation (see Foucault, 1977a: 34).

Let us return to our hypothetical 'human rights' case. The case built by our legal practitioner turned decisively on an accusation concerning 'forced exile'. Yet we can turn everything on its head here by pointing out how the legal practitioner, in accusing certain parties of violating or transgressing 'human rights' law, could, herself, be shown to be engaging in a transgressive act – that is, in an act of violation and infringement. This, of course, would be a useful tactic for those who would seek to defend the rights of the accused against the prosecution's assumption of guilt (after all, the dictum 'innocent until proven guilty' is, for example, built into Article 6 of *The European Convention on Human Rights*).

Imagine that the prosecution have produced enough evidence for the defence to accept the claim of 'forced exile'. There is a sense in which a defence lawyer could work innovatively with the terms surrounding this claim (namely, that the exile really took place) in order to bring into account other pertinent considerations that could, in this view, enable the court to exonerate the accused. Suppose that the defence lawyer sets to work providing evidence that the supposedly maltreated individual was a member of a 'politically subversive' organisation whose 'terrorist' activities threaten the very stability of the social order in its present sovereign form – that her exile amounted not to a flight from persecution but from the law and its authority. We should note that the defence (assuming, of course, that they could make these accusations stick) is on solid legal ground here. There is provision in Article 15 of *The European Convention on Human Rights* for a sovereign body to take 'measures derogating from its obligations under [the] convention' in 'a time of war or any other public emergency threatening the life of the nation' (quoted in Clements, 1994: 233).

From the perspective of the prosecution, the actions of those engaged in 'forcible exile' are transgressive – that is, they are clear infringements or violations of international law. In this sense, international 'human rights' law provides the legal practitioner with a series of codes and conventions with which to critique, judge and, consequently, limit violations. Clearly, things begin to get complicated when this very limit (namely, the codes and conventions of international law) is used by the defence in order to accuse the prosecution of violating and infringing (in short, transgressing) the right of, in this case, a sovereign nation to protect itself from dangers of life threatening 'terrorism'.

The crucial point to keep in mind is that the relationship between transgression and limit is complicated because they are products of conceptual innovation. To rephrase a slogan used earlier: *there is no reality of transgression or limit that has not been assembled or invented through the concept*. Thus, the prosecution, in the example above, assembled a concept of transgression in accordance with a specific 'human rights violation' (making the connection between 'forced exile and 'genocide'). The defence, in response, assembled a concept of transgression in accordance with the suggestion that the prosecution case violated codes and conventions of international law which underpin the right of a sovereign nation to protect itself from danger (by making the specific conceptual connection between the supposedly 'maltreated individual' and 'subversive' or 'terrorist' activity threatening 'national security').

The double sense of transgression as we initially defined it (both limiting infringement and movement beyond it) is preserved here. Clearly, the prosecution and the defence are engaged in a conceptual struggle and, as a consequence, they are seeking to infringe and violate the sanctity of the other's perspective. This is transgressive, in the second sense, precisely because it seeks to move beyond the limits set by the thought of the other. Or, more accurately, the prosecution and defence conceptually set up the limiting barriers which they take to be inherent in the position of the other while simultaneously cutting through them. Such a gesture is at once *critical* and *singular*. It is *critical* in as much as it refuses to merely accept, and insists in moving beyond, what the thought of the other bequeaths (the defence does not merely accept the prosecution's assumption of guilt; the prosecution, let us say, will not accept the justification of individual maltreatment in the name of 'national security'). It is *singular* – to repeat – precisely because of its irreducibility to the specific and unique conceptual terms ('forced exile', 'genocide', 'terrorist' and so on) through which it is assembled.

Certain consequences follow from theorising transgression in a way that emphasises the critical and singular. For instance, although it is quite accurate to say that transgression is always already defined by a limit, it is a mistake to say that both terms are the same. If transgression and limit are products of the singular conceptual innovation through which they are assembled, then we must take seriously the notion that the singularity of this act can never be predetermined (remembering, of course, that one of the defining characteristics of singularity is that nothing in it is determined in advance). So it is never accurate enough to say that 'wherever there is transgression there will be limit' or that 'transgression can never constitute a pure space outside limits'. Such conceptual generalities tell us nothing. What, from a Deleuze-Guattarian perspective, remains crucial is the singular consistency and impact given to the (transgressive, limiting) concept in the social-political field (for example, in the interaction between the prosecution and defence in an international court of law).

By merely pointing out that we should remain critically sensitive to the singular consistency and impact of the concept as used in the social-political field is to immediately content ourselves with the hollowness of another generality. In these terms, thought (the thought of being critically sensitive) exhausts itself as mere contemplation or reflection of a possibility (of being a critic). Yet, to be a political critic, to think critically about the concept of the political, is never to remain within the passivity of such contemplation or reflection; criticism, on the contrary, is always a positive activity which involves taking what has become sedimented in thought and breathing new life into it.

Our legal prosecutor took what was given to her in thought (for example, legal convention and witness evidence) in order to breathe life into an accusation of 'forced exile'. Or, to take but one other example, the proponent of 'politically motivated violence' breathes life into a thought (for instance, the unavoidable political predicament that follows from a history of colonial oppression) that can be strategically deployed as a justificatory tactic. These positive critical gestures can never be abstracted from the singular terms in which they limit and order the social-political field. Can the singular intervention of a proponent of 'politically motivated violence' retroactively justify and convince us that the present 'armed struggle' is a necessary product of a history of suppression? Can the singular intervention of the legal practitioner convince the judges presiding over the case she is presently formulating? These are the crucial questions.

Conclusion

Let us conclude our discussion by considering what lessons and insights can be taken from using Deleuze and Guattari's notion of singularity in the service of thinking critically about the concept of the political. Immediately connected to the strategy of issuing lessons is a task which is both *pedagogical* and *ethical*. We can focus on each of these issues (the issue of pedagogy and the issue of ethics) by formulating them in conjunction with the following questions:

   1. How can a Deleuze-Guattarian logic of singularity pedagogically guide us and help us in thinking critically about the political?
   2. How useful is such guidance when considered from an ethical point of view?

Let us begin by (re)focusing on certain terms that we have used to designate the activity of thinking critically about the political. The idea of a political critic has, thus far, been implicitly presented according to a double – on the one hand, as *prohibitive* and, on the other hand, as *constructive*. Our critical remarks with respect to Platonic, Kantian and Habermasian thought were, for instance, clearly of a *prohibitive* nature. That is to say, our critique wanted to prohibit Plato, Kant and Habermas from claiming that the 'problem position' they adopt vis-à-vis the political (for instance, the Platonic problem of accessing or gravitating toward the 'Form' of the 'good' or, to take another example, the Habermasian problem of morally legitimising political norms in accordance with a reciprocal and inclusive communicative exchange) is independent of the concept or conceptual innovation in which it is realised and given sense.

Such a critical-prohibitive gesture is guided by a logic of singularity in as much as it seeks to bring into focus the unique terms in which the problem of the political is determined. The point of this critical focus was not to show that Plato and others failed to think hard enough about their conceptual presuppositions, but to show how the process of conceptually positing an image of the political is instantly caught up in an ordering complex and how, consequently, this surrounds us with certain dangers. In other words, a logic of singularity can guide us in thinking critically about the political by giving us an awareness of the power of the concept or conceptual imperative as used by the political activist in ordering the social field.

Of course, to register an awareness of the power of the concept (for example, the power of a concept of 'moral law' which is used to justify the actions of a 'suicide bomber') is not enough. This is because a desire for prohibition (a desire to thwart the power that is exercised through the concept) must be assembled – it is a *constructive* activity. That is to say, to be a political critic, to think critically about the concept of the political, is – to repeat – always positively and constructively to take what has been sedimented in thought and breathe new life into it (think again of our legal prosecutor taking what was given to her in legal convention, witness evidence and so on in order to breath life into a case prohibiting 'forced exile'). In a sense, the awareness of the power of the concept is a prelude to political empowerment – that is, to a process of involvement or participation in ideas that can be strategically deployed with a singular purpose in mind (for a legal conviction, for example).

To imply, as we seem to be, that thinking according to a logic of singularity allows us to *empower* ourselves through participating in the concept is not, let us be clear, simply to lend this notion an approvable ethical sense. This would be naive in the extreme. Let us return to an important principle concerning the singular logic we have been using here. We have consistently stressed that the reality mediated through the concept is never determined in advance of its unique assemblage as such. This logic equally applies to the reality of ethics. That is to say, the reality of ethics is nothing but its invention through an assembled concept that is never predetermined.

In this regard, the concept (of the political) is not a good or bad thing, a thing to be cherished or lamented. Rather, it is something through which the good and bad, the cherished or lamentable are singularly assembled. Further, the limits and ordering demands hidden in conceptualisations (of the political) are not simply unacceptable barriers in need of ethical transgression. Ethically approving the transgression of limits or barriers involves their specific construction in a conceptual struggle. In other words, transgression is not necessarily good, limits are not necessarily bad. They are, however, necessarily put together as such (On the 'questionable association' between transgression and ethics, see Foucault, 1977a: 35). 'Good and bad', as Deleuze and Guattari put it, 'are only the product of an active and temporary selection, which must be renewed' (Deleuze and Guattari, 1988: 10).

The (Deleuze-Guattarian) lesson is to actively and positively select the 'good' – to engage in the empowering activity or, what Deleuze calls, 'true freedom' of participating in a concept (of the 'good') that will decidedly impact on the political reality you *desire* (see Deleuze, 1991: 15). Guattari and, particularly, Deleuze are close to Spinoza's view that what is considered to be ethically good is immediately related to desire. Ethics, in a sense, gains its *active* and *temporary* consistency in a desire for the 'good'. Consider the following passage from Spinoza's *The Ethics*:

> It is plain ... that in no case do we strive for, wish for, long for, or desire anything, because we deem it to be good, but on the other hand, we deem a thing to be good, because we strive for it, wish for it, long for it, or desire it. (Spinoza, 1909: 137)

Let us be clear, this is not a matter of merely saying 'ethics is simply what I want it to be!'. Desire, from a Deleuze-Guattarian perspective, is not understood as a 'festival' of individual will and pleasure. Rather, it is the product of an assemblage that always already enters into a negotiation with a social matrix (Deleuze and Parnet, 1987: 96). This was one of the first points we made concerning the 'human rights' case introduced at the beginning of the chapter. It was made clear that the desire expressed by the legal prosecutor to build a case against 'human rights abuses' involved the negotiation of a social matrix (an international court of law, evidence compiled on behalf of the victims of 'human rights abuses', a determinable notion of what constitutes a 'human rights abuse' and so on) re-actualised for the purposes of the specific task at hand – that is, the task of gaining a conviction.

If desire is a negotiated and organised assemblage, then only in these terms does it become something over which responsibility can be exercised. Deleuze and Guattari categorically reject the notion of desire as a spontaneous drive, irresponsibly prompting us in conscious life (Deleuze and Parnet, 1987: 96–7). Consider, for example, the circumstances of a man who is caught having an extra-marital affair and ends up in court haggling over a financial settlement. Now, we could imagine a skilled legal practitioner defending his client's infidelity according to a logic of the spontaneous and irresponsible drive ('There is no malice in my client's extra marital affair, only a psycho-biological weakness over which he can exert no responsibility or control. After all he is a 'sex addict', clearly sorry for the pain he has caused ...'). The critical point here is that the concept of 'psycho-biological weakness' is assembled by the legal practitioner in the hope of displacing, rather than acknowledging, responsibility as produced by desire ('It is not my client's fault, it was his spontaneous and uncontrollable drive!').

Let us return explicitly to the related questions formulated above. Firstly, we asked, how can a Deleuze-Guattarian logic of singularity pedagogically guide us and help us in thinking critically about the political? By following Deleuze and Guattari, we are guided to focus specifically on the potential power of the concept, as used by the political activist in ordering the social field. So the lesson is to look around, to see how concepts are being used in accordance with certain political imperatives or orders. What, for example, does it mean for Tony Blair to characterise 'New Labour' in accordance with the concept of the 'Radical Centre'? Connected to this concept of the 'Radical Centre' is, as Žižek points out, the notion of abandoning old and outmoded political outlooks (the traditional outlook which thinks the term 'radical' should be reserved for the 'hard left' or 'extreme right') in favour of the supposedly *radical* concept that we should pragmatically use ideas in the service of what works best in existing political conditions (Žižek, 1999: 198–9). The critical lesson here is that, while Blairism justifies itself as pragmatically able to deal with the demands and conditions of realpolitik, it is all the while constructing, intervening and changing this reality in conjunction with a series of implicit demands or imperatives of its own (the demand for economic prudence, the imperative of not upsetting the markets too much by drastically increasing public expenditure and so on).

Secondly, we asked how useful is such guidance when considered from an ethical point of view? It is again important to emphasise (in accordance with the logic of singularity) how the 'ethical point of view' can never exist independently of the conceptual innovation through which it is realised. Ethics, in other words, is an assemblage. This is precisely what gives ethics its 'desiring quality' (see Deleuze and Guattari, 1986: 49). That is to say, ethics is a matter of desire in so far as it is assembled and organised in conjunction with a social field that it seeks to reconstitute. The ethical lesson seems simple – actively assemble the ethic (that is, believe and participate in the power of the 'ethical' concept) that will decidedly impact on the political reality you *desire*. In guiding us in this manner, Deleuze and Guattari are clearly not advocating a 'festival' of individual want or pleasure but, rather, a process of socially informed and sober negotiation and empowerment. This, again, is *constructive criticism – the constructive and innovative activity in which the singularity of the political is brought to life.*

13

Genres, Technologies and Spaces of Being-in-Common

MICHAEL J. SHAPIRO

Introduction

Of all the genres treating public life, explicitly political treatises have been among the most insensitive to changing circumstances. Political theorists persist, for example, in referring to private versus public interests as if the boundary practices constructing these domains are historically stable. A simple narrative has dominated influential, canonical political texts – 'private life' precedes civic life, which, in turn, creates the conditions of possibility for the state as a political realisation of popular will. In one version, associated with the writings of John Locke, the state is a contractual extension of the civic order, which is composed of an aggregate of individual, private interests. In the Lockean narrative, civil society precedes the state. It is a naturally constituted, pre-political community that has no public interests until the state, as a contractual extension of the civic domain, creates a public interest, associated primarily with the exercise of a domestic policing function. The state defends the interests of each (propertied) individual from predatory violence and individuals reciprocate with allegiance in the form of an implicit agreement to forego autonomous violence in exchange for the state's protection.

Hegel's model of the relationship is organic rather than contractual. His departure from the Lockean model is owed, in part, to his steadfast rejection of contingency. Although, in Hegel's legendary narrative, the state is an extension of both the family and community and is the exemplary expression of the ultimate public interest – the ethical life – that extension is not the result of implicit contractual reciprocity. The state cannot be the result of a contract because that would imply that associative connections are 'the transient and utterly chaotic accidents of contingent agreement'. For Hegel, the family possesses a 'natural unity' that is threatened when civil society 'tears the individual from his family ties' and 'estranges the members of the family from one another, and recognizes them as self-subsistent persons' (Hegel, 1945: 148). And, worse, civil society displaces that natural unity with contingency.

> For the paternal soil and the external inorganic resources of nature from which the individual formerly derived his livelihood, it substitutes its own soil and subjects

the permanent existence of even the entire family to dependence on itself and to contingency. (Hegel, 1945: 148)

Ultimately, however, the state reasserts a non-contingent ethicality. As the representative of the historical evolution of the 'idea', it constitutes the realisation of the ethical life that begins in the family. Hegel's 'family' is the first 'ethical root of the state' – it contains an 'objective universality in a substantial unity' (ibid.: 154). Because universally emerging mind governs all levels, from the family through to larger levels of aggregation, the state, as the ultimate level of organisation is 'the end immanent within them' (ibid.: 161).

Inasmuch as Hegel's state effects a coincidence of private and public interests, his narrative, paradoxically, locates the state in two seemingly incompatible places. The state initiates what it ultimately consummates. It is 'not so much the result as the beginning' of the natural ethical life – 'It is within the state that the family is first developed into civil society, and it is the Idea of the state itself which disrupts itself into these two moments' (Hegel, 1945: 155).

What can we make of Hegel's story of the emergence of the state? At a minimum, it is a piece of fiction in which 'nature' plays a paradoxical role. First, nature is left behind – as the civil society substitutes contingency for the organic solidarity of the family – and then nature returns – as the state restores the ethical life that is dissipated in civil society. Hegel's resolution of the paradox is to substitute immanence for chronology. He locates the state both at the beginning – where it creates the conditions of possibility for the moral family – and at the end – where it embodies the enlargement of an ethical life begun within the family.

Hegel's family/state story fits within the genre that Etienne Balibar has called 'fictitious universalities' (1995: 56). Contending with earlier, religious constructions of personhood, Hegel's philosophical project was an attempt to replace a religious universality with a political one. But the stories are homologous. While religious and political modes of conceptual mastery differ in terms of what they regard as being 'essential to human personality', both aspire to a universal community of meaning that unites the status of each unit within a common understanding (Balibar, 1995: 58–9).

More specifically, the political universality, which Hegel saw as a common historical destiny for all peoples (although some, he thought, still resided in earlier temporal stages), was ultimately a historically inevitable world of state citizens, whose national allegiances would be enlarged versions of those that structure the natural (and, therefore, ethical) solidarity of the family.

While Hegel's fiction was aimed at substituting historical necessity for contingency, the analysis here has the reverse aim – to restore contingency. More specifically, I want to show that the domains of the private and the public are historically unstable practices of space, contingent upon a variety of disjunctive forces, and that the political discourse of 'interests' has unstable and disjunctive referents as well (although one, often suppressed, referent –

death – lends an important measure of stability). At a minimum, to understand the politics of public and private interests in 'our time', it is necessary to identify the ways in which contemporary technologies have re-inflected the boundaries of the private and public domains and, accordingly, have called into question the traditional discourses of public versus private interests.

Before turning to the present, however, I want to note that Hegel's discourse on the relationship between the family and state was wholly inapposite for treating the relationship both in his historical period, as well as since then. Jacques Donzelot's (1980) analysis of the production of the modern family, based on historical inquiry rather than moralistic fantasy, provides a challenge to Hegel's fictitious universality. Among other things, it treats the changing relationships between the 'private' interests of the family (which have become increasingly 'public') and the public interests shaped by the modern state.

Donzelot's investigation begins with the late seventeenth century, when the most significant impacts on the family were associated with changing structures of occupational recruitment. As work became increasingly supplied outside of extended family structures, families continued to regulate marriages but they did so with a different rationale. When work and domestic setting coincided, the marriage bond was aimed at preserving the family order as a working unit. However, by the nineteenth century, as work was increasingly supplied by extra-familial structures, the family became increasingly concerned with preparing children for marriages that would help furnish their offspring with the credentials necessary for fitting into orders outside the family.

At the same time, states were intervening to transform families. With the development of nationally regulated economies, they sought to regulate the way the family helped to produce children destined for a national work force and to control the effects on families of fluctuations in the economy. This, increasingly, involved the state in interventions in the health, education and fiscal conditions of family members.

Ultimately, as a result of changes in economic structures and the related development of a state-manipulated social order, 'a tactical collusion' developed between states and families.

> What troubled families was adulterine children, rebellious adolescents, women of ill-repute – everything that might be prejudicial to their honour, reputation, or standing. By contrast, what worried the state was the squandering of vital forces, the unused or useless individuals (Donzelot, 1980: 25).

The issue of the family emerges again in this analysis, in connection with a reading of Atom Egoyan's film, *The Sweet Hereafter* (1997), which focuses on an issue more vital than qualifying children for life outside the family – the concern with keeping them alive. At this juncture, however, I turn to a piece of fiction, a detective story, that, despite its imaginative inventions, is far more adequate to an appreciation of modernity as a shifting terrain of private and public spaces than a Hegelian, fictitious universality, in which public life consummates the natural morality of private life.

Gypsies and Repo Men

There are good reasons to turn to detective fiction as a vehicle for mapping modern space. Tom Gunning has summarised them well:

> The narrative form of the detective story, rather than serve simply as an exercise in puzzle solving, depends explicitly upon the modern experience of circulation. While circulation relies on an evolving process of rationalization of time and space, the very intricacy and speed of those routes of transfer and exchange create a counter-thrust in which stability and predictability can be threatened. The detective story maps out two positions in this dialectical drama of modernity: the criminal who preys upon the very complexity of the system of circulation; and the detective, whose intelligence, knowledge, and perspicacity allow him to discover the dark corners of the circulatory system, uncover crime, and restore order. (Gunning, 1995: 20)

Joe Gores's *32 Cadillacs* (1992) is a crime novel version of a historical episode: 'Once upon a time a band of Gypsies really did rip off thirty-two cars from a large Bay Area bank in a single day' (Gores, 1992: xi.). The story pits a detective agency, specialising in auto repossession, against a band of Gypsies who have 'ripped off' the Cadillacs. And, as Gunning suggests, the story maps San Francisco and other cities, treating spatio-temporal structures that define the modern city as an intricate and complexly normative 'system of circulation'. Moreover, and also in accord with Gunning's insights into the genre, it shows the way the criminal 'preys upon the very complexity of the system of circulation' and how 'the detective[s], whose intelligence, knowledge, and perspicacity allow him to discover the dark corners of the circulatory system, uncover crime, and restore order' (Gunning, 1995).

There are, however, special features of this crime story. The personae occupy unusual positions in the normative order of the modern city. Since the emergence of both modern law enforcement and criminality, crime investigators and a 'criminal element' have had an intimate relationship with structures of legality/illegality, as well as with each other. The same enforcement structures that produce a surveillance of criminality have created what Michel Foucault calls 'a delinquent milieu', a domain of 'fabricated delinquency' or 'controlled illegality' that produces the informants necessary to the function of policing (1977b: 277–9).

Ordinary private detectives lack the intimacy of police detectives with the system of legal norms but maintain it with the delinquent milieu. In this crime story, however, both the repo men and their targets, the Gypsies, operate largely outside of this structure of intimacy with the legal system and mostly outside of the domain of delinquency connected to policing (although the repo men do make use of one Gypsy informant). As a result, their encounters provide insights into the spaces and tempos of the city – both public and private – that are not afforded by following interactions between policing and criminal personae who function within more recognised and normatively ordered city spaces.

Michel de Certeau's concepts are appropriate for identifying what is peculiar to the characters in this tale. Because they do not control their spaces of operation, Gypsies and repo men cannot employ what de Certeau calls 'strategies', which involve

> the calculation (or manipulation) of power-relationships that becomes possible as soon as a subject with will and power (a business, an army, a city, a scientific institution) can be isolated. [A strategy] postulates a place that can be delimited as its own and serve as a base from which the relations of an exteriority composed of targets or threats (for example, customers, competitors, enemies, the country sur- rounding the city, objectives and objects of research) can be managed (1984: 35–6).

Instead, because they are 'others' – people without the institutionalised con- trol of space from which strategies can be deployed – Gypsies and repo men employ 'tactics' which require temporal more than spatial strategies. 'The space of the tactic is the space of the other; it must play on and with a terrain imposed on it and organized by the law of a foreign power' (de Certeau, 1984: 37). Because the field of this 'other' is more temporal than spatial:

> It takes advantage of opportunities, and depends on them, being with out any base where it could stockpile its winnings, build its position ... it must vigilantly make use of the cracks that particular conjunctions open in the surveillance of the proprietary powers. (de Certeau, 1984: 37)

Given their positions outside the spheres of the 'proprietary powers', the Gypsies and repo men in 32 Cadillacs employ a 'mobile infinity of tactics' (de Certeau, 1984: 41). At the same time, the novelistic genre, within which their encounter unfolds, provides not only a perspective on the circuits of movement and exchange within the city but also on the disjunctions between the idioms and sites of enunciation of the different types involved in the circulation and exchange. Each word, as M. M. Bakhtin has put it, 'tastes of the context and contexts in which it has lived its socially charged life' (1981: 293). And, more generally, as a genre the novel is distinguished, Bakhtin asserts, by its 'heteroglossia' – the plurality of contending voices. It is well suited to resisting the de-pluralising political discourses that reference fixed and universal models of 'private interests' and 'the public interest' (Bakhtin, 1981: 259–422).

Countering the de-pluralising tendencies of official discourses, the novel is ideationally centrifugal – it maps a world of differences, which pull away from the verbal-ideological centre of the social domain. As a result, the novel is stylistically suited to disrupt the political codes that deny difference and promote the fiction of a stable set of relations between public and private domains.

In the case of Gores's novel, the cast of characters adds to the genre's stylistically-induced centrifugal tendencies. The culture of Gypsies is disjunctive with the boundary practices of public versus private characterising their more mainstream US consociates. Gores is sensitive to the ways the Rom radically distinguish themselves from outsiders, the 'gadje'. They practise, among other things, a different relationship to consumption: 'Buying ... is a sucker's game, and no Rom, ever, believes he is a sucker'. For dealing with the straight world, the gadje world, the non-Gypsy (*sic*) motto is: Gidje gadje, zi lai ame Rom san – outsiders are outsiders, but we are the Rom.

This boundary practice articulates itself in various ways. Gypsies maintain a separation between how they actually live and what they reveal. For example, the extreme cleanliness they practise in their daily lives – women will not speak to men in the morning until they have washed their faces, and all loners and outsiders are regarded as unclean – is belied by the exteriors of the dwellings. And, in general, they avoid allowing what is seen or heard by outsiders to reveal what is practised among insiders. Indeed, they take pleasure (as well as profit) in the fabulous relationship they have with the outside world.

The Gypsy practices of the exoteric versus esoteric reveal much more than the peculiarities of their culture. Historically, their use of some technologies and their resistance to others provide insights into the way those technologies have altered the public domain. In *32 Cadillacs*, it is noted in passing, for example, that many of the Gypsies involved in the car scam do not read. Designated readers among the Gypsies are required to manage parts of the theft – just as, more generally, some Gypsies have felt it distasteful but necessary to adopt some gadje practices and/or have various kinds of intimacy with outsiders whom they regard as unclean (for example, the car scam in *32 Cadillacs* is enabled, in part, by the sexual seduction of gadje men and women by Gypsies).

To appreciate that Gypsy resistance to written language has been a survival strategy rather than a disability, it is necessary to understand the complicated spatial implications of writing technologies. On the one hand, the emergence of writing technologies has helped to produce a public sphere outside of the tutelage of former hegemonic institutions. Certainly, for example, the development of print in the fifteenth century was essential to the gains of a 'critical humanism' and, thus, to the production of a vernacular language, which was instrumental in aspects of democratisation that followed from the

Reformation (see Martin, 1994). Writing technologies helped, in short, to dissolve the hegemony of a vertical model of space, based on a strict boundary between the domains of the sacred and the profane. And, as Benedict Anderson (1994) has argued, they helped to displace that vertical world with a horizontal one – a nation-state geographic imaginary.

On the other hand, writing technologies in general, and in particular the written text as an extension of the self, became increasingly bound up with structures of proprietary control. Ever since the various struggles to establish copyright laws and install the author as a 'proprietor', writing technologies have significantly altered the boundaries of the public versus the private sphere. However, written documents have been enabling for some and disabling for others. In the form of property recordings, they constitute records that give proprietorial power a tangible warrant. In the form of stored dossiers, they have been part of the growing surveillance structures of state societies. Among other things, writing provides the normative codes through which modern space has been, in Deleuze and Guattari's terms, 'striated' – densely coded such that unauthorised movement can be tracked and contained. Because the state 'does not dissociate itself from a process of capture of flows of all kinds, populations, commodities or commerce, money or capital, etc.' (Deleuze and Guattari, 1987: 385–6), it has attempted vigorously to sedentarise Gypsies (for example, with anti-vagabond and anti-vagrancy laws), and writing has been one of the primary instruments of surveillance. As Foucault has noted in his analysis of the segmenting of space and the proliferation of technologies to fix identities and surveil them from centres of power, 'an uninterrupted work of writing links the centre and periphery in which power is exercised without division' (1997: 197).

Because the Gypsies' raison d'être has been, in part, the resistance to surveillance and sedentarisation, they have been resistant to writing. They have always operated outside of the state capture of space and, ironically, have found it easier to cross borders without passports and other written documents. Moreover, they have been generally resistant to written language. Their language, Romany, has no words for 'to write' or 'to read' (Fonseca, 1995: 11) and they regard reading as a strange and idle practice (ibid.: 53).

The disjuncture between the Gypsy and gadje cultures becomes apparent early in the novel. The repo men speak constantly of working on the 'Gypsy file', a dossier which they fix and expand in their pursuit. In contrast, insofar as Gypsies read, it is a matter of tactics – the exigencies of the moment. For example, in Gores's novel, while working a scam on a fortune-telling client, the Gypsies read the contents of his trash in order to create an impression that their intimacy with spiritual power is allowing them to know something about their client's destiny.

Because Gypsies are always moving, this kind of reading practice creates no paper trail – it is a tactic that articulates with the rest of their mobile practices, organised to live within the crevices and around the margins of the social order. Most significantly, the differential relationships of Gypsies and gadje to writing technologies reveal the ways in which writing has organised the contemporary spatial order – the domains of public versus private.

The central scam of the story, the ripping-off of the thirty-two Cadillacs, involves the tactical use of written documents. A Gypsy manages to dress in expensive clothes, book a high-priced hotel room and adopt a plausible credit history by stealing the identity papers from a wealthy person while he is visiting his vacation home. The timing of the scam is linked to a variety of temporalities – their victim's vacation practices, among others. The most challenging bit of timing of the scam involves opening several bank accounts and depositing and withdrawing the same $10,000 amount several times. These moves are predicated on a knowledge of the temporalities of banking practices. The Gypsies arrange the car purchases on a Friday so that the banks do not learn that the cheques are not backed by sufficient funds until they reopen on the following Monday.

Moreover, and most significantly for this analysis, the use of temporally oriented tactics and writing technologies by the Gypsies cannot be easily reciprocated by authorities, because the Gypsies' private spaces are not coded in official documents. Their relationship to the writing practices that organise the modern city are fugitive. For this reason, the repo men, who serve these authorities – in this case the banks that have been stung – must also function in the domain of the tactic, seizing the right moments. For example, they look for Gypsies at race tracks and at certain bars that they know to be familiar Gypsy haunts. And each 'score' involves precise timing – for example, stealing a car back from a Gypsy by bribing the garage man and using his uniform to pretend to be the one delivering the car from the garage to the front of the hotel, where the Gypsy has been staying under an alias.

The various venues of encounter between Gypsies and repo men help, ultimately, to map the circuits of the city and, at the same time, to map a social space that is a hybrid composite of the private and public. A certain bar and lounge, for example, is known by the repo men to be a Native American gathering place. Because one Gypsy they are tracking is known to use a false Native American identity to work a charity scam, they are able to find her stolen Cadillac parked there. Such spaces – bars, hotels, motels, stores and banks – linked by roads, elevators and telephones, constitute a structure of relationships between not so much clear separations of public and private spaces as between forces seeking to retain degrees of privacy and those attempting to impose a public mode of control.

The contingencies of these structures, the combinations of surveillance and haphazardness in the forms and timing of their connections, are precisely what determine the tactics of those who seek to profit from others. The various rigidities of the forms in the modern city produce 'free spaces' –

'The combination of formal requirements of a certain order ... permits all kinds of freedom or disorder within the interstices'. Thus the action in *32 Cadillacs* maps the interstices as well as the structures of the city and challenges any view of an orderly structuring of private and public domains.

But, to appreciate the disorder within the order of the modern city, it is necessary to recognise the historical emergence of yet another domain of technology that has reconfigured the interconnections of the public and private spheres – technologies of the visual associated with modern architecture. Walter Benjamin and Asja Lacis were among the first to theorise the 'porosity' of the private-public boundary that modern architecture had wrought: 'Just as the living room reappears on the street ... so the street migrates into the living room' (quoted in Buck-Morss, 1989: 26).

The ambiguity of the public-private boundary, which Benjamin and Lacis saw, has become increasingly an effect of the architectural forms of the modern city. A variety of technologies have enabled these forms, not the least of which are various forms of lighting and other media that enhance visibility. For example, the window, which is implicated in the visual porosity of structures, and television which, as a 'window on the world', introduces an even more radical 'confusion over inside and out' (Keenan, 1993: 130) and thus over the distinction between public and private.

However, technologies alone cannot alter structures of social interaction. Other forces have provided the context for the forces involved in the management of vision that structures contemporary orders of association. Not the least of these are the commercial forces shaping both class structures and the modern, bourgeois sphere of consumption. As Habermas noted in his investigation of historical changes in the public sphere, the pre-bourgeois, aristocratic order staged its station in public space with displays of insignia, dress and demeanour (1989: 8). Although it is certainly the case that the contemporary bourgeois public sphere involves display, much of that display is based on a technologically- and architecturally-aided display of commodities. Commercial concerns employ 'colour, glass and light' (Leach, 1993: 39–70) to attract a clientele that is driven less by an ascribed status to which appropriate insignia attest than by rules of normality with respect to body weight, clothing styles, investment practices and rules of sociability. And they are impelled by a social logic of distinction, which prescribes different practices for different age groups, genders, and social 'fractions' (Bourdieu, 1984).

While Gypsies operate largely outside of the pressures of both the dominant commercial structures and the related normalising judgements that help them function, the tactics enabled by modern zones of visibility are not lost on them. A bank scene in *32 Cadillacs*, in which a Gypsy is working his loan scam, effectively maps the way in which the architecture of the contemporary commercial bank reflects a set of shaping forces on and a set of relays between the zones of the public and private. In a key scene, a well-dressed Gypsy, Rudolph Marino, enters the main branch of 'California Citizens Bank at One Embarcadero (Now Open Nine to Five Every Weekday to Serve you Better)' and is able to see all his relevant opportunities:

> Since a man was handling New Accounts, Marino scanned the other bank officers behind the metal and Formica railing. He chose a pretty, early-40's, round faced woman with pouty lips. She wore floral perfume and pink-tinted glasses that magnified her eyes into a slightly surprised expression. She did not wear a wedding band. Her nameplate said HELEN WOODING (Gores, 1992: 34).

The bank, laden with signs and spaces organised to seduce a clientele and governed by a rigid temporal structure (fixed opening hours, consistent durations for check clearing), turns out to be an easy mark for one prepared to be the seducer rather than the seduced. Just as the temporal structure is spelled out, the subordinate-superordinate structure – and the personalities and life styles of the personnel – are available to direct vision. The points and moments of attack are wholly readable (even to one who eschews literacy).

As the Gypsy rip-off and the repo men counter-attack unfolds, the city's streets, highways, bars, hotels and motels, banks, and car dealerships are described in detail. What, on a casual reading, appears to be mere background becomes pertinent to a reading of the spaces of modernity when foregrounded. It becomes evident that the city's circuits of exchange function in a built social domain. The windows, elevators, automobiles, telephones, filing systems, open hotel lobbies and motel complexes are expressive of technological developments that have increasingly reconfigured the boundaries between public and private space.

Moreover, because the primary personae in the detective story make use of the increased porosity between the public and private domains and, most essentially, use the city's temporal rhythms to make the right moves in the right places at the right times, the moments and venues of their interactions reveal complexities of the public-private relationships that are fugitive in the more abstract genres of social or political theory.

Nevertheless, in some ways, the staging of the Gypsy/repo men encounter in this detective story conceals a profound and pervasive incompatibility between the commercial life of the city – the derivative, monetary interests to which individuals and groups are connected – and a deeper set of 'interests' that attach to what might best be termed the 'ethical life'. To treat this second domain of interests it is appropriate to summon Hegel once more, this time for a more appreciative hearing.

Although the later Hegel saw the state as a vehicle of history's ineluctable capacity to reconcile contradictions, an earlier Hegel was convinced of an irreconcilable conflict between the commercial and 'ethical life' (*Sittlichkeit*). He referred to the relationship between the two as 'tragic' because, from the point of view of the ethical life, the commercial life is both necessary and destructive (Hegel, 1962: 94–5). Because Hegel's observation provides a framing for the connection between the spatial practices of public-private and interests, we need to find a story and genre that is even more sensitive to the connection between spatiality and interests.

Atom Egoyan's film, *The Sweet Hereafter*, provides the appropriate vehicle. As a filmic story about a town's tragedy – many families have lost children in a school bus accident – it operates within the more pervasive, Hegelian tragedy because carriers of a primarily commercially-driven motivation invade the moral-communitarian space of the town. Moreover, the conjunctures and disjunctures in the film reveal the contingencies of interests. On the one hand, a deep, common interest in protecting children connects the characters – the people of the town and a personal injury lawyer – on different sides of an encounter central to the film. But, on the other hand, this encounter evokes disparate motivations. It pits a mutual support structure of grieving parents (part of the local *Sittlichkeit*) against a lawyer whose interest is in amplifying their anger and muting their grief – he wants to articulate their economic vulnerability and anger to produce a class action suit, whereas before they had struggled to maintain a community based on the bonds of grief-produced mutual sympathy.

Egoyan's *Sweet Hereafter*

The critical insights deriving from Atom Egoyan's treatment of Russell Banks's novel (1992) owe as much to his use of the film genre as they do to the storyline of the screenplay. There is, first of all, a productive relationship between the spatial practices involved in the story and the spatiality of film in general. The story begins when a lawyer, Mitchell Stephens, enters the town of Sam Dent. Whereas Stephens is first shown – with zooming and framing shots – in the confined space of his car, the town is presented continually with panning and tracking shots that explore the town's extension and boundaries. Sam Dent's surrounding mountains give it, at least physically, a definitive boundary and the camera leaves viewers with the impression that the life world enclosed by the mountains is more or less available to direct vision.

We learn early on, however, that the invading lawyer is a representative of shaping forces outside of the town. The story then proceeds in what Noel Burch has identified as two kinds of filmic space, 'that included within the frame and that outside the frame' (1973). A world of predatory commercial interests outside of the town has become cognisant of the town's tragedy. Mountains are no barrier to media and air routes and roads also make the town rapidly accessible. As a result, the various parents who have lost children cannot be left to grieve within the isolation of the community. The personal injury lawyers on their way in, seeking to profit from the town's tragedy, are attempting to turn an 'accident' into a form of responsible agency. They want to find 'deep pockets' belonging either to the town or the bus manufacturer.

Other forces outside the frame are also apparent in the filmic story. The Walkers, the first set of parents encountered by Stephens, run a failing motel that cannot compete with publicly owned motel chains on the same route that connects the town with various others. There is, therefore, a homology between the structure of the film and the situation of the town. They have the forces of political economy pressing at their frame and boundary respectively. The duality of filmic space is well suited, then, to represent the 'outside' as a set of commercial forces, an outside anonymous public (the aggregated shareholders in motel corporations who cannot be assembled to effect the management of corporations much less the life spaces on which they impact).

In addition to its treatment of space, however, the temporal structure of cinema contributes to its critical perspective. Egoyan's film thinks with time images as well as with its shot-produced spatiality. Although the camera is often trained on the lawyer, Mitchell Stephens, the implications the film generates are a function of the sequence of shots. As Gilles Deleuze points out, the 'time image' constitutes a way of reading events that is more critical than mere perception (1989: 24). As long as the camera merely followed action, the image of time was indirect, presented as a consequence of motion. The new 'camera consciousness' is no longer defined by the movements it is able to follow. Now, 'even when it is mobile, the camera is no longer content to follow the character's movement' (Deleuze, 1989: 23). The thinking articulated through a film, whose shots shift among a variety of scenes and alter their depth of focus, constitutes meaning not on the basis of the experiences of individual characters but on the basis of the way an ensemble of shots are connected. These practices of filmic composition resist the simple chronologies that were the basis of 'organic film narration', a storyline produced when the camera simply follows the action (ibid.: 127).

In contrast with organic film narration is 'crystalline film narration' which structures *The Sweet Hereafter*. It is a mode of filmic description that creates its objects. Chronological time – that which is imposed by following the actors – is displaced by 'non-chronological time' (ibid.: 129). Instead of composing movement images to treat the tensions explicitly acknowledged by Mitchell Stephens and the various persons with whom he interacts, movement is subordinated to temporality and the encounter becomes a critical event providing insights into 'our time'.

Certainly Banks's novel generates critical insight as well. But its insights, given the novelistic genre, are a function of the way it composes various different voices. Throughout Banks's *Sweet Hereafter*, there are shifts in voice, as different characters take over the narration. In Egoyan's version, narrative voice is displaced by the composition of camera shots. The absence of a narrator's voice is wholly appropriate to Egoyan's demonstration that the tensions evinced in encounters of difference are less a matter of the incommensurate forms of consciousness of the various characters than a matter of a difference of spatio-temporal 'habitus'. Egoyan shows a community whose 'horizon of experience' is, at least in part, spatially confined – it is bounded by its physical separation from other places.

In contrast, Mitchell Stephens's domain of experience is shown to be horizonless. When he is not in the town, he spends his time on his cell phone, in his car and on a plane. And even when he is in the town, he is partly outside of it – in one scene, for example, he excuses himself from a face-to-face conversation to answer a call on his cell phone from his daughter. Stephens's horizonless habitus is not a matter of idiosyncrasy. He reflects an aspect of modernity – the dissolution of space in favour of a temporal simultaneity – that has not yet dominated the town of Sam Dent.

As the quintessential modern person, Mitchell Stephens inhabits the life world as an information processing node. In the opening scenes, it is his cell phone that connects him to people, both an impersonal operator, whom he calls when he is stuck in a car wash and his daughter Zoë, who calls him frequently to ask for money to manage her drug habit. On the occasions when he must negotiate space – for example, hurrying from a house in Sam Dent to his car to fetch legal forms – his movements are the awkward ones of persons accustomed to having mechanical and informational prostheses to connect them with what is distant.

Stephens's uncomfortable management of space and face-to-face encounters is part of a pervasive aspect of modern life. He is a product of what Paul Virilio calls 'the urbanization of time'; his 'perceptual faculties' have been 'transferred one by one to machines' (1997: 10). He is part of a modernity whose most significant alterations are owed to a collapse of local time and space that began perhaps when the first time signal was sent around the world from the Eiffel Tower in 1913 (Kern, 1983: 14).

In sum, Mitchell Stephens's bodily gestures have seemingly atrophied through the prolonged use of informational equipment and motorised vehicles. Once unplugged or unseated, he has difficulty transacting in a world of spatial inhibitions and barriers to effortless motion or contact. For example, he resists interacting with his seat mate on a plane by resorting to his headset that connects him with the plane's entertainment programmes. Moreover, his lack of continuity in a spatial location has shattered the coherence of his personal experiences. When he learns that his seat mate is a childhood friend of his daughter Zoë, he is unable to recollect that the woman's father was once his business partner.

Only a switch in genres allows him to refocus on the continuity of his life world. When he abandons his headset and gets absorbed into a conversation with his daughter's friend, he tells a story about a traumatic episode in the life of his young family. He had to transport his infant daughter from a remote cabin to a hospital after she had been bitten by a scorpion to which she was allergic. As the film shows his frantic trip to a hospital in flashback, during which he had to be prepared to perform a tracheotomy, we see him staring intently at his daughter. If her reaction to the scorpion's poison caused her throat to close, he would have to become an amateur surgeon, based on a doctor's instructions over the phone. As it turns out, keeping his daughter alive has been Stephens's lifelong task ever since, although he no longer has her in sight – indeed, it is the primary 'interest' that he has in common with the parental couples of Sam Dent.

However, before exploring that common interest, it is important to note the most significant difference between Stephens's world and that of the community he invades for profit. Unlike Stephens, the residents of Sam Dent exist in a frontier between modern forces of simultaneity and the face-to-face world of spatially enclosed communities. They function in a sphere that has not been fully absorbed by modern, global corporations. In some cases, family space and work space coincide – for example, Stephens's first visit is to the Walker couple, who have lost a child in the school bus accident and live in a motel they own and manage. And the Ottos, who have also lost a child, live primarily off the crafts that Wanda Otto makes in their home.

Nevertheless, the wider world is impinging on Sam Dent. Paul Sarossy, the cinematographer, uses a wide screen format to connect this story of a small town to the larger world. And this format, which permits close-ups and the wider context in the same frame, allows Egoyan to achieve his plan of fitting the terrain of the face ... in the context of the greater geography. A composition of perceptions images within a spatially-oriented filmic enunciation shows how personality is subordinated to a geographically situated habitus.

However, the life space of the small town is under a technological assault that precedes Mitchell Stephens. Wendell Walker, the motel owner, is first encountered when he is summoned from in front of his television set to converse with Stephens. He is a hockey fan and it becomes evident that his sports fanaticism has him connected to a global mediascape. It is doubtless not incidental, moreover, that Walker, a virtual recluse, whose sociality is primarily a function of his distant connection with other television viewers, utters disparaging remarks about the other grieving parents that are a function of his prejudices rather than direct experience. When, for example, he expresses an inference that the Ottos are drug users, his wife Risa retorts, 'you don't know that'.

The town's mountain horizon does not, therefore, constitute the entire horizon of experience. Competing with the 'topical' place is the 'teletopical' place (Virilio, 1997: 26). This is a more general tendency of modernity, for, as Virilio puts it, 'the skyline that once limited the perspective of our movements is today joined by the square horizon of the TV set' (ibid.: 90), with the result that 'contemporaneity' is privileged over local citizenship as the 'live broadcast' dominates 'the geopolitical reality' (ibid.: 47) of much of the town (although the town's annual fair is an instance of reaffirmation of locality).

Although some couples in Sam Dent succumb to Mitchell Stephens's strategy of amplifying anger (and ignoring the mutual support structure) to collect grievances, some of the parents and one survivor of the accident, Nicole, manage to resist. That Dolores Driscoll, the school bus driver, heeds her husband Abbott's injunction to rely on peers rather than legalities is doubtless a function of her connection with everyone – she saw all the children and their parents almost daily when she did her pickups and drop-offs.

In addition, the parent most resistant to the class action suit is Billy Ansell, the widower who followed the school bus daily in his truck, seemingly reluctant to let his children out of sight. It is ultimately his resistance to the suit, expressed to Nicole's parent within her hearing, that makes Nicole resolve to testify in a way that destroys Stephens's litigation (she lies and claims that she saw the speedometer reading 70 mph before the accident).

Indeed, the key encounter of the film is between Stephens and Ansell. When Ansell finds Stephens examining the damaged bus in the yard of his garage, he tries to dissuade him from pursuing the suit and threatens to assault him. In response, Stephens evokes a shared interest – he tells Ansell that he is also a grieving parent. His daughter is a drug addict. Ansell asks why he is telling him this but doubtless he knows that it is a gesture designed to unite their concerns. In any case, Stephens is partially correct. He and the parents of the town have had a common interest – both have striven, largely unsuccessfully, to keep their children alive (Stephens learns near the end of the film that his daughter is HIV positive).

Despite their differences, then, the one who is connected to his child by phone and the other who tried not to let his children out of sight, they have had a common interest. They are both trying to deal with the presence of death in life. Moreover, both have been defeated by unmanageable contingencies. Like the rest of the bereaved parents, both have struggled with modernity's primary parental ambivalence, holding on to their children's affectionate dependence while, at the same time, qualifying them to survive outside the home.

The ambivalence is most evident in the case of Nicole, whose father had tried to foster her singing career but, at the same time, had drawn her into an incestuous sexual relationship. She is destined to remain at home because she is left paralysed by the bus accident. Nevertheless, she is given a technology that will provide her with a virtual escape. Mitchell Stephens, the man who lives primarily as a global information node, has given her a computer as a gift.

Nicole's situation, along with a number of other examples of troubled families and unhappy inter-familial encounters canvassed during the filmic montage of the story, makes it clear that an enclosed horizon of experience is not an unmitigated advantage for producing a felicitous connection between private and public interests. Technologies, which re-inflect the distribution of spaces, operate along with other contingencies, to disturb attempts at naturalising and moralising modes of social organisation.

Conclusion: ambiguated spheres and the fate of the ethical life

> Death is the sanction of everything that the storyteller can tell. He has borrowed his authority from death. (Benjamin, 1968: 94)

There is a genre of expression embedded in Egoyan's *The Sweet Hereafter*, story telling, which breaks through the enclosed horizon of experience of the people of Sam Dent and opens up the horizonless world of immediacy of Mitchell Stephens. In particular, two stories told in the film, one read by Nicole and one told by Stephens are the kind of 'heterotopias' (spaces of other-ness) to which Foucault refers when he notes that some acts of imagination 'create a space of illusion that exposes every real space ... as still more illusory' (1986: 26).

In Nicole's case, her reading of 'The Pied Piper of Hamelin' to Billy Ansell's children (a scene repeated throughout the film with flashbacks) has special resonance with her situation. Just as the children in the story (with the exception of the crippled one left behind) are liberated to a sweet hereafter, outside of the mean-spiritedness of the town, Nicole is left behind, a cripple now confined to an incestuous household. But her acts of imagination, evinced at first in her reading of the story, have liberated her from the enclosed horizon of experience of both her home and Sam Dent. And her ultimate act of imagination, an invention of a speeding bus, saves the children of the town, allowing them to remain in the 'sweet hereafter', rather than being brought back for an unseemly litigious encounter. Her participation in spaces of illusion (stories) takes her outside of the stifling privacy of her home, as well as outside of legalities that would draw the children into a space of informational immediacy and out of the special place within which they reside in the town people's memories.

Nicole's reading of the Pied Piper story turns out to be allegorical – among other things it fulfils the vocation of the storyteller to which Benjamin refers. Storytelling allows death a presence. It is the genre of imagination that recognises the pervasive presence of death in life. Temporally, death is at once contingent and non-contingent. Its ultimate presence is inevitable but the when of its appearance is a matter of uncontrollable contingencies. For Benjamin, displacement of the death-presencing craft of the storyteller by informational genres constitutes a degradation of experience.

Mitchell Stephens's existence in the world of information is intimately tied to his attempt to degrade the experience of death of the people of Sam Dent. Virilio's distinction between the roles of information and memory captures very well Stephens's disposition throughout most of the film. Virilio notes – in a remark that locates Stephens in dramatic contrast with the people of Sam Dent, who enjoy a visible connection with their horizon of experience – that, with remote control and long distance 'telepresence', we approach a 'transparent horizon' and become a society with 'no extension and no duration' (1997: 25), only an intense and immediate presence.

Technologies have, in effect, confiscated Mitchell Stephens's depth of field (an insight that is captured cinematically throughout Egoyan's film in which perception shots from Stephens's vantage point rarely achieve a long focus). He lives in a world of instantaneous information or, what Virilio calls, 'immediate memory' (ibid.: 26). It is, therefore, not surprising that, at the outset of his conversation with his daughter's childhood friend on the plane, he cannot recall her name or even the name of her father, who was his business partner.

Stephens's practice of an immediate instead of a durational memory provides the most significant contrast with the bereaved people of Sam Dent. The bus driver, Dolores Driscoll, for example, keeps the dead children in her memory with pictures of them on the wall of her living room and struggles to keep them alive with her grammar. In her conversation with Stephens her choice of tenses wavers between the past and present when she refers to the children individually.

But, again, the strongest contrast is between Mitchell Stephens and Billy Ansell. In a conversation with his paramour, Risa Walker, Ansell speaks about an important episode of duration, 'the pleasure of the interval' (Virilio, 1997: 55) that he has enjoyed while waiting (sometimes in vain) for her to join him for their liaisons in a motel room. The period of waiting had created a space for him to recall his past life, to summon in memory how life had been when before his wife had died. Significantly, motel rooms are neither distinctly private nor public. Foucault includes them among his heterotopias (1986: 27) – they are spaces of respite, allowing for contemplation outside of life's more familiar, temporally restricted zones of interaction. Finally, however, Mitchell Stephens's experience of duration/memory turns out not to be a lost cause. As he tells the story of his frantic trip with his daughter to a hospital, he is extracted from the world of information and absorbed into memory. He has abandoned his headset and has used the duration of his flight to tell a story whose details are aided by camera flashbacks. The filmic montage provides a reinforcement of the time images in the story, as Stephens's predatory commercial aims seem to be temporarily suspended while he tells the personal story of a near-tragedy. Like the assemblage of camera shots from different periods of his life, telling the story locates him in a duration that reminds us what he and the people of Sam Dent have as an ultimate common interest – participating in life and providing each other with solace, in the recognition that everyone's life is ultimately intimate with death.

Bibliography

Adorno, T. and M. Horkheimer (1985), *Dialectic of Enlightenment*, London: Verso.

Agamben, G. (1993), *Infancy and History: Essays on the Destruction of Experience*, London: Verso.

Agamben, G. (1998), *Homo Sacer*, London: Meridian.

Aglietta, M. (1998), 'Capitalism at the Turn of the Century: Regulation Theory and the Challenge of Social Change', *New Left Review*, No. 232, Nov./Dec. 41–90.

Algazy, J. (1989) *L'Extrême-Droite en France de 1965 à 1984*, Paris: L'Harmattan.

Althusser, L. (1971), *Lenin and Philosophy and other essays*, London: New Left Books.

Althusser, L. (1984), *Essays on Ideology*, trans. Ben Brewster, London: Verso.

Althusser, L. (1990), *Reading Capital*, trans. Ben Brewster, London: Verso.

Altier, J.-P. (1999), 'FN-MN: Premier test public jeudi à Paris pour Bruno Mégret', *Yahoo-Actualités*, 17 February.

Amin, A. and J. Hausner (eds) (1997), *Beyond Market and Hierarchy: Interactive Governance and Social Complexity*, Cheltenham: Edward Elgar.

Anderson, B. (1991), *Imagined Communities*, (2nd edn) London: Verso.

Anderson, B. (1994), *Imagined Communities*, London: Verso.

Ashley, R. K. (1988), 'Untying the Sovereign State: A Double Reading of the Anarchy Problematique', *Millennium*, 17: 2, 227–62.

Ayer, A. J. (1971), *Language, Truth and Logic*, Harmondsworth: Penguin.

Ayoob, Mohammed (1995), *The Third World Security Predicament: State Making, Regional Conflict and the International System*, Boulder, CO: Lynne Rienner.

Bacqué, R. et al., 'Les dix jours qui ont déchiré la droite', *Le Monde*, 26 March 1998.

Bakhtin, M. M. (1981), 'Discourse and the Novel', in M. Holquist, (ed.), *The Dialogic Imagination*, Austin: University of Texas Press, pp. 259–422.

Balibar, E. (1991), 'Citizen Subject', in Eduardo Cadava et al. (eds), *Who Comes After The Subject?*, London and New York: Routledge, pp. 33–57.

Balibar, E. (1994), 'Subjection and Subjectivation', in Joan Copjec (ed.), *Supposing the Subject*, London: Verso, 1–15.

Balibar, E. (1995), 'Ambiguous Universality', *Differences*, 7, 48–74.

Banks, R. (1992), *The Sweet Hereafter*, New York: HarperCollins.

Barry, A., et al. (eds) (1996), *Foucault and Political Reason: Liberalism, neo-liberalism and rationalities of government*, London: UCL Press.

Bartelson, J. (1995), *A Genealogy of Sovereignty*, Cambridge: Cambridge University Press.

Bastow, S. (1997), 'Front national economic policy: from neo-liberalism to protectionism?', *Modern and Contemporary France*, 5: 1, 61–72.

Bastow, S. (1998), 'The radicalisation of Front National discourse: a politics of the "third way"?', *Patterns of Prejudice*, 32: 3.

Bastow, S. (2000), 'The Mouvement National Républicain: Moderate Right-wing Party or a Party of the Extreme Right', *Patterns of Prejudice*, April 2000.

Bauman, Z. (1989), 'Modernity and Ambivalence', *Theory, Culture and Society*, 7: 3, 141–169.

Bauman, Z. (1992), *Intimations of Postmodernity*, London: Routledge.

Baumgartner, F. and B. Jones (1993), *Agendas and Instability in American Politics*, Chicago: University of Chicago Press.

Beck, U. (1992), *Risk Society: Towards a New Modernity*, London: Sage.

Bell, D. (1965), *The End of Ideology*, Basingstoke: Macmillan.

Benjamin, W. (1968), 'The Storyteller', in H. Zohn (trans.), *Illuminations*, New York: Schocken, pp. 83–109.

Benveniste, E. (1971), *Problems in General Linguistics*, Coral Gable: University of Miami Press.

Bertramsen, R. B., J. P. F. Thomsen, J. Torfing (1991), *State, Economy and Society*, London: Unwin Hyman.

Besset, J.-P., 'Quand Bruno Mégret part la recherche laborieuse des vrais gens', *Le Monde*, 13 February 1999.

Betz, H-G. (1994), *Radical Right-Wing Populism in Western Europe*, London: St Martin's Press.

Bevir, M. and R. Rhodes (1999), 'Studying British government: reconstructing the research agenda', *British Journal of Politics and International Relations*, 1: 2, 215–39.

Biersteker, T. J. and C. Weber (eds) (1996), *State Sovereignty as Social Construct*, Cambridge, Cambridge University Press.

Birenbaum, G. (1992), *Le Front National en Politique*, Paris: Editions Balland.

Bloom, William (1990), *Personal Identity, National Identity and International Relations*, Cambridge: Cambridge University Press.

Blyth, M. M. (1997), '"Any More Bright Ideas?" The Ideational Turn of Comparative Political Economy', *Comparative Politics*, 29: 2, 229–50.

Booth, Ken (1991), 'Security and emancipation', *Review of International Studies*, 17, 313–27.

Booth, Ken (1995), 'Human wrongs and international relations', *International Affairs*, 71, 103–26.

Bourdieu, P. (1984), *Distinction: A Social Critique of the Judgment of Taste*, Cambridge, MA: Harvard University Press.

Boyer, R. (1997), 'French Statism at the Crossroads', in Crouch, C. and W. Streeck (eds), *The Political Economy of Modern Capitalism: Mapping Convergence and Diversity*, London: Sage.

Bréchon, P. and S. Mitra (1992), 'The National Front in France: the Emergence of an Extreme-Right Protest Movement', *Comparative Politics*, 4.

Brockman, J. (ed.) (1995), *The Third Culture: Beyond the scientic revolution*, New York: Simon and Schuster.

Brunkhorst, H. (1999), *Adorno and Critical Theory*, Cardiff: University of Wales Press.

Buchanan, D. and R. Badham (1999), *Power, Politics and Organizational Change: Winning The Turf Game*, London: Sage.

Buck-Morss, S. (1989), *The Dialectics of Seeing*, Cambridge, MA: MIT Press.

Burch, N. (1973), *Theory of Film Practice*, New York: Praeger.

Burchell, G. et al. (eds) (1991), *The Foucault Effect: Studies in Governmentality*, London: Harvester Wheatsheaf.

Butler, J. (1997), *The Psychic Life of Power: Theories in Subjection*, Stanford: Stanford University Press.

Butler, J. (1999), *Subjects of Desire*, New York: Columbia University Press.

Buzan, Barry (1991), *People, States and Fear: An Agenda for International Security Studies*, London: Harvester Wheatsheaf.

Buzan, Barry, Ole Waever and Jaap de Wilde (1998), *Security: A New Framework for Analysis*, Boulder, CO: Lynne Rienner.

Buzzi, P. (1991), 'Le Front national entre national-populisme et extrémisme de droite', *Regards sur l'actualité*, 169.

Byrne, D. (1998), *Complexity Theory and the Social Sciences*, London: Routledge.

Cadava, Eduardo, et al. (eds) (1991), *Who Comes After the Subject?*, London: Routledge.

Campbell, David (1994), 'The deterritorialization of responsibility: Levinas, Derrida, and ethics after the end of philosophy', *Alternatives*, 19, 455–84.

Campbell, David and Michael Shapiro (1999), 'Introduction: From Ethical Theory to the Ethical Relation', in Campbell and Shapiro (eds), *Moral Spaces: Rethinking Ethics and World Politics*, Minneapolis: Minnesota University Press, pp. vii–xx.

Camus, J.-Y. (1985), 'Les familles de l'extrême-droite', *Projet*, 193, 29–38.

Camus, J.-Y. (1996), *Le Front National*, Paris: Editions Olivier Laurens.

Caruth, Cathy (1995), *Trauma: Explorations in Memory*, Baltimore: Johns Hopkins University Press.

Caruth, Cathy (1996), *Unclaimed Experience: Trauma, Narrative and History*, Baltimore: Johns Hopkins University Press.

Caruth, Cathy (1999), presentation at *Testimonial Culture and Feminist Agendas*, University of Lancaster.

Cavell, S (1995), 'What did Derrida Want of Austin?' in Cavell, S. *Philosophical Passages: Wittgenstein, Emerson, Austin and Derrida*, Oxford: Blackwell.

Cefkin, M. (1998), 'Toward A Higher Order Merger: A Middle Manager's Story', in G. Marcus (ed.), *Corporate Futures: The Diffusion of the Culturally Sensitive Corporate Form*, Chicago: University of Chicago Press, pp. 89–112.

Chatterjee, P. (1990), 'A Response to Taylor's Modes of Civil Society', *Public Culture*, 3, 119–132.

Chebel d'Appollonia, A. (1990), *L'extrême-droite en France*, Paris: Editions Complexe.

Chia, R. (1998), 'From Complexity Science to Complex Thinking: Organization as Simple Location', *Organisation*, 5: 3, 341–69.

Chombeau, C. (1996a), 'M. Le Pen: "Oui, je crois à l'inégalite des races"', *Le Monde*, 1–2 September.

Chombeau, C. (1996b), 'M. Le Pen récidive sur "l'inegalité des races"', Le Monde, 11 September.

Chombeau, C. (1996c), 'Le syndicalisme officiel n'est plus légitime', Le Monde, 24 October.

Chombeau, C. (1996d), 'Plusieurs groupuscules d'extrême droite se rapprochent du Front national', Le Monde, 12 November.

Chombeau, C. (1997a), 'Une victoire locale qui renforce le délégué général du FN', Le Monde, 11 February, p. 6.

Chombeau, C. (1997b), 'Une forte délégation d'invités des extrêmes droites européennes', Le Monde, 29 March, p. 6.

Chombeau, C. (1997c), 'Un ancien dirigeant OAS parmi les candidats du FN', Le Monde, 30 April.

Chombeau, C. (1998a), 'La nébuleuse Mégret', Le Monde, 28 April, p. 14.

Chombeau, C. (1998b), 'Le Front national est menacé d'implosion', Le Monde, 9 December.

Chombeau, C. (1999a), 'Les mégrétistes sont majoritaires dans le Front national', Le Monde, 12 January.

Chombeau, C. (1999b), 'Le Front national de Bruno Mégret préconise une politique de sécurité ultra-répressive', Le Monde, 20 February.

Chombeau, C. (1999c), 'Les querelles d'influence recommencent parmi les dirigeants du Front national', Le Monde, 1 September.

Chombeau, C. (1999d), 'Au FN, Samuel Maréchal quitte la direction de la communication', Le Monde, 29 October.

Chombeau, C. (1999e), 'Le Mouvement national se divise sur le nom et la stratégie du parti', Le Monde, 2 October.

Chombeau, C. (1999f), 'Etats d'âme et défections dans les rangs du Mouvement national de M. Mégret', Le Monde, 6 November.

Chombeau, C. (2000), 'L'extrême droite est en plein marasme un an après la scission de M. Mégret', Le Monde, 4 January.

Cilliers, P. (1998), Complexity and Postmodernism: Understanding Complex Systems, London: Routledge.

Clarke, J. and J. Newman (1997), The Managerial State, London: Sage.

Clements, L. J. (1994), European Human Rights: Taking A Case Under The Convention, London: Sweet & Maxwell.

Cohen, A. P. (1985), The Symbolic Construction of Community, London: Routledge.

Coleman, W. (1998), 'From protected development to market liberalism: paradigm change in agriculture', Journal of European Public Policy, 5: 4, 632–51.

Cooke, M. (1999), 'Habermas, Feminism and Autonomy', in Peter Dews (ed.), Habermas: A Critical Reader, Oxford: Blackwell.

Coole, D. (1999), Negativity and Politics, London: Routledge.

Copjec, J. (1994), Read My Desire: Lacan Against the Historicists, Cambridge, MA: MIT Press.

Cornell, D. et al. (eds) (1992), Deconstruction and the Possibility of Justice, New York and London: Routledge.

Coward, R. and J. Ellis (1977), Language and Materialism, London: Routledge and Kegan Paul.

Crick, B. (1993), *In Defence of Politics*, London: Penguin.

Critchley, S. (1992), *The Ethics of Deconstruction: Derrida and Levinas*, Oxford: Blackwell.

Critchley, S. (1996), 'Ethics? Subject as trauma/philosophy as melancholy', in *Literature and Ethics*, Conference held in Aberystwyth: July.

Critchley, S. (1997), *Very Little … Almost Nothing: Death, Philosophy, Literature*, London: Routledge.

Critchley, S. (1999), *Ethics, Politics, Subjectivity*, London: Verso.

Critchley, S. and P. Dews (eds) (1996), *Deconstructive Subjectivities*, Albany: State University of New York Press.

Culler, J. (1983), *On Deconstruction: Theory and Criticism after Structuralism*, London: Routledge.

Culler, J. (1985), *Saussure*, London: Fontana.

Daly, G. (1991), 'The Discursive Construction of Economic Space', *Economy and Society*, 20: 1, pp. 79–102.

Daly, G. (1994), 'Post-metaphysical Culture and Politics: Richard Rorty and Laclau and Mouffe', *Economy and Society*, 23: 2, pp. 173–200.

de Certeau, M. (1984), *The Practice of Everyday Life*, Berkeley: California Press.

DeLanda, M. (1991), *War in the Age of Intelligent Machines*, New York: Zone Books.

Deleuze, G. (1988), *Michel Foucault*, London: Athlone Press.

Deleuze, G. (1989), *Cinema 2*, London: Athlone.

Deleuze, G. (1991), *Bergsonism*, New York: Zone Books.

Deleuze, G. (1993), *The Fold, Leibniz And The Baroque*, London: Athlone Press.

Deleuze, G. (1995), *Negotiations: 1972–1990*, New York: Columbia University Press.

Deleuze, G. and F. Guattari (1986), *Kafka: Toward A Minor Literature*, Minneapolis: University of Minnesota Press.

Deleuze, G. and F. Guattari (1984), *Anti-Oedipus: Capitalism and Schizophrenia*, London: Athlone.

Deleuze, G. and F. Guattari (1988), *A Thousand Plateaus: Capitalism And Schizophrenia*, London: Athlone Press.

Deleuze, G. and F. Guattari (1994), *What Is Philosophy?*, London: Verso.

Deleuze, G. and C. Parnet (1987), *Dialogues*, London: Athlone Press.

Dely, R. (1998), 'Les coulisses du complot', *Libération*, 10 December.

Department of the Environment, Transport and the Regions (1999), *Guidance on Local Housing Strategies*, www.housing.detr.gov.uk.

Department of Health (1998a), *Modernising Social Services: Promoting Independence, Improving Protection, Raising Standards*, London: HMSO.

Department of Health (1998b), *Meeting the Childcare Challenge*, London: HMSO.

Department of Health (1999a), *Saving Lives: Our Healthier Nation*, London: HMSO.

Der Derian, J. and M. J. Shapiro (eds) (1989), *International/Intertextual Relations: Postmodern Readings of World Politics*, Lexington, MA: D.C. Heath.

Derrida, J. (1974), *Of Grammatology*, Baltimore: Johns Hopkins University Press.

Derrida, J. (1982), *Margins of Philosophy*, London: Harvester Wheatsheaf.

Derrida, J. (1987), *Positions*, London: Athlone Press.

Derrida, J. (1987), *The Post Card: From Socrates to Freud and Beyond*, Chicago: University of Chicago Press.

Derrida, J. (1988), *Limited Inc.*, Evanston, Illinois: Northwestern University Press.

Derrida, J. (1991), 'Eating Well, or the Calculation of the Subject: An Interview with Jacques Derrida', in Cadava, E., P. Connor and J.-L. Nancy (eds), *Who Comes After the Subject*, London and New York: Routledge.

Derrida, J. (1992a), 'Force of Law: The "Mystical Foundation of Authority"', in Carlson, David Gray, Drucilla Cornell and Michel Rosenfeld (eds), *Deconstruction and the Possibility of Justice*, New York: Routledge, pp. 3–67.

Derrida, J. (1992b), *The Other Heading: Reflections on Today's Europe*, Bloomington, IN: Indiana University Press.

Derrida, J. (1994), *Spectres of Marx*, New York: Routledge.

Derrida, J. (1997), *Politics of Friendship*, London: Verso.

Descartes, R. (1968), *Discourse on Method and Other Writings*, Harmondsworth: Penguin.

Descombes, V. (1980), *Modern French Philosophy*, trans. J. M. Harding and L. Scott-Fox, Cambridge, MA: Cambridge University Press.

Devenney, M. (2001), *Ethics and Politics in Post-Marxist Theory*, London, Routledge.

Dillon, Michael (1996), *Politics of Security*, London: Routledge.

Donzelot, J. (1980), *The Policing of Families*, London: Hutchinson.

Dudley, G. (1999), 'British Steel and Government Since Privatisation: Policy "Framing" and the Transformation of Policy Networks', *Public Administration*, 77: 1.

Dudley, G. and J. Richardson (1999), 'Competing advocacy coalitions and the process of "frame reflection": a longitudinal analysis of EU steel policy', *Journal of European Public Policy*, 6: 2, 225–48.

Dunn, J. (ed.) (1994), 'Contemporary Crisis of the Nation State?', *Political Studies*, Special Issue, vol. 42, 51–71.

Dunsire, A. (1996), 'Tipping the Balance: Autopoiesis and Governance', *Administration and Society*, 28: 3, 299–334.

Durkheim, E. (1933), *The Division of Labour in Society*, New York: The Free Press.

Durkheim, E. (1976), *The Elementary Forms of the Religious Life*, London: George Allen and Unwin.

Durkheim, E. (1987), *Selected Writings*, Anthony Giddens (ed.), Cambridge: Cambridge University Press.

Duval, R.-L. (1996), 'Le pouvoir face à l'explosion sociale', *National-Hebdo*, 3–9 October.

Dyrberg, T. B. (1997), *The Circular Structure of Power: Politics, Identity, Community*, London: Verso.

Eatwell, R. (1995), *Fascism: A History*, London: Chatto & Windus.

Eccleshall, Robert (1990), *English Conservatism since the Restoration: an introduction and anthology*, London: Unwin Hyman.

Edkins, Jenny (1996), 'Legality with a vengeance: Famines and humanitarian intervention in "complex emergencies"', *Millennium*, 25, pp. 547–75.

Edkins, Jenny (1999), *Poststructuralism and International Relations: Bringing the Political Back In*, Boulder, CO: Lynne Rienner.

Edkins, Jenny and Véronique Pin-Fat (1999), 'The Subject of the Political', in Jenny Edkins, Nalini Persram and Véronique Pin-Fat (eds), *Sovereignty and Subjectivity*, Boulder, CO: Lynne Rienner.

Esposito, E. (1991), 'Paradoxien als Unterscheidungen von Unterscheidungen', in Gumbrecht, U. H. and K. L. Pfeiffer (eds), *Paradoxien, Dissonanzen, Zusammenbruche: Situationen offener Epistemologie*, Frankfurt: Suhrkamp Verlag.

Eve, R. A., S. Horsfall and M. E. Lee (1997), *Chaos, Complexity and Sociology: Myths, Models, and Theories*, London: Sage.

Fish, S. (1994), *There's No Such thing as Free Speech and it's a Good Thing Too*, Oxford: Oxford University Press.

Fitzpatrick, P. (1991), *Dangerous Supplements: Resistance and Renewal in Jurisprudence*, London: Pluto.

Fitzpatrick, P. and A. Hunt (eds) (1987), *Critical Legal Studies*, New York and London: Basil Blackwell.

Fitzpatrick, T. (1996), 'Postmodernism, Welfare and Radical Politics', *Journal of Social Policy*, 25: 3, 303–20.

Fonseca, I. (1995), *Bury Me Standing*, New York: Vintage.

Foucault, M. (1972), *The Archaeology of Knowledge*, London: Tavistock.

Foucault, M. (1974), *The Order of Things: An Archaeology of the Human Sciences*, London: Routledge.

Foucault, M. (1977a), 'A Preface To Transgression', in Bouchard, D. (ed.), *Language, Counter-Memory, Practice: Selected Essays And Interviews By Michel Foucault*, New York: Cornell University Press.

Foucault, M. (1977b), *Discipline and Punish: The Birth of the Prison*, Harmondsworth: Penguin.

Foucault, M. (1980), 'Truth and Power', in C. Gordon (ed.), *Power/Knowledge: Selected Interviews and Other Writings 1972–1977*, London: Harvester Wheatsheaf.

Foucault, M. (1981), *The History of Sexuality: An Introduction*, Harmondsworth: Penguin.

Foucault, M. (1982), 'The Subject and Power', in H. C. Dreyfus and P. Rabinow, *Beyond Structuralism and Hermeneutics*, Brighton: Harvester Wheatsheaf.

Foucault, M. (1986), 'Of Other Spaces', *Diacritics*, Vol. 16, pp. 22–7.

Foucault, M. (1991), 'Governmentality', in G. Burchell, C. Gordon and P. Miller (eds), *The Foucault Effect: Studies in Governmentality*, London: Harvester Wheatsheaf.

Front National (1985), *Militer au Front*, Paris: Editions Nationales.

Front National (1990), *300 Mesures*, Paris: Editions Nationales.

Fukuyama, F. (1992), *The End of History and the Last Man*, Harmondsworth: Penguin.

Fysh P. and J. Wolfreys (1992), 'Le Pen, the National Front and the Extreme Right in France', *Parliamentary Affairs*, 45, 309–26.

Gamble, Andrew (1988), *The Free Economy and the Strong State: The Politics of Thatcherism*, London: Macmillan.

Gane, M. and T. Johnson (eds) (1993), *Foucault's New Domains*, London: Routledge.

Gasché, R. (1986), *The Tain of the Mirror: Derrida and the Philosophy of Reflection*, Cambridge, MA: Harvard University Press.

Gell-Mann, M. (1994), *The Quark and the Jaguar: Adventures in the Simple and the Complex*, London: Abacus.

Geras, Norman (1990), *Discourses of Extremity: Radical Ethics and Post-Marxist Extravagances*, London: Verso.

Giddens, A. (1998), *The Third Way: The Renewal of Social Democracy*, Cambridge: Polity Press.

Giddens, A. (2000), *The Third Way and its Critics*, Cambridge: Polity Press.

Gleick, J. (1987), *Chaos: Making a New Science*, Harmondsworth: Penguin.

Goertzel, B. (1994), *Chaotic Logic: Language, Thought, and Reality from the Perspective of Complex Systems Science*, London: Plenum Press.

Goldhill, S. (1986), *Reading Greek Tragedy*, Cambridge: Cambridge University Press.

Goldhill, S. (1987), 'The Great Dionysia and Civic Ideology', *Journal of Hellenic Studies*, 107, pp. 58–76.

Goodrich, P. (1986), *Reading the Law: A Critical Introduction to Legal Method and Techniques*, Oxford: Blackwell.

Gordon, C. (1991), 'Governmental rationality: an introduction', in G. Burchell et al. (eds), *The Foucault Effect: Studies in Governmentality*, London: Harvester Wheatsheaf.

Gores, J. (1992), *32 Cadillacs*, New York: Time Warner.

Goux, J. J. (1997), 'Values and Speculations: The Stock Exchange Paradigm', *Cultural Values*, 1: 2, pp. 22–40.

Gramsci, A. (1976), *Selections from the Prison Notebooks*, London: Lawrence and Wishart.

Griffin, R. (1991), *The Nature of Fascism*, London: Pinter.

Griggs, S. and D. Howarth (1998), '"Vegans and Volvos": Problematising and Explaining the Campaign Against Manchester Airport's Second Runway', *Essex Papers in Politics and Government*, No. 131, Colchester: University of Essex.

Grosz, P. (2000), 'France: Further Fascist Fragmentation', *Searchlight*, February.

Gunning, T. (1995), 'Tracing the Individual Body,' in L. Charney and Vanessa R. Schwartz (eds), *Cinema and the Invention of Modern Life*, Berkeley: University of California Press, pp. 15–45.

Haas, P. (1992), 'Introduction: Epistemic Communities and International Policy Co-ordination', *International Organisation*, 46: 1, pp. 1–36.

Habermas, J. (1987), *The Philosophical Discourse of Modernity*, Cambridge, MA: MIT Press.

Habermas, J. (1989), *The Structural Transformation of the Public Sphere*, Cambridge, MA: MIT Press.

Habermas, J. (1990), *Moral Consciousness and Communicative Action*, Cambridge: Polity Press.

Habermas, J. (1997), *Between Facts and Norms*, Cambridge: Polity Press.

Hacking, I. (1991), 'How should we do the history of statistics?', in G. Burchell et al. (eds), *The Foucault Effect: Studies in Governmentality*, London: Harvester Wheatsheaf.

Hahn, L. E. (ed.) (1992), *The Philosophy of A. J. Ayer*, La Salle, IL, Open Court.

Hall, P. (1993), 'Policy Paradigms, Social Learning and the State. The Case of Economic Policymaking in Britain', *Comparative Politics*, 25: 3, pp. 275–94.

Hall, P. (1997), 'The Role of Interests, Institutions, and Ideas in the Comparative Political Economy of the Industrialised Nations', in M. Irving and A. Zuckerman (eds), *Comparative Politics: Rationality, Culture and Structure*, Cambridge: Cambridge University Press.

Hall, Stuart (1987), 'Gramsci and Us', *Marxism Today*, June, pp. 16–21.

Hall, S. (1988), *The Hard Road to Renewal: Thatcherism and the Crisis of the Left*, London: Verso.

Hall, Stuart (1992), 'The Question of Cultural Identity', in Stuart Hall, David Held and Tony McGrew (eds), *Modernity and its Futures*, Cambridge: Polity Press in association with the Open University.

Hambleton, R., S. Essex et al. (1995), *The Collaborative Council: A Study of Inter-agency Working in Practice*, London: Joseph Rowntree Foundation.

Hann, A. (1995), 'Sharpening Up Sabatier: Beliefs Systems and Public Policy', *Politics*, 15: 1, pp. 19–26.

Haraway, D. (1997), *Modest_Witness@Second_Millennium.FemaleMan©_Meets_OncoMouse?: Feminism and Technoscience*, New York and London: Routledge.

Hawkes, T. (1977), *Structuralism and Semiotics*, London: Methuen.

Hayles, N. K. (1990), *Chaos Bound: Orderly Disorder in Contemporary Literature and Science*, Ithaca: Cornell University Press.

Hayles, N. K. (1999), *How We Became Posthuman: Virtual Bodies in Cybernetics, Literature and Informatics*, Chicago: University of Chicago Press.

Hegel, G. W. F. (1945), *Philosophy of Right*, Oxford: Oxford University Press.

Hegel, G. W. F. (1975), *Natural Law*, Philadelphia: University of Pennsylvania Press.

Held, D. (1989), *Political Theory and the Modern State: Essays on State, Power and Democracy*, Cambridge: Polity Press.

Held, David (1991), 'Democracy, the Nation State and the Global System', in David Held (ed.), *Political Theory Today*, Cambridge: Polity Press.

Hilferding, R. (1940), 'State Capitalism or Totalitarian State Economy', *Socialist Courier*, New York (reprinted in *Modern Review*, 1, 1947).

Hilferding, R. (1985), *Finance Capital*, London: Harvester Wheatsheaf.

Hillyard, P. and S. Watson (1996), 'Postmodern Social Policy: A Contradiction in Terms?', *Journal of Social Policy*, 25: 3, 321–46.

Hirschman, A. O. (1982), *Shifting Involvements: Private Interest and Public Action*, Princeton: Princeton University Press.

Hirst, P. (1976), 'Althusser and the Theory of Ideology', *Economy and Society*, 5: 4, 385–412.

Hobbes, T. [1651] (1991), *Leviathan*, Cambridge: Cambridge University Press

Hobsbawm, E. J. (1973), *Revolutionaries: Contemporary Essays*, London: Weidenfeld and Nicholson.

Hoffman, J. (1998), *Sovereignty*, Buckingham: Open University Press.

Howarth, D. (1988), 'Post-Marxism', in A. Lent (ed.), *New Political Thought: An Introduction*, London: Lawrence and Wishart.

Howarth, D. (1995a), 'Complexities of Identity/Difference', *Journal of Political Ideologies*, 2: 1, 55–78.

Howarth, D. (1995b), 'Discourse Theory', in D. Marsh and G. Stoker, *Theory and Methods in Political Science*, London: Macmillan, pp. 15–33.

Howarth, D. (1996), 'Theorising Hegemony', in I. Hampsher-Monk and J. Stanyer (eds), *Contemporary Political Studies 1996*, Glasgow: PSA UK, pp. 944–56.

Howarth, D. (2000a), *Discourse: An Approach to Social and Political Analysis*, Buckingham: Open University Press.

Howarth, D. (2000b), 'Representing Blackness: Black Consciousness Discourse and the Media', in L. Switzer (ed.), *South Africa's Resistance Press: Subaltern Texts and Communities in the Last Generation of the Apartheid Era*, Cambridge: Cambridge University Press.

Hudson, B., B. Hardy, M. Henwood and G. Wistow (1999), 'In Pursuit of Inter-Agency Collaboration in the Public Sector: what is the contribution of theory and research?', *Public Management: An International Journal of Research and Theory*, 1: 2, 235–60.

Husbands, C. (1992), 'The Other Face of 1992: the Extreme-Right Explosion in Western Europe', *Parliamentary Affairs*, 45: 3, 267–84.

Jameson, F. (1972), *The Prison House of Language*, Princeton, NJ: Princeton University Press.

Jameson, F. (1992), 'Postmodernism and Space', *Assemblage*, 17, pp. 32–7.

Jessop, B. (1990), *State Theory: Putting Capitalist States in their Place*, Cambridge: Polity Press.

Jessop, B. (1998), 'The rise of governance and the risks of failure: the case of economic development', *International Social Science*, 155 (March), 29–45.

Jessop, B. (1999a), 'The Social Embeddedness of the Economy and its Implications for Economic Governance' (draft), published by the Department of Sociology, Lancaster University at : *http://www.lancaster.ac.uk/sociology/soc016rj.html*.

Jessop, B. (1999b), 'Narrating the Future of the National Economy and the National State' (draft), published by the Department of Sociology, Lancaster University at: *http://www.lancaster.ac.uk/sociology/soc014rj.html*.

Jobert, B. (1992), 'Représentations sociales controverses et débats dans la conduite des politiques publiques', *Revue Française de Science Politique*, 42: 2, pp. 219–34.

John, P. (1998), *Analysing Public Policy*, London: Pinter.

John, P. (1999), 'Ideas and interests; agendas and implementation: an evolutionary explanation of policy change in British local government finance', *British Journal of Politics and International Relations*, 1: 1, 39–62.

Johnson, T. (1993), 'Expertise and the state', in M. Gane and T. Johnson (eds), *Foucault's New Domains*, London: Routledge, pp. 139–52.

Kampis, G. (1991), *Self-Modifying Systems in Biology and Cognitive Science: A New Framework for Dynamics, Information and Complexity*, Oxford: Pergamon Press.

Kant, I. [1949] (1993), *Critique of Practical Reason*, New York: Macmillan.

Keenan, T. (1993), 'Windows of Vulnerability,' in B. Robbins (ed.), *The Phantom Public Sphere*, Minneapolis: University of Minnesota Press, pp. 121–41.

Kern, S. (1983), *The Culture of Time and Space 1800–1918*, Cambridge, MA: Harvard University Press.

Keynes, J. M. (1936), *The General Theory of Employment, Interest and Money*, London: Macmillan Press.

Kickert, W. J. M., E.-H. Klijn et al. (eds) (1997), *Managing Complex Networks: Strategies for the Public Sector*, London: Sage.

Kiel, L. D. and E. Elliot (1995), *Chaos Theory in the Social Sciences: Foundations and Applications*, Michigan: University of Michigan Press.

Kingdon, J. (1995), *Agendas, Alternatives and Public Policies* (2nd edn), New York: HarperCollins.

Kolb, D. (1986), *The Critique of Pure Modernity: Hegel, Heidegger and After*, Chicago: University of Chicago Press.

Kooiman, J. (ed.) (1993), *Modern Governance: New Government-Society Interaction*, London: Sage.

Krause, K. and M. C. Williams (eds) (1996), *Critical Security Studies*, Boulder, CO: Lynne Rienner.

Kristeva, J. (1975), 'The System and the Speaking Subject', in T. A. Sebeok (ed.), *The Tell-Tale Sign: A Survey of Semiotics*, Lisse, Netherlands: Peter de Ridder Press.

Kristeva, J. (1991), *Strangers to Ourselves*, New York: Columbia University Press.

Kristeva, J. (1998), 'The Subject in Process', in P. ffrench and R. F. Lack (eds), *The Tel Quel Reader*, London: Routledge.

Kuhn, T. S. (1970), *The Structure of Scientific Revolutions*, Chicago: University of Chicago Press.

Lacan, J. (1977), *Écrits: A Selection*, London: Routledge.

Laclau, E. (1979), *Politics and Ideology in Marxist Theory: Capitalism, Fascism, Populism*, London: Verso.

Laclau, E. (1990), *New Reflections on the Revolution of our Time*, London: Verso.

Laclau, E. (ed.) (1994), *The Making of Political Identities*, London: Verso.

Laclau, E. (1996), *Emancipation(s)*, London: Verso.

Laclau, E. (2000a), 'Identity and Hegemony', in Judith Butler, Ernesto Laclau and Slavoj Žižek (eds), *Contingency, Hegemony, Universality*, London: Verso.

Laclau, E. (2000b), 'Structure, History and the Political' in Judith Butler, Ernesto Laclau and Slavoj Žižek, *Contingency, Hegemony, Universality*. London: Verso.

Laclau, E. and C. Mouffe (1985), *Hegemony and Socialist Strategy*, London: Verso.

Laclau, E. and C. Mouffe (1990), 'Post-Marxism Without Apologies', in E. Laclau, *New Reflections on the Revolution of Our Time*, London: Verso.

Lash, S. and J. Urry (1987), *The End of Organised Capitalism*, Cambridge: Cambridge University Press.

Lash, S. and J. Urry (1994), *Economies of Signs and Space*, London: Sage.

Latham, Robert (1996), 'Getting out from under: rethinking security beyond liberalism and the levels-of-analysis problem', *Millennium*, 25: 1, pp. 77–108.

Latour, B. (1993), *We Have Never Been Modern*, New York: Harvester Wheatsheaf.

Latour, B. (1996), *Aramis or The Love of Technology*, Cambridge, MA: Harvard University Press.

Le Monde (1998), document 'fn981211.htm' on the Le Monde website.

Le Monde (1999a), 'De l'Ain à la Savoie, les mutins préparent le congrès de Marignane', 12 January 1999.

Le Monde (1999b), 'Interview with A. Chebel d'Appollonia', 24 January 1999.

Le Monde (1999c), '"Le délinquant est un prédateur nuisible"', 20 February 1999.

Le Pen, J.-M. (1984), *Les Français d'abord*, Paris: Carrre/Laffont.

Le Pen, J.-M. (1989), 'Editorial', *Identité*, No.1 (May–June), p. 1.

Le Pen, J.-M. (1994), 'Ma vérité sur l'Europe', *National-Hebdo* (12–18 May), p. 7.

Leach, W. (1993), *Land of Desire*, New York: Pantheon.

Lechte, J. (1994), *Fifty Key Contemporary Thinkers: From Structuralism to Post-modernity*, London: Routledge.

Lefort, C. (1986), *Political Forms of Modern Society: bureaucracy, democracy, totalitar-*

ianism (edited and introduced by J .B. Thompson), Cambridge: Polity Press.

Lefranc, D. (1989), 'La confiscation de la démocratie', *Identité*, No. 2, juillet-août 1989.

Lévi-Strauss, C. (1963), *Structural Anthropology*, London: Penguin.

Lévi-Strauss, C. (1997), 'Selections from Introduction to the Work of Marcel Mauss', in A. D. Schrift (ed.), *the logic of the gift: Toward an Ethic of Generosity*, London: Routledge.

Lipschutz, Ronnie D. (ed.) (1995), *On Security*, New York: Columbia University Press.

Lipsky, M. (1980), *Street-level Bureaucracy: Dilemmas of the individual in public services*, New York: Russel Sage Foundation.

Lipsky, M. (1993), 'Street-level Bureaucracy: an introduction', in M. Hill (ed.), *The Policy Process*, London: Harvester Wheatsheaf.

Loraux, Nicole (1986), *The Invention of Athens: the funeral oration in the classical city*, Cambridge, MA: Harvard University Press.

Luhmann, N. (1982), *The Differentiation of Society*, New York: Columbia University Press.

Luhmann, N. (1988), 'Closure and Openness: On Reality in the World of Law', in G. Teubner (ed.), *Autopoietic Law: A New Approach to Law and Society*, New York: de Gruyter.

Luhmann, N. (1990), *Essays on Self Reference*, New York: Columbia University Press.

Luhmann, N. (1994), '"What Is the Case?" and "What Lies Behind It?" The Two Sociologies and The Theory of Society', *Sociological Theory*, 12: 2, pp. 126–39.

Luhmann, N. (1995), *Social Systems*, Palo Alto: Stanford University Press.

Luhmann, N. (1998), *Observations on Modernity*, Stanford, CA: Stanford University Press.

Lukes, Steven (1974), *Power*, Basingstoke: Macmillan.

Lyotard, J.-F. (1984), *The Postmodern Condition: A Report on Knowledge*, Minneapolis: University of Minnesota Press.

Lyotard, J.-F. (1993), *Libidinal Economy*, London: Athlone.

Majone, G. (1989), *Evidence, Argument and Persuasion in the Policy Process*, New Haven: Yale University Press.

Marcus, G. (1998), *Corporate Futures: The Diffusion of the Culturally Sensitive Corporate Form*, Chicago: University of Chicago Press.

Martin H.-J. (1994), *The History and Power of Writing*, L. G. Cochrane (trans.), Chicago: University of Chicago Press.

Martin, J. (1998a), *Gramsci's Political Analysis: A Critical Introduction*, Basingstoke: Macmillan.

Martin, J. (1998b), 'Crisis and Incompletion: Interpreting the Italian State', in A. Dobson and J. Stanyer (eds), *Contemporary Political Studies 1998*, Vol. 2, Nottingham: Political Studies Association, pp. 703–13.

Marx, Karl and Friedrich Engels (1970), *The German Ideology: Part One*, London: Lawrence and Wishart.

Marx, Karl (1981), *Capital: Vol. 3*, Harmondsworth: Penguin.

Maturana, H. (1988), 'Reality: The Search for Objectivity or the Quest for a Compelling Argument', *The Irish Journal of Psychology*, 9, pp. 25–82.

Maturana, H. and F. Varela (1987), *The Tree of Knowledge: The Biological Roots to Human Understanding*, Boston: Shambhala.

McClellan, David (ed.) (1988), *Karl Marx: Selected Writings*, Oxford: Oxford University Press.

McNally, D. (1993), *Against the Market*, London: Verso.

McSweeney, Bill (1996), 'Identity and security: Buzan and the Copenhagen school', *Review of International Studies*, 22: 1, pp. 81–93.

Mégret, B. (1990), *La Flamme: les voies de la renaissance*, Paris: Robert Laffont.

Mégret, B. (1997), *La Troisième Voie: pour un nouvel ordre économique et social*, Paris: Edition Nationales.

Mendus, Susan (1992), 'Kant: "An Honest but Narrow-Minded Bourgeois"?', in Ruth Chadwick (ed.), *Immanuel Kant: Critical Assessments, Vol. 3: Kant's Moral and Political Philosophy*, London: Routledge, pp. 370–88.

Miller, P. and N. Rose (1993), 'Governing Economic Life', in M. Gane and T. Johnson (eds), *Foucault's New Domains*, London: Routledge.

Milza, P. (1987), *Fascisme Français: Passé et Présent*, Paris: Flammarion.

Mingers, J. (1995), *Self-Producing Systems*, New York: Plenum.

Mintz, S. L. (1962), *The Hunting of Leviathan*, Cambridge: Cambridge University Press.

Mol, A. (1999), 'Ontological Politics: A word and some questions', in J. Law and J. Hassard (eds), *Actor-Network Theory and After*, Oxford: Blackwell.

Monzat, R. (1996), 'FN, les mots pour le dire', *Le Monde*, 18 September.

Mouffe, C. (1981), 'Hegemony and the Integral State in Gramsci: Towards a New Concept of Politics', in G. Bridges and R. Brunt (eds), *Silver Linings: Some Strategies for the Eighties*, London: Lawrence & Wishart.

Mouffe, C. (1993), *The Return of the Political*, London: Verso.

Mouffe, C. (ed.) (1996), *Deconstruction and Pragmatism*, London: Routledge.

Mouzelis, N. P. (1990), *Post-Marxist Alternatives: The Construction of Social Orders*, Basingstoke: Macmillan.

Mudde, C. (1996), 'The War of Words: Defining the Extreme-Right Party Family', *West European Politics*, 19: 2, April, 225–48.

Nancy, J.-L. (1991), *The Inoperative Community*, Minneapolis: University of Minnesota Press.

Nancy, J.-L. (1993), *The Birth to Presence*, Stanford: Stanford University Press.

NASDAQ (1999), 'A truly global stock market? Perhaps sooner than you think', *The Wall Street Journal*, 12 November.

National-Hebdo (1997), 'La préférence nationale est le cœur nuclaire de notre programme' (interview with Le Gallou), *National-Hebdo*, 10–16 April, p. 2.

Negt, O. and A. Kluge (1993), *The Public Sphere and Experience*, P. Labanyi, J. Daniel and A. Oksiloff (trans.), Minneapolis: University of Minnesota Press.

Noblecourt, M. (1997), 'Lionel Jospin accuse la droite de «récupérer l'extrême droite au lieu de la combattre»', *Le Monde*, 23–24 March, p. 7.

Nocon, A. (1994), *Collaboration in Community Care in the 1990s*, Sunderland: Business Education Publishers.

Nolte, E. (1966), *Les mouvements fascists: L'Europe de 1919–1945*, Paris: Calmann-Levy.

Norris, C. (1997), 'Why Strong Sociologists Abhor a Vacuum: Shapin and Schaffer on the Boyle/Hobbes Controversy', *Philosophy and Social Criticism*, 23: 4, pp. 9–40.

Norval, A. (1996), *Deconstructing Apartheid Discourse*, London: Verso.

Olson, M. (1965), *The Logic of Collective Action*, Cambridge, MA: Harvard University Press.

Osborne, G. and T. Gaebler (1992), *Reinventing Government: How the Entrepreneurial Spirit is Transforming the Public Sector*, Reading, MA: Addison-Wesley.

Osborne, P. (1991), 'Radicalism without limit', in P. Osborne (ed.), *Socialism and the Limits of Liberalism*, London: Verso, pp. 201–26.

Payne, S. (1983), *Fascism: Comparison and Definition*, Madison, WI: University of Wisconsin Press.

Peltier, M. (1997), 'La cohérence nationale', *National-Hebdo*, 10–16 April, pp. 2–3.

Penna, S. and M. O'Brien (1996), 'Postmodernism and Social Policy: A Small Step Forwards?', *Journal of Social Policy*, 25: 1, 39–61.

Perrineau, P. (1997), *Le Symptôme Le Pen*, Paris: Fayard.

Perrineau, P. (1998), 'La desespérance nourrit la dynamique électorale du FN', *Le Monde*, 20 March, p. 9.

Pierson, C. (1993), 'Democracy, Markets and Capital: Are there Necessary Economic Limits to Democracy?', in D. Held (ed.), *Prospects for Democracy*, Cambridge: Polity Press.

Pippin, R. B. (1991), *Modernism as a Philosophical Problem*, Oxford: Blackwell.

Plato (1976), *The Republic*, Letchworth: Aldine Press.

Pocock, J. G. A. (1975), *The Machiavellian Moment*, Princeton, NJ: Princeton University Press.

Pocock, J. G. A. (1989), *Politics, Language and Time*, Chicago: University of Chicago Press.

Poulantzas, N. (1978), *State, Power, Socialism*, London: New Left Books.

Prigogine, I. and I. Stengers (1984), *Order Out of Chaos: Man's New Dialogue with Nature*, London: Heinemann.

Pringle, R. and S. Watson (1992), '"Women's Interests" and the Post-Structuralist State', in M. Barrett and A. Philips (eds), *Destabilizing Theory: Contemporary Feminist Debates*, Cambridge: Polity Press.

Radaelli, C. (1995), 'The role of knowledge in the policy process', *Journal of European Public Policy*, 2: 2.

Radaelli, C. (1997), *The Politics of Corporate Taxation in the European Union: Knowledge and International Policy Agendas*, London: Routledge.

Rancière, J. (1999), *Disagreement: Politics and Philosophy*, Minneapolis: Minnesota University Press.

Rawls, John (1971), *A Theory of Justice*, Oxford: Oxford University Press.

Rawls, John (1993), *Political Liberalism*, New York: Columbia University Press.

Rein, M. and D. Schön (1991), 'Frame-reflective policy discourse', in P. Wagner, C. Hirschon Weiss, B. Wittrock and H. Wollman (eds), *Social Sciences and Modern States: National Experiences and Theoretical Crossroads*, Cambridge: Cambridge University Press, pp. 262–89.

Ripley, H. S. (1998), 'Corporate Punishment', *Harper's*, Vol. 296, March, p. 4.

Roland-Lévy, F. (1997), 'La droite cherche sa voie entre le PS et le Front national', *Le Monde*, 21 March, p. 6.

Rollat, A. (1985), *Les hommes de l'extrême droite*, Paris: Calmann-Levy.

Rorty, R. (1989), *Contingency, Irony and Solidarity*, Cambridge: Cambridge University Press.

Rorty, R. (1991), *Objectivity, Relativism and Truth*, Cambridge: Cambridge University Press.

Rose, M. (1988), 'The Author as Proprietor: Donaldson v. Beckett and the Genealogy of the Modern Author', *Representations*, 23, pp. 51–85.

Rose, N. (1987), 'Beyond the Public/Private Division: Law, Power and the Family', in P. Fitzpatrick and A. Hunt (eds), *Critical Legal Studies*, New York and London: Blackwell.

Rose, N (1996a), 'Re-figuring the territory of government', *Economy and Society*, 25: 3, pp. 327–56.

Rose, N. (1996b), 'Governing "advanced" liberal democracies', in A. Barry et al. (eds), *Foucault and Political Reason: Liberalism, neo-liberalism and rationalities of government*, London: UCL Press.

Rose, N. (1999), *Powers of Freedom*, Cambridge: Cambridge University Press.

Rose, N. and P. Miller (1992), 'Political power beyond the state: problematics of government', *British Journal of Sociology*, 43: 2, pp. 172–205.

Rossi, E. (1995), *Jeunesses française des années 80–90: la tentation néo-fasciste*, Paris: LGDJ.

Rouse, J. (1994), 'Power/Knowledge', in G. Gutting (ed.), *The Cambridge Companion to Foucault*, Cambridge: Cambridge University Press.

Safran, W. (1993), 'The Front National in France: from Lunatic Fringe to Limited Respectability', in P. Merkl and L. Weinberg (eds), *Encounters with the Contemporary Radical Right*, Boulder, CO: Westview Press.

Samson, M. (1998), 'Déconstruire le discours du FN', *Le Monde*, 22–23 March, pp. 1–15.

Sandel, Michael J. (1982), *Liberalism and the Limits of Justice*, Cambridge: Cambridge University Press.

Sarup, M. (1993), *An Introductory Guide to Post-structuralism and Postmodernism*, Brighton: Harvester Wheatsheaf.

Saussure, Ferdinand de (1966), *Course in General Linguistics*, New York: McGraw Hill.

Saux, J.-L. (1997a), 'M. Léotard récuse d'un même mouvement le FN et le "Front populaire"', *Le Monde*, 18 March.

Saux, J.-L. (1997b), 'Les dirigeants de la droite récusent toute compromission avec le FN', *Le Monde*, 1 June.

Saward, M. (1998), *The Terms of Democracy*, Cambridge: Polity Press.

Scotto, M. (1997a), 'Le RPR et l'UDF font front commun pour denoncer les thèses de l'extrême droite', *Le Monde*, 28 March, p. 10.

Scotto, M. (1997b), 'M. Jospin veut renvoyer l'extrême-droite «à sa marginalité ancienne»', *Le Monde*, 2 April, p. 6.

Shackley, S., C. Waterton and B. Wynne (1996), 'Imagine Complexity! The Past, Present, and Future Potential of Complex Thinking', *Futures*, 28, 201–25.

Shapin, S. (1996), *The Scientific Revolution*, Chicago: University of Chicago Press.

Shapin, S. and S. Schaffer (1985), *Leviathan and the Air-Pump: Hobbes, Boyle, and the Experimental Life*, Princeton NJ: Princeton University Press.

Silverman, K., (1983), *The Subject of Semiotics*, New York: Oxford University Press.

Skinner, Q. (1988), 'Meaning and Understanding in the History of Ideas', in J. Tully (ed.), *Meaning and Context: Quentin Skinner and his Critics*, Cambridge: Polity Press.

Skinner, Q. (1989), 'The State', in T. Ball et al. (eds), *Political Innovation and Conceptual Change*, Cambridge: Cambridge University Press.

Skinner, Q. (1996), *Reason and Rhetoric in the Philosophy of Hobbes*, Cambridge: Cambridge University Press.

Skinner, Q. (1999), 'Hobbes and the Purely Artificial Person of the State', *The Journal of Political Philosophy*, 7: 1, pp. 1–29.

Spinoza, Benedict De (1909), *The Ethics*, London: Chiswick Press.

Staheli, U. (1995), *Latent Places of the Political in Niklas Luhmann's Systems Theory*, Working Paper No. 5, Centre for Theoretical Studies, University of Essex.

Staten, Henry (1984), *Wittgenstein and Derrida*, Oxford: Blackwell.

Sturrock, J. (1979), *Structuralism and Since: From Lévi-Strauss to Derrida*, Oxford: Oxford University Press.

Sturrock, J. (1993), *Structuralism*, London: Fontana.

Taggart, P. (1995), 'New Populist Parties in Western Europe', *West European Politics*, 18: 1, 34–51.

Taguieff, P.-A. (1985), 'Les droites radicales en France: Nationalisme révolution-naire et national libéralisme', *Les Temps Modernes*, Avril.

Taplin, O. (1996), 'Fifth-Century Tragedy and Comedy', in Erich Segal (ed.), *Oxford Readings in Aristophanes*, Oxford: Oxford University Press, pp. 9–28.

Taylor, Charles (1992), 'The Politics of Recognition', in Amy Gutmann and Charles Taylor (eds) *Multiculturism on the Politics of Recognition*, Princeton, NJ: Princeton University Press, 25–73.

Taylor-Gooby, P. (1994), 'Postmodernism and Social Policy: a great leap backwards?', *Journal of Social Policy*, 23: 3, 385–405.

Teubner, G. (1993), *Law as an Autopoietic System*, Oxford: Blackwell.

Thrift, N. (1999), 'The Place of Complexity', *Theory Culture and Society*, 16: 3, pp. 31–69.

Torfing, J. (1991), 'A Hegemony Approach to Capitalist Regulation', in R. B. Bertramsen, J. P. F. Thomsen and J. Torfing (eds), *State, Economy and Society*, London: Unwin Hyman.

Torfing, J. (1998), *Politics, Regulation and the Modern Welfare State*, Basingstoke: Macmillan.

Torfing, J. (1999), *New Theories of Discourse: Laclau, Mouffe and Žižek*, Oxford: Blackwell.

Tsoukas, H. (1998), 'Introduction: Chaos, Complexity and Organization Theory', *Organization*, 5: 3, 291–313.

Tucker, R. C. (1978), *The Marx-Engels Reader*, New York: Norton.

Varela, F. (1979), *Principles of Biological Autonomy*, New York: North Holland.

Virilio, P. (1997), *Open Sky*, London: Verso.

Viroli, M. (1992), *From Politics to Reason of State*, Cambridge: Cambridge University Press.

Waever, Ole (1995), 'Securitization and desecuritization', in Ronnie D. Lipschutz (ed.), *On Security*, New York: Columbia University Press, pp. 46–86.

Waever, Ole, Barry Buzan, Morten Kelstrup and Pierre Lemaitre (1993), *Identity, Migration and the New Security Agenda in Europe*, London: Pinter.

Walker, R. B. J. (1995), 'From International Relations to World Politics', in J. A. Camilleri et al. (eds), *The State in Transition: Reimagining Political Space*, Boulder, CO and London: Lynne Rienner.

Walker, R. B. J. (1997), 'The Subject of Security', in Keith Krause and Michael C. Williams (eds), *Critical Security Studies*, Boulder, CO: Lynne Rienner, pp. 61–82.

Walz, K. (1959), *Man, the State and War*, New York: Columbia University Press.

Ward, H. (1997), 'The Possibility of an Evolutionary Explanation of the State's Role in Modes of Regulation', in J. Stanyer and G. Stoker (eds), *Contemporary Political Studies 1997*, Nottingham: Political Studies Association, pp. 125–37.

Webster, P. (1998a), 'Gaullists split on local alliances with Le Pen', *The Guardian*, 20 March, p. 14.

Webster, P. (1998b), 'Le Pen fails in Marseille', *The Guardian*, 24 March, p. 12.

Williams, Caroline (1999), 'Structure, Language and Subjectivity: Lacan', in S. Glendinning (ed.), *The Edinburgh Encyclopaedia of Continental Philosophy*, Edinburgh: Edinburgh University Press.

Wittgenstein, Ludwig (1961), *Tractatus Logico-Philosophicus*, London: Routledge and Kegan Paul.

Wood, Ellen (1998), *The Retreat from Class: A New 'True' Socialism*, London: Verso.

Wyn-Jones, R. (1995), 'Critical security studies and the emancipatory project', paper presented to the British International Studies Association Annual Conference, Southampton, December.

Zahariadas, N. (2000), 'Ambiguity, Time and Multiple Streams', in P. Sabatier (ed.), *Theories of the Policy Process*, Boulder, CO: Westview Press, pp. 73–93.

Zarb, F. G. (1999), 'The Coming Global Digital Stock Market', speech given before the National Press Club, Washington, DC, Wednesday, 23 June.

Zeleny, M. (1980), *Autopoiesis, Dissipative Structures, and Spontaneous Social Order*, Boulder, CO: Westview Press.

Žižek, Slavoj (1989), *The Sublime Object of Ideology*, London: Verso.

Žižek, Slavoj (1990), 'Beyond Discourse Analysis', in E. Laclau (ed.), *New Reflections on the Revolution of Our Time*, London: Verso.

Žižek, Slavoj (1991), *Looking Awry: An Introduction to Jacques Lacan through Popular Culture*, Cambridge, MA: MIT Press.

Žižek, Slavoj (1992), *Enjoy your Symptom: Jacques Lacan in Hollywood and Out*, New York: Routledge.

Žižek, Slavoj (1993), *Tarrying with the Negative: Kant, Hegel and the Critique of Ideology*, Durham, NC: Duke University Press.

Žižek, Slavoj (1997), *The Plague of Fantasies*, London: Verso.

Žižek, Slavoj (1999), *The Ticklish Subject: The Absent Centre Of Political Ontology*, London: Verso.

Index

Adorno, Theodor, 187
Agamben, Giorgio, 179–80, 184
Aglietta, Michael, 114, 119–20
Althusser, Louis, 1, 24
    and Foucault, 25
    and ideology, 5, 26, 28, 84
    and Lacan, 25, 41, 115
    and Reading Capital, 25–6
    and theory of subject, 25–7
Anderson, Benedict, 212
Aristotle, 10, 163–4, 171
Ashley, Rick, 55–6
Autopoiesis, 119–22, 152–4, 156
Ayer, A. J., 180–1

Bakhtin, Mikhail, 210
Balibar, Etienne, 37, 38, 207
Banks Russell, 216
Bateson, Greg, 151
Baudrillard, Jean, 2
Benjamin, Walter, 214, 221
Bentham, Jeremy, 29
Benveniste, Emile, 42–4
Betz, H.-G., 91
Blair, Tony, 101, 205
Boyer, R., 114
Boyle, Robert, 146–8, 158
Brittan, Samuel, 104
Burch, Noel, 216
Burke, Edmund, 162
Butler, Judith, 35, 36, 184
Buzan, Barry, 66–9, 73–4, 76–8, 89

Campbell, David, 77
Cavell, Stanley, 180
Certeau, Michel de, 210
Chaos Theory, 150–1

Conservatism, 162
Cooke, Maeve, 184–5
Coole, Diana, 189
Crick, Bernard, 177–80
Critchley, Simon, 71, 172–3

Deconstruction, 2, 13, 32–4
    and the economy, 116–19
    and law, 56–8, 113
    and state theory, 54–8
Deleuze, Gilles, 2, 126
Deleuze and Guattari, 3, 145, 193–205
    passim
    and complexity theory, 154–5
    and concept of the political, 196–9
    and desire, 204
    and film, 217
    and singularity, 200–2
Derrida, Jacques, 1, 2, 3, 13, 24, 73, 76, 77,
    97, 101, 102, 113, 123, 127, 129
    and theory of the subject, 32–4
Descartes, Rene, 37–40, 100
Dillon, Mick, 67, 72
Donzelot, Jacques, 208
Durkheim, Emile, 48, 169–70

Egoyan, Atom, 208, 216, 221
Einstein, Albert, 157
European Convention on Human Rights,
    200

Foucault, Michel, 1, 2, 28–30, 41, 51, 67, 97,
    113, 209, 222
    and Althusser, 25
    genealogical approach, 58–61
    and psychoanalysis, 30
    and theory of subject, 28–30

Friedman, Milton, 105
Fukuyama, Frances, 116, 129

Galileo, 147
Genealogy
    and theory of the state, 58–61
Giddens, Anthony 14, 131
Globalisation, 124–8
Goertzel, Ben, 150–1
Gores, Joe, 209
Goux, J. J., 125
Governmentality, 2, 59–60
Gramsci, Antonio, 1, 6, 114, 117–19, 128
    and state theory, 61–4
Griffin, Roger, 88
Guattari, Felix, 125 see also Deleuze and
    Guattari
Gunning, Tom, 209–10

Habermas, Jurgen, 49, 126, 165–6, 170,
    183, 185, 187–8, 189, 191, 193, 197,
    198–202, 214
Hall, Stuart, 5, 63, 67, 92
Haraway, Donna, 148–9
Hayek, Friedrich Von, 104, 163
Hayles, Katherine, 156–7
Hegel, G. W. F., 100, 206–7, 215–16
Hegemony
    and Gramsci, 117–18
    and logic of in policy, 108–10
    and state theory, 61–4, 103
Heidegger, Martin, 113, 116–17, 171
Hilferding, Rudolf, 114, 116–17, 128
Hobbes, Thomas, 4, 23, 38–41
    and dispute with Boyle, 196, 197–8, 180
    and theory of state sovereignty, 54
Hobsbawm, Eric, 99
Horkheimer, Max, 187
Husserl, Edmund, 100, 113

Ideology, 5, 83–96 passim
    Althusser's theory of, 25–7
    Žižek on, 32
International Relations
    and constructivism, 66–9
    and security, 66–80 passim
    and state theory, 55–7
Interpellation, 27, 84

Jessop, Bob, 120–1

John, Peter, 97, 108–9

Kant, Immanuel, 23, 121, 165, 193, 198–9,
    202
Keynes, J.-M., 99–100, 114
Kingdon, J. 108
Kristeva, Julia, 12, 70

Lacan, Jacques,1, 2, 25, 48–50, 69–72, 79,
    118, 126
    and Althusser, 24
    theory of modernity, 44–50
    theory of the subject, 30–2
Lacis, Asja, 214
Laclau, Ernesto, 1, 50, 84–6, 92–3, 97, 103,
    162, 184, 186–7
Laclau and Mouffe, 1, 62–63, 85–6, 92–3,
    102, 114, 115, 116, 118–19, 122, 124–5,
    129
Language
    Benveniste's theory of, 42–4
    and Derridean deconstruction, 33
    and Lacanian theory of the subject, 30–
    32, 44–7
    Saussure's theory of, 8–9
    and structuralism, 10–11
Lash, Scott, 124
Lefort, Claude, 7, 172, 183
Leibniz, G. W., 149
Lenin, V. I., 116
Le Pen, J.-M., 94–5, 96
Lessnoff, Michael, 2–3
Lévi-Strauss, 10–11, 177
Lipietz, Alain, 114
Locke, John, 4, 23, 106
Loraux, Nicole, 163
Luhmann, Niklas, 120–1, 126, 128–9, 130,
    142–3, 146, 149, 151
    and autopoiesis, 53–4
Lyotard, J.-F., 127

Machiavelli, N., 179
Mannheim, Karl, 100
Marx, Karl, 24, 99–100
    and globalisation, 122, 124–5, 126–7, 167
    and political economy, 113, 114
McSweeney, Bill, 18
Mégret, B., 91, 93, 94, 95
Mirror stage, 30–1, 45
Mouffe, Chantal, 1, 97

Mudde, C., 89

Nancy, J.-L., 171–2
Nazism, discourse of, 123
Newton, Isaac, 147, 149–50
Nietzsche, F., 29, 198
Nolte, E., 88
Norris, Christopher,148–9
Norval, Aletta, 64

Panopticon, 29–30
Patton, Paul, 3
Payne, S., 88
Plato, 100, 161, 193, 197, 202–3
Populism, 84–6, 90–1, 92, 94
Poulantzas, Nicos, 60–1, 84, 115
Prigogine, I., 151, 155
Proudhon, P., 125

Rancière, Jacques, 7, 173–4
Rational Choice, 105–6
Rawls, John, 23, 166–7, 184, 187
Regulation Theory, 119–21
Rights, 194–6, 200–1
Rorty, Richard, 129
Rose, Nik, 2, 14, 60
Rousseau, J.-J., 4, 13, 161, 186

Saussure, Ferdinand de, 1
    and Benveniste, 42–4, 70
    and Lacan, 31, 45
    structural linguistics, 8–9
Saward, Michael, 178–9, 180
Schaffer, S., 146–8
Schmitt, Carl, 179
Shannon, Claude, 146
Shapin, S., 146–8
Simmel, G., 114

Skinner, Quentin, 101
Smith, Adam, 112, 126
Sovereignty
    and exception, 180
    and subject, 182–4
    theory of, 54–8, 72
Spinoza, Benedict, 204
Strauss, Leo, 7
Structuralism
    and Levi-Strauss, 10–11
    linguistic, 8–9
    and subject, 42–4
Sweet Hereafter, The, 216–21
Systems theory, 119–23

Taggart, P., 90
Taylor, Charles, 188
Third Way, 141–2
    Giddens, 131
    New Labour, 101
    in FN, 89, 94
32 Cadillacs, 209–16
Thrift, Nigel, 156
Torfing, Jacob, 64
Tracy, Destutt de, 100

Undecidability, 13, 14, 76
Universal Declaration of Human Rights,
    194–5
Urry, John, 124

Varela, F., 152–3
Virlio, Paul, 218–19, 221–2

Walker, R. B. J., 65, 68
Weber, Max, 99–100
Wittgenstein, Ludwig 100, 101, 113

Zarb, F. G., 126
Žižek, Slavoj, 1, 32, 69–70, 80, 167, 205

From Kant to Lévi-Strauss
The Background to Contemporary Critical Theory

Jon Simons
Lecturer in Critical Theory at the University of Nottingham

This introductory textbook provides students and other readers with an accessible basic guide to key figures in 'The Tradition of Critique' – critical post-Enlightenment European thinking.

The intellectual tradition covered by the book is broadly the Continental philosophy and theory which has had a significant impact on many theoretical innovations in the humanities and social sciences. Yet many students and non-philosophers have little understanding of the tradition on which such thinking draws. The book therefore covers those thinkers whose work serves as the background for many contemporary thinkers such as Derrida, Foucault and Habermas.

There are individual chapters on: Kant, Hegel, Marx, Nietzsche, Weber, Freud, Lukacs, Adorno and Horkheimer, Husserl, Heidegger, Gadamer, Wittgenstein, Arendt and Lévi-Strauss. Each chapter offers some contextualisation, presents and explains key concepts, explains the thinker's relevance to an ongoing tradition and offers suggestions for further reading.

The volume provides readers with sufficient background knowledge to study more contemporary theorists whose work draws on, or assumes knowledge of, these earlier or more foundational thinkers. Thus the book is aimed specifically at students and scholars who do not have a philosophical training and who study literary, cultural, social or political theorists who engage with this European intellectual tradition.

Features
- Introduces 15 key figures in modern Western philosophy
- Enables students to study individual thinkers from one handy reference resource
- Explains the relevance of philosophical tradition to contemporary thought
- Accessible to beginners and non-philosophers
- Explains the main ideas and concepts which contemporary thinkers address
- Oriented to the philosophical, social and political aspects of the critical tradition

October 2002	Pb 0 7486 1506 7 £15.99

Order from
Marston Book Services, PO Box 269, Abingdon, Oxon OX14 4YN
Tel 10235 465500 • Fax 01235 465555
Email: direct.order@marston.co.uk

Polemicization
The Contingency of the Commonplace

Benjamin Arditi, Political Theorist at Universidad Nacional
Autonoma de Mexico and **Jeremy Valentine**, Lecturer in
Cultural Studies at Queen Margaret University College,
Edinburgh

The distinctive feature of this book is its ingenious argumentative strategy: it
takes on the political by developing a practice and a thought the authors call
'polemicization'. They draw from the recent work of the political philosopher
Jacques Rancière, for whom a polemic or disagreement does not refer to the case
when one interlocutor says white and another black. Instead, it designates the
conflict arising when, for example, both parties say white, yet each understands
something different by whiteness. This situation forces the interlocutors to
construe the scene of the validity of their claims, which is just another way of
saying that the given or commonplace is never settled once and for all.

The authors generalise the logic of this encounter and claim that disagreement is
the very process through which objectivity is instituted. They develop the
contours of polemicization and deepen its philosophical implications through a
critical engagement with the work of leading contemporary theorists, such as
Lefort, Schmitt, Laclau, Derrida and Žižek. In particular, the authors interrogate
commonplace narratives of modernity, identity, difference, universality,
antagonism and subjectivity. The result is a provocative text whose broad
disciplinary appeal cuts across the boundaries between political thought,
cultural studies and social theory.

August 1999	Pb 0 7486 1064 2
176pp	£9.95

Critical Political Theory in the Media Age
Jon Simons
Lecturer in Critical Theory at the University of Nottingham

September 2003	Hb 0 7486 1583 0 £40.00
256pp	Pb 0 7486 1582 2 £14.99

Order from
Marston Book Services, PO Box 269, Abingdon, Oxon OX14 4YN
Tel 10235 465500 • Fax 01235 465555
Email: direct.order@marston.co.uk

Visit our website www.eup.ed.ac.uk

Third Way Discourse
The Crisis of European Ideologies in the 20th Century

Steve Bastow, Senior Lecturer in Politics at Kingston University, London; and James Martin, Lecturer in Politics at Goldsmiths College, University of London

The 'Third Way' has been hailed by European social democrats as the ideology of the 'radical centre'. Steering a route between state collectivism on the one hand, and market-led neo-liberalism on the other, it promises a new form of governance based on principle not dogma. But third way thinking is not a new phenomenon, and nor is it exclusively of the left. Similar ideas were developed throughout the twentieth century and across the political spectrum, from fascism to ecologism. This book introduces the history of third way ideology, surveys its various contrasting forms and locates it within the context of a recurrent crisis of modern European ideologies.

The authors apply a theoretical approach that draws upon contemporary theories of discourse. Understood discursively, third way ideas seek to displace received ideological dichotomies and fashion a sense of common moral purpose and identity at times of accumulated social dislocation. Rather than focus narrowly on issues of public policy, Bastow and Martin analyse the third way as an ideological structure, highlighting in particular its rhetorical features and diverse forms.

Features
- Draws upon contemporary post-structuralist discourse theory
- Offers a new interpretive frame to understand the complexity and diversity of third way discourse
- Includes chapters on New Labour, Italian Liberal Socialism, Ecologism, and Neo-Fascism
- Explores the relationship between current third way theory and radical politics

The aim of this book is to offer an informed introduction to the key variants of third way thinking in Europe as they have developed over the course of the 20th century, ranging from right to left on the political spectrum, thereby widening students' theoretical and historical understanding of current arguments within European Social Democracy.

February 2003	Hb 0 7486 1560 1 £45.00
224pp	Pb 0 7486 1561 X £14.99

Cinematic Political Thought
Narrating Race, Nation and Gender

Michael J. Shapiro, Professor of Political Science at the University of Hawaii

This book has two aims: to offer a series of investigations into aspects of contemporary politics such as race, nation and gender; and to articulate a critical philosophical perspective with politically disposed treatments of contemporary cinema. What the author offers is a politics of critique, inspired by Kant, in which he attempts to show what it can mean to think the political.

The interventions into aspects of contemporary political issues, as reflected in films including *Hoop Dreams, Lonestar, Father of the Bride II , The Adventures of Priscilla, Queen of the Desert*, and *To Live and Die in LA*, are also influenced by Deleuze, Derrida, Foucault and Lyotard: theorists loosely regarded by the author as post-Kantian. This is a polemical work, aimed at encouraging critical, ethico-political thinking. Its breadth of theoretical scope and empirical reference, and the innovative style of presentation will make it vital reading for all those with an interest in the linking of culture and politics.

August 1999	Pb 0 7486 1289 0
192pp	£9.95

Post-Marxism: A Reader

Stuart Sim, Professor of English, University of Sunderland

"A very useful pedagogic tool for teachers of theory seeking to explain the twists and turns of Marxist thought in a period of relative eclipse. Sim's introduction is lucid, accessible and free from the jargon that often plagues volumes of this sort."   *The Year's Work in Critical and Cultural Theory*

This is the first source-book for this cross-disciplinary area. It takes students through a wide range of readings from philosophy, politics, and sociology, to human geography, international relations, and feminist studies. Bringing together statements from leading twentieth-century thinkers such as Derrida, Lyotard, Baudrillard, and Laclau and Mouffe, and with the editor's substantial introduction, this is an ideal teaching text, inspiring debate about the future of Marxism as a cultural theory.

August 1999	Hb 0 7486 2043 X	£43.50
176pp	Pb 0 7486 1044 8	£10.50